# Marketing on the Internet
## Second Edition

# Marketing on the Internet
## Second Edition

**Jill H. Ellsworth, Ph.D.**
**Matthew V. Ellsworth**

**Wiley Computer Publishing**

**John Wiley & Sons, Inc.**

New York • Chichester • Brisbane • Toronto • Singapore • Weinheim

Executive Publisher: Katherine Schowalter
Editor: Tim Ryan
Managing Editor: Mark Hayden
Text Design & Composition: SunCliff Graphic Productions

Designations used by companies to distinguish their products are often claimed as trademarks. In all instances where John Wiley & Sons, Inc. is aware of a claim, the product names appear in initial capital or all capital letters. Readers, however, should contact the appropriate companies for more complete information regarding trademarks and registration.

This text is printed on acid-free paper.

This publication is designed to provide accurate and authoritative information in regard to the subject matter covered. It is sold with the understanding that the publisher is not engaged in rendering legal, accounting, or other professional service. If legal advice or other expert assistance is required, the services of a competent professional person should be sought.

*Library of Congress Cataloging-in-Publication Data*

Ellsworth, Jill H.
    Marketing on the Internet, 2nd ed. / Jill H. Ellsworth, Matthew V. Ellsworth
        p.    cm.
    Includes bibliographical references.
    ISBN 0-471-16504-2 (pbk. : alk. paper)
    1. Internet advertising..   2. Internet marketing.   I. Title.
HF6148.I58E44    1997
658.8'4- -dc20                                        96-41394
                                                     CIP

ISBN: 0471-16504-2

Printed in the United States of America

10 9 8 7 6 5 4 3 2 1

# Contents

# Acknowledgments

We want to acknowledge the help of several people who worked to make this a better book:

Tim Ryan
Jodi Beder
Cliff Fischbach

and the patience and support of our families:

Rose Anne Pool
Claire and Jack Harrison
Dan and Judy Ellsworth

# *Introduction*

## Who Is This Book For?

This book was written to help businesses, nonprofit organizations, and other groups of people discover how to use the World Wide Web to promote their organizations or to advertise and market their products. Information is provided for:

- Businesses that have had little experience with the Internet, but are interested in modernizing
- Businesses currently using some portions of the Internet, that want to use the World Wide Web for marketing and sales
- Nonprofit groups or organizations that want better contact with their members and the public at large
- Individuals interested in knowing how to use the World Wide Web for any reason

## The Internet—User-Friendly for Business

The Internet has become user-friendly both for individuals and for businesses. In the past, business activities on the Internet were indeed limited, but now, not only *can* business be done on the Internet, it *is* being done by tens of thousands of businesses.

Business access, previously confined mostly to businesses dealing with government contracts, is now readily and inexpensively available to all businesses. Businesses can now be online 24 hours a day, worldwide, with World Wide Web sites (the colorful multimedia portion of the Internet); monthly costs are from as low as $10 for a small business site to thousands for intricate sites with full-time staffs.

Another required marketing component is on the Internet, too: people—lots of them. While no one knows exactly, there may be as many as 50 million people worldwide on the Internet now. It has been predicted that there will be 100 million Internet users by 1998—with most Internet growth statistics showing an increase of 10% per month, this seems easily possible.

# The Internet—User-Friendly for People

Until recently, an individual had to learn about many different Internet systems to make full use of the Internet's resources. This included learning the nature of, and commands for: FTP, Archie, Gopher, Veronica, and WAIS. Now, however, fueled by the growth of the World Wide Web on the Internet, programs have been written that act as an interface between you and the Internet. These programs, called "browsers," provide a uniform, easy-to-learn way of dealing with the diverse systems and resources on the Internet.

Access to the World Wide Web on the Internet has also greatly improved, with toll-free local Internet access numbers in many areas, and individual monthly rates as low as $15. Internet access providers are also making online sessions easier through use of custom-configured communications software designed to interact with the provider's system and with the Internet.

# The World Wide Web—Excellent for Marketing and Sales

The Web is a system on the Internet that allows anyone to have a 24-hour-a-day "presence" on the Internet. Specially written files are placed on a computer connected full time to the Internet. Others on the Internet then can, by using one of the browser programs, view these files. Those "browsing" the Internet can be presented with much more than words—the files can contain full-color pictures, movies, sound, and interactive programs. Viewers indicate their choices of items on a Web page by pointing and clicking with their computer's mouse. These choices can be for other pictures, audio, lists, or even on-screen fill-out forms that can be used to send responses to the business or individual that owns the Web page.

Here are just a few of the possibilities for marketing and sales using the World Wide Web:

- Full-color virtual catalogs with formatted pages of text and pictures—easily updated, with updates available to others immediately
- On-screen order forms
- Online customer support with graphics, photographs, sound, and text information
- Worldwide distribution of product and other business announcements, without printing or mailing costs
- Customer feedback, request, and survey forms, with data collected in files for you to use whenever you want

## How Businesses Are Using the World Wide Web

Today, for business on the Internet, the absolute hot spot is the World Wide Web. From kitchen table entrepreneurs to multinational conglomerates, businesses are creating their own business presence in cyberspace on the Web. There are numerous business functions and activities that can be pursued by using the Web online. These include communication (both internal and external), information management and distribution, public relations, customer service, technical assistance, cost containment, and, of course, marketing and sales.

### What Is a Web Page?

You will find numerous reference to Web "pages" and "homepages" throughout this book and on the Internet. A "page" is the World Wide Web name for a particular kind of document designed to be displayed on a browser, such as the one shown in the computer screen image in Figure I.1. A "homepage" is the main or top page offered by an individual or business on which are listed choices that lead to all of the other pages that they are offering.

Not only are there a large number of businesses and institutions using the World Wide Web, they are very diverse. Here's a small sampling of the range and diversity currently on the Web:

## Sugarloaf

*http://www.sugarloaf.com/*

Sugarloaf, a winter ski resort and summer outdoor activities resort in Maine, has an excellent site that demonstrates well what a business can do to make an interesting useful business marketing site. The page (Figure I.1) is made up of three sections: a column of buttons to get information on various topics, a row of frequently changing pictures at the top which can lead to information on golf, mountain biking, and other activities, and the main part of the screen with news, weather, and events information about Sugarloaf (including an online audio report). This is a site primarily directed at marketing, not direct sales of a product.

**Figure I.1 Sugarloaf's homepage.**

> ## What Is a URL?
>
> Each Web site has its own "URL" (Uniform Resource Locator—an Internet type of address). The URL begins with *http://*. If you don't know what a URL is yet, don't worry—later in this book you will learn about using these long strings of characters to visit these and other Internet sites.

## Ann Hemyng's Chocolate Factory

*http://mmink.com/mmink/dossiers/choconon.html*

In rural Buck's County, Pennsylvania, Ann Hemyng's Chocolate Factory (Figure I.2) offers access to many kinds of chocolate candies and custom-molded chocolate products (including a chocolate tool assortment with chocolate hammer, wrench, pliers, and screwdriver).

**Figure I.2 The Chocolate Factory homepage.**

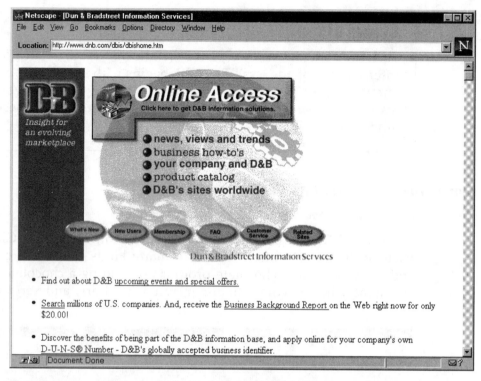

**Figure I.3 The Dun & Bradstreet Information Services homepage.**

Custom orders for unique shapes are also offered. Orders are taken via 800 number, fax, e-mail, and postal mail, and directly online using software that provides protection of the payment and ordering information. This is a good example of a small-town business that has used the Internet to expand its sales reach nationally.

## Dun & Bradstreet

*http://www.dnb.com/dbis/dbishome.htm*

Well-known, large, established businesses are using the Internet for part of their marketing effort. Dun & Bradstreet, for example, offers a site (Figure I.3) with general information about financial matters for businesses as well as information on their line of services. Categories of online information include:

- business how-to's
- news, views, and trends

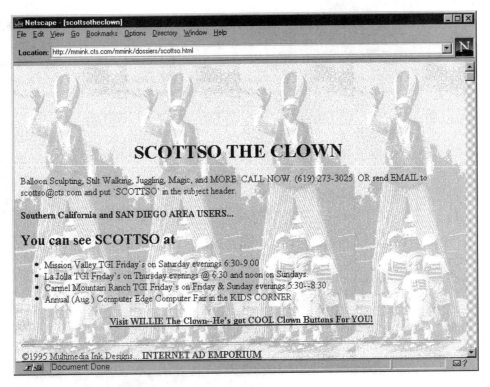

**Figure I.4  Scottso the Clown's homepage.**

- D & B sites worldwide
- product catalog
- online access
- D & B events

## Scottso the Clown

*http://mmink.cts.com/mmink/dossiers/scottso.html*

Even if you are more of a rubber nose, floppy shoe type of business than a three-piece suit establishment, the Internet can be of value. Scottso the Clown, for example, has maintained an ongoing presence on the Internet (Figure I.4). He offers balloon sculpting, stilt walking, juggling, magic, and more. In southern California he does events and parties, and announces his public appearances and contact information with his Web page.

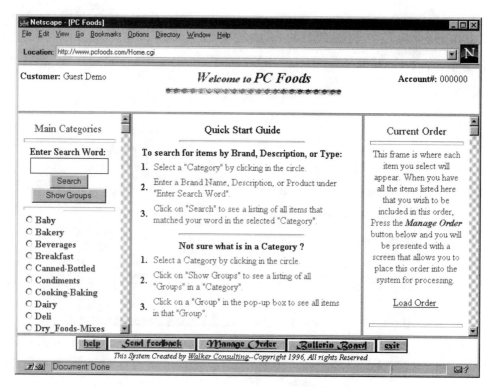

**Figure I.5 PC Foods Market page for placing an online grocery order.**

## PC Foods

*http://www.pcfoods.com/Home.cgi*

While the Internet's potential to market even unusual products worldwide shouldn't be overlooked, businesses with common products sold in every community can use the Internet to get a greater market share. PC Foods, for example, provides a shopping and delivery service for groceries in the Austin, Texas area. Orders can be placed by phone, by fax, or by online electronic order through their Web site.

## Real Audio

*http://www.realaudio.com*

Books, software, photos, and database information have regularly been sold and distributed through the Internet, and now audio products can be delivered as well. Any digital recording can be sent over the

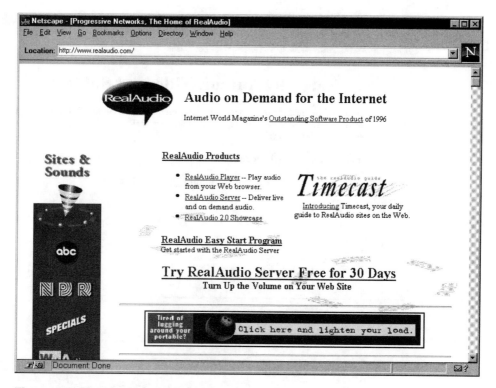

**Figure I.6  RealAudio's homepage.**

Internet, and real-time audio such as that produced by a radio station can also be delivered.

This opens up opportunities for businesses to provide local or worldwide distribution of any audio product. RealAudio provides one type of software for sending and receiving audio over the Internet, and also provides a site that some businesses use to distribute their own audio.

## Amazon.com

*http://www.amazon.com/*

Many bookstores are online now—small bookstores, specialty bookstores, and large online book sellers such as Amazon.com. Amazon.com offers over a million book titles available for direct purchase via the Internet.

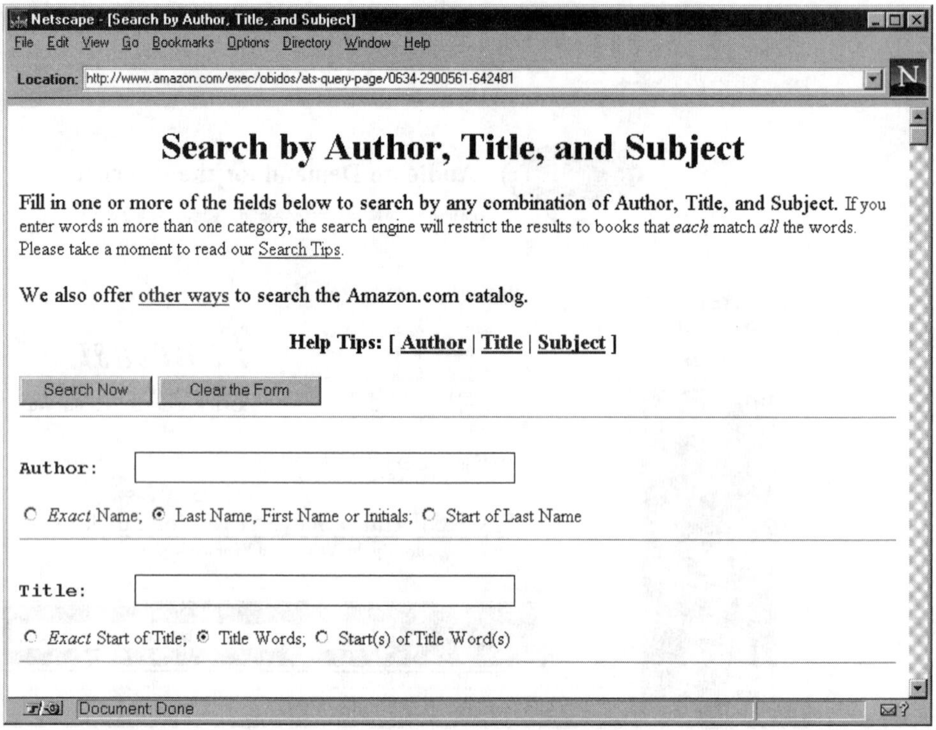

```
┌─────────────────────────────────────────────────────────────────────┐
│ ⋙ Netscape - [Search by Author, Title, and Subject]        _ □ X │
│ File  Edit  View  Go  Bookmarks  Options  Directory  Window  Help    │
├─────────────────────────────────────────────────────────────────────┤
│ Location: │http://www.amazon.com/exec/obidos/ats-query-page/0634-2900561-642481│ ▼ │ N │
└─────────────────────────────────────────────────────────────────────┘
```

# Search by Author, Title, and Subject

Fill in one or more of the fields below to search by any combination of Author, Title, and Subject. If you enter words in more than one category, the search engine will restrict the results to books that *each* match *all* the words. Please take a moment to read our Search Tips.

We also offer other ways to search the Amazon.com catalog.

**Help Tips: [ Author | Title | Subject ]**

[ Search Now ]  [ Clear the Form ]

---

Author: [_____]

○ *Exact* Name;  ● Last Name, First Name or Initials;  ○ Start of Last Name

---

Title: [_____]

○ *Exact* Start of Title;  ● Title Words;  ○ Start(s) of Title Word(s)

---

Document: Done

**Figure I.7 One of Amazon.com's book search pages.**

## Chambers of Commerce

*http://online-chamber.org/*

The Web allows organizations that are often limited by expenses and availability of volunteer help a chance to communicate with members, and to extend the reach of their messages and goals to non-members. This site, for example, lists chambers of commerce nationwide that have a presence on the Internet; you can visit any of the listed online sites with just a click of the mouse button.

## Kaleidospace—Independent Artists

*http://kspace.com/*

Web sites for groups of individuals can be developed on the Internet. Kaleidospace, for example, is an online marketplace where independent artists can sell their work. This site contains links to a variety

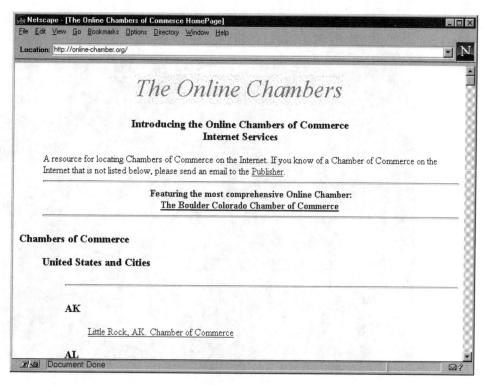

**Figure I.8 Part of the national list of Online Chambers of Commerce.**

of artists' homepages, and a set of icons used to get information on announcements, consulting, ordering, and signing up. Kaleidospace has a page showing a kaleidoscope (see Figure I.9) with choices for selecting the Tool Shop, Art studio, Center Stage, Cyberfaire, interactive media, music, news, readings, the screening room, and spotlighted items.

## Grants Flowers

*http://branch.com/flowers*

Online virtual malls are offered by some companies on the Internet. They offer full packages of services that make it easy for businesses to get online and receive payments from customers. Grants Flowers, for example, can be found in the Branch Mall, where they offer fresh flowers that can be purchased online. The homepage provides links to full-color pictures of the flowers and arrangements that are available. They

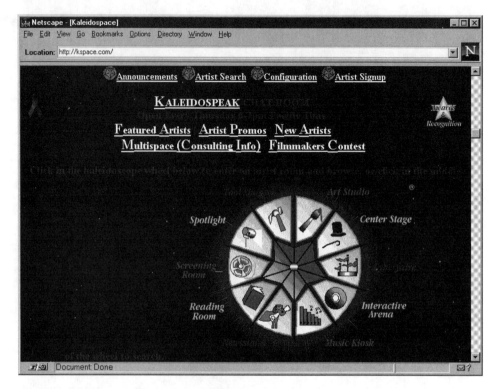

**Figure I.9  The Kaleidospace kaleidoscope.**

even have a reminder service to help you keep on top of anniversaries and birthdays. Once you have made your choice, click on "order" and you are presented with a page containing several purchase alternatives. Figure I.10 shows an order page at *http://branch.com/flowers/order-flowers.html*.

## The White House

*http://www.whitehouse.gov/WH/Welcome.html*

And finally, just to prove that no organization is too big to use the Web, here's the U.S. government in the form of The White House site (Figure I.11). Actually, this site provides more than a tourist's view of the White House; it also offers access to many government sites through guides and a government site database.

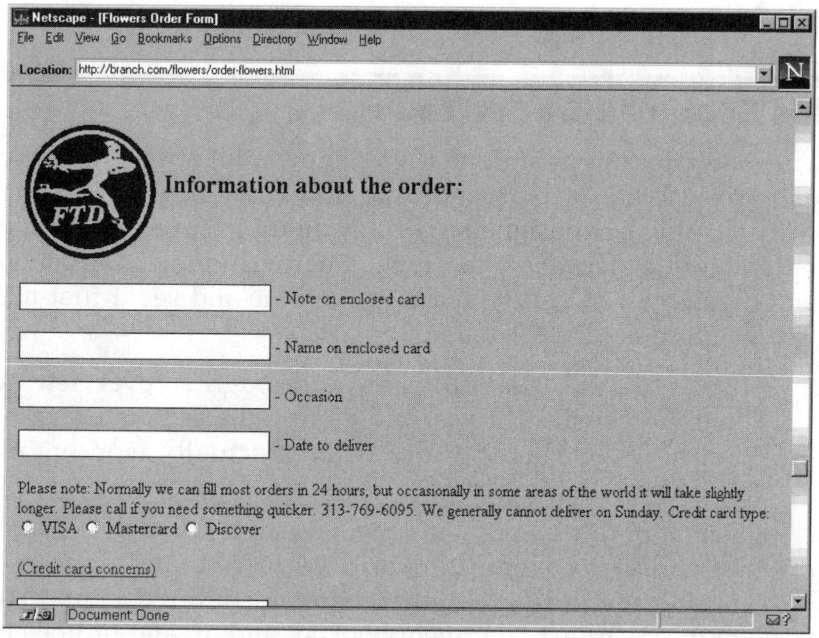

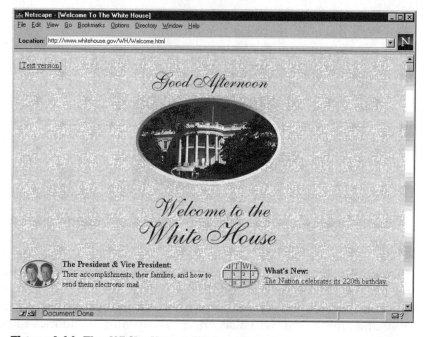

**Figure I.10  A Grants Flowers order page.**

**Figure I.11  The White House Welcome page.**

## What This Book Will Do for You

This book doesn't assume that you know a lot about what the Internet and World Wide Web are, nor that you know how to use them, so the early chapters are designed to bring you up to speed on these topics. In order to understand how to use the Internet, and to comprehend its size and diversity, you really have to get online and see it first-hand. What will you find here?

- Part I of this book will take you through an overview of Internet and Web business tools, and getting the big picture of marketing on the Web. This includes what is actually working out on the Net, and what is selling.

- Part II of this book focuses on how to market on the Internet successfully. It covers the World Wide Web and how to use it for business, effective Web marketing, including Net and Web demographics, how to get them hooked, and on and offline channel integration. In addition, this Part covers security and issues surrounding secure transactions.

- Part III describes the basics of effective web sites, how to create Web documents, how to add and effectively use graphics and sound, plus good Web page practices specifically for marketing. This Part discusses the use of tools such as RealAudio, Java, Shockwave and other technologies.

- Part IV covers the variety of online resources for marketing, including Web searching, marketing and advertising resources. It includes information on Net audio and videoconferencing, Web chat, and group Web site touring software.

- The Appendices take you through gaining access to the Internet, and the practicalities of getting on the Net, and browsers.

Instead of spending many chapters explaining how to use the various Internet "protocols," systems, and software, this book focuses on how to get access to the Internet's resources by learning to use one program, a Web "browser." This is a practical approach to techniques for using the World Wide Web on the Internet for sales, marketing, and research (including extensive listings of online resources for businesses large and small). You will also find cautions and guidelines to help keep your business from getting into trouble or damaging its reputation.

On the Internet, the 4 Ps of marketing—product, price, place, and promotion—are being played out quite differently than they normally are offline:

- **Products** marketed on the Internet can now include almost any goods or services.
- **Price** on the Internet involves many of the same concerns as price offline, but with savings brought about by online marketing. Companies are finding that price can be adjusted for greater competitiveness when selling via the World Wide Web.
- **Place** is, of course, a focus of this book—creating methods for using the World Wide Web to market and sell.
- **Promotion** is also a focus of this book—the Web as a vehicle for promotion—including advertising, sales, marketing, and public relations. Offline promotional modalities must be adapted to make the transition to the Net.

Marketing on the Internet deals with the implications of each of these issues for online marketing and sales.

## From Here . . .

Chapter 1 will explain what the Internet is, how large it is, where it is, who is on it, and how the World Wide Web is related to it.

# PART I

# Leveraging the Web for Marketing—A Preview

# *Internet Overview*

The Internet is a large network formed by the interconnection of computer networks and individual computers all over the world, via phone lines, satellites, and other telecommunications systems. While you don't need a history course on its development to use the Internet, a brief overview of how the Internet works, and why it is the way it is now, can definitely help in making your business a power user.

Historically, the Internet has it roots in ARPAnet, established by the Advanced Research Projects Agency. It was a research and defense network created by the U.S. Department of Defense in the early 1970s to research network systems and to allow scientists and researchers better communication and data exchange for other projects. One of the early outcomes of this initiative was the development of new ways of routing data via multiple paths using units of data called *packets;* the destination address of each packet was built into its structure. These methods became the standards known today as Transmission Control Protocol/Internet Protocol (TCP/IP), and form the common language of the Internet allowing different types of computers and different types of networks to interact.

The National Science Foundation (NSF) expanded upon ARPAnet with the NSFnet, which was initially designed primarily to connect universities and research centers. Increasingly these connections were also used for maintaining communication among individuals in these institutions through e-mail, data file transfers, discussion groups, and other

**3**

uses. As this network of networks grew, it became what we now call the Internet.

As the growth continued, new understandings about the purposes of the network and its potential were being forged, particularly as NSF ended its involvement. Broader access was created through regional networks that linked to the Internet. Policy changes by the government, NSFnet, and privitization later allowed commercial Internet service providers (ISPs) to offer Internet access to those who were not part of an institution or educational organization. These changes opened the floodgates to the current very rapid commercialization of much of the Internet.

## What is the World Wide Web (the "Web")?

The Web is a system that makes the exchange of data on the Internet easy and efficient. It consists of two basic components:

- The Web *server:* a computer and software ("server" can refer to either) that stores and distributes data to other computers throughout the Internet that request the information.
- The Web *browser:* software running on an individual's ("client") computer that requests information from the Web server and displays it in a manner directed in the data file itself.

To use the Web, an individual needs a computer with Web browser software and a modem installed (the modem is a hardware device that converts computers signals to sounds and vice versa to enable the computer to communicate via normal phone lines). After the Web browser is launched (started), the computer is directed to dial an Internet service provider (with which an account has been arranged). The browser is then given the address of a Web "site" where a Web server will respond by sending a "page" of information. This "page" may have text of various sizes and styles, with pictures and other graphics intermixed. Certain pictures and text will have special highlights or underlines. These special highlights indicate that further information is available. All the individual needs to do is to move the mouse indicator over the highlighted item and click, and the remote Web server will respond with the appropriate information.

More than text and pictures can be offered:

- Movies and animation
- Moving graphics
- Sound files and real-time sound
- Databases and catalogs
- Programs that run directly on your computer
- Opportunities to send information to the owner of the Web site

If you've been "surfing" the Web, this is obvious to you by now; if you haven't been online yet, read Appendix B for information on how to get online.

## How Big Is the Internet?

The Internet is experiencing incredible growth in terms of the number of users, the number of computers, and the number of networks connected to it. This growth over the last three years and the increasing commercialization have created extreme changes in the Internet.

Depending upon whose data you use and how you interpret it, there are anywhere from 30 to 60 million people worldwide who have some kind of Internet connectivity.

Here are some interesting recent trends and statistics:

- Growth in number of people on the Internet is estimated to be over 10 percent a month.
- Growth of the commercial sectors has been increasing by over 60% per quarter.
- The World Wide Web, the multimedia portion, is growing faster than any other part of the Internet.

The growth of the Internet has been dramatic in the last three years, and phenomenal in the last year. The graph in Figure 1.1 shows that growth in hosts from the end of 1985 to the end of 1995.

Vinton Cerf, one of the early creators of the Internet, testified to the U.S. House of Representatives that "there is reason to expect that the user population will exceed 100 million by 1998."

Media attention has both followed Internet growth and encouraged it. Four years ago U.S. newspapers carried about three articles per

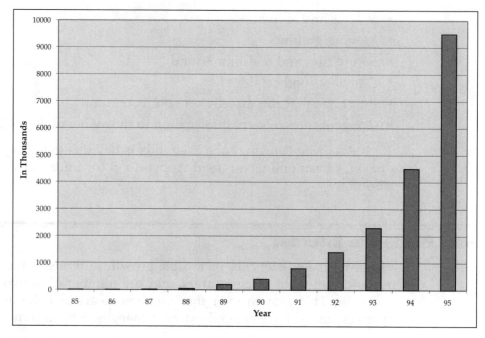

**Figure 1.1 The growth of Internet hosts 1985-1995.**

month mentioning the Internet; two years ago there were about 300 articles per month. Currently, the two of us review about 300 articles a day, and that's just a small portion of those available. There is a flood of individual magazine articles and radio and TV features about the Internet, as well as entire radio and TV shows and magazines dedicated to covering the Internet phenomena. You see URLs everywhere—more about those below.

The media are contributing to the growth of the Internet in another way—not by just observing and reporting, but by participating. Several thousand newspapers, as well as magazines such as *Time* and *Newsweek*, offer their articles as well as other content specifically written for online use. Individual TV stations and networks have also become part of the Internet story they are covering.

## Who Is Really on the Internet?

The Internet, in its broadest meaning, includes individuals, groups, organizations, grade schools, universities, commercial services, companies, governments, and free-nets who use the standard TCP/IP protocols and usually maintain full-time connections to the Net.

There are a variety of opinions about what is meant by "being on the Internet." For the purposes of this book, "being on the Internet" means having access to all of the main Internet systems such as FTP, Gopher, Telnet, e-mail, and the World Wide Web. There are many commercial Internet access providers who offer access to all of those systems via normal telephone lines (see Appendix A). Commercial information services such as America Online and CompuServe have in the past only offered e-mail access to the Internet. Now they are very actively offering access to most Internet systems, as well as maintaining proprietary information and services available only to their customers. Their addition of tools for creating Web pages, and the access they provide from the whole Web to these pages, make these services useful to online business startups who want to explore online marketing.

For the most part, communication over the Internet has been in English. Servers in Europe, Asia, and South America are usually reached via English menus. Recently, however, browsers that can display the character sets used by many other languages have become available. These are making the Web accessible to a much larger worldwide audience. Businesses that are seriously interested in international markets should now consider developing online sites in multiple languages.

Table 1.1 shows international Internet codes for countries with Internet connectivity.

**Table 1.1 International Internet codes for countries currently on the Internet.**

| Code | Country |
| --- | --- |
| AL | Albania (Republic of) |
| DZ | Algeria (People's Democratic Republic of) |
| AS | American Samoa |
| AD | Andorra (Principality of) |
| AO | Angola (People's Republic of) |
| AI | Anguilla |
| AQ | Antarctica |
| AG | Antigua and Barbuda |
| AR | Argentina (Argentine Republic) |

*(continues)*

**Table 1.1** (*Continued*)

| | |
|---|---|
| AM | Armenia |
| AW | Aruba |
| AU | Australia |
| AT | Austria (Republic of) |
| AZ | Azerbaijan |
| BS | Bahamas (Commonwealth of the) |
| BH | Bahrain (State of) |
| BD | Bangladesh (People's Republic of) |
| BB | Barbados |
| BY | Belarus |
| BE | Belgium (Kingdom of) |
| BZ | Belize |
| BJ | Benin (People's Republic of) |
| BM | Bermuda |
| BT | Bhutan (Kingdom of) |
| BO | Bolivia (Republic of) |
| BA | Bosnia-Herzegovina |
| BW | Botswana (Republic of) |
| BV | Bouvet Island |
| BR | Brazil (Federative Republic of) |
| IO | British Indian Ocean Territory |
| BN | Brunei Darussalam |
| BG | Bulgaria (Republic of) |
| BF | Burkina Faso (formerly Upper Volta) |
| BI | Burundi (Republic of) |
| KH | Cambodia |
| CM | Cameroon (Republic of) |
| CA | Canada |
| CV | Cape Verde (Republic of) |
| KY | Cayman Islands |
| CF | Central African Republic |
| TD | Chad (Republic of) |
| CL | Chile (Republic of) |
| CN | China (People's Republic of) |
| CX | Christmas Island (Indian Ocean) |

CO  Colombia (Republic of)
KM  Comoros (Islamic Federal Republic of the)
CK  Cook Islands
CR  Costa Rica (Republic of)
CI  Cote d'Ivoire (Republic of)
HR  Croatia
CU  Cuba (Republic of)
CY  Cyprus (Republic of)
CZ  Czech Republic
DK  Denmark (Kingdom of)
DJ  Djibouti (Republic of)
DO  Dominican Republic
TP  East Timor
EC  Ecuador (Republic of)
EG  Egypt (Arab Republic of)
SV  El Salvador (Republic of)
GQ  Equatorial Guinea (Republic of)
ER  Eritrea
EE  Estonia (Republic of)
ET  Ethiopia (People's Democratic Republic of)
FO  Faroe Islands
FJ  Fiji (Republic of)
FI  Finland (Republic of)
FR  France (French Republic)
GF  French Guiana
PF  French Polynesia
GM  Gambia (Republic of the)
GE  Georgia (Republic of)
DE  Germany (Federal Republic of)
GH  Ghana (Republic of)
GI  Gibraltar
GR  Greece (Hellenic Republic)
GL  Greenland
GD  Grenada
GP  Guadeloupe (French Department of)
GU  Guam
GT  Guatemala (Republic of)

*(continues)*

**Table 1.1** (*Continued*)

| | |
|---|---|
| GN | Guinea (Republic of) |
| GY | Guyana (Republic of) |
| HT | Haiti (Republic of) |
| HN | Honduras (Republic of) |
| HK | Hong Kong |
| HU | Hungary (Republic of) |
| IS | Iceland (Republic of) |
| IN | India (Republic of) |
| ID | Indonesia (Republic of) |
| IR | Iran (Islamic Republic of) |
| IE | Ireland |
| IL | Israel (State of) |
| IT | Italy (Italian Republic) |
| JM | Jamaica |
| JP | Japan |
| JO | Jordan (Hashemite Kingdom of) |
| KZ | Kazakhstan |
| KE | Kenya (Republic of) |
| KI | Kiribati (Republic of) |
| KR | Korea (Republic of ) |
| KW | Kuwait (State of) |
| KG | Kyrgyz Republic |
| LA | Lao People's Democratic Republic |
| LV | Latvia (Republic of) |
| LB | Lebanon (Lebanese Republic) |
| LS | Lesotho (Kingdom of) |
| LI | Liechtenstein (Principality of) |
| LT | Lithuania |
| LU | Luxembourg (Grand Duchy of) |
| MO | Macau (Ao-me'n) |
| MK | Macedonia (former Yugoslav Republic of) |
| MG | Madagascar (Democratic Republic of) |
| MW | Malawi (Republic of) |
| MY | Malaysia |
| ML | Mali (Republic of) |

| | |
|---|---|
| MT | Malta (Republic of) |
| MH | Marshall Islands (Republic of the) |
| MU | Mauritius |
| MX | Mexico (United Mexican States) |
| MD | Moldova (Republic of) |
| MC | Monaco (Principality of) |
| MN | Mongolia |
| MA | Morocco (Kingdom of) |
| MZ | Mozambique (People's Republic of) |
| NA | Namibia (Republic of) |
| NR | Nauru (Republic of) |
| NP | Nepal (Kingdom of) |
| NL | Netherlands (Kingdom of the) |
| AN | Netherlands Antilles |
| NC | New Caledonia |
| NZ | New Zealand |
| NI | Nicaragua (Republic of) |
| NE | Niger (Republic of the) |
| NG | Nigeria (Federal Republic of) |
| NU | Niue |
| NO | Norway (Kingdom of) |
| PK | Pakistan (Islamic Republic of) |
| PA | Panama (Republic of) |
| PG | Papua New Guinea |
| PY | Paraguay (Republic of) |
| PE | Peru (Republic of) |
| PH | Philippines (Republic of the) |
| PL | Poland (Republic of) |
| PT | Portugal (Portuguese Republic) |
| PR | Puerto Rico |
| RE | Réunion (French Department of) |
| RO | Romania |
| RU | Russian Federation |
| LC | Saint Lucia |
| VC | Saint Vincent and the Grenadines |
| WS | Samoa (Independent State of) |
| SM | San Marino (Republic of) |

*(continues)*

**Table 1.1 (*Continued*)**

| | |
|---|---|
| SA | Saudi Arabia (Kingdom of) |
| SN | Senegal (Republic of) |
| SC | Seychelles (Republic of) |
| SL | Sierra Leone (Republic of) |
| SG | Singapore (Republic of) |
| SK | Slovakia |
| SI | Slovenia |
| SB | Solomon Islands |
| ZA | South Africa (Republic of) |
| ES | Spain (Kingdom of) |
| LK | Sri Lanka (Democratic Socialist Republic of) |
| SD | Sudan (Democratic Republic of the) |
| SR | Suriname (Republic of) |
| SJ | Svalbard and Jan Mayen Islands |
| SZ | Swaziland (Kingdom of) |
| SE | Sweden (Kingdom of) |
| CH | Switzerland (Swiss Confederation) |
| TW | Taiwan |
| TJ | Tajikistan |
| TZ | Tanzania (United Republic of) |
| TH | Thailand (Kingdom of) |
| TG | Togo (Togolese Republic) |
| TO | Tonga (Kingdom of) |
| TT | Trinidad and Tobago (Republic of) |
| TN | Tunisia |
| TR | Turkey (Republic of) |
| TM | Turkmenistan |
| TV | Tuvalu |
| UG | Uganda (Republic of) |
| UA | Ukraine |
| AE | United Arab Emirates |
| GB | (UK) United Kingdom (United Kingdom of Great Britain and Northern Ireland) |
| US | United States (United States of America) |
| UY | Uruguay (Eastern Republic of) |

UZ    Uzbekistan

VU    Vanuatu (Republic of) (formerly New Hebrides)

VA    Vatican City State (Holy See)

VE    Venezuela (Republic of)

VN    Vietnam (Socialist Republic of)

VI    Virgin Islands (U.S.)

YU    Yugoslavia (Socialist Federal Republic of)

ZM    Zambia (Republic of)

ZW    Zimbabwe (Republic of)

## Who Owns the Internet and the Web?

The Internet is a voluntary undertaking. The networks connected to the Internet have all agreed on certain communication protocols regarding how packets are sent and received, e-mail addressing, and so on. There are groups and committees that work on this cooperation, such as the Internet Engineering Task Force, the Internet Assigned Number Authority, the Federal Networking Council, Network Information Centers, the Internet Architecture Board, and the Internet Society. One of these groups that a business is likely to communicate with is InterNic (currently operated by Network Solutions, Inc.), which keeps track of, and avoids duplication of, top-level Internet addresses (domain names). Applications and fees must be paid if you want your business to have a unique top-level address (though you can also provide access to your business using your Internet service provider's site address).

A network joining the Internet becomes part of the Internet, but retains control and ownership of its own network. Control is therefore shared among the thousands of networks currently connected to the Internet. Businesses joining the Internet often find that this cooperative venture is different from any other organization that they work with. It has an unusual history, and is not governed in the way that other organizations are. On the Internet, there is a significant community culture of cooperation, sharing data, and providing services and information for free. In the United States, however, it is good to remember that in general, no matter how the data is stored, transferred, or displayed, its ownership is retained by the group or individual that provides it, unless that ownership is specifically waived (see Chapter 5 for details).

## From Here . . .

If you are new to the Internet and the World Wide Web, take a direct trip to Appendix B for information on how to get on the Internet. If you've already gone online, proceed directly to Chapters 2, 3, and 4 for specific information on how businesses can use the Internet for marketing and sales.

# CHAPTER 2

# *Marketing on the Internet: The Big Picture*

Some say that marketing on the Internet is like the Wild West, but increasingly, it is becoming a more mature medium. Yet it is an exciting medium for marketing, offering a new and different channel. This chapter is designed to give some context for Internet marketing. Chapter 3 will introduce the concepts of the Web and how to use it for business, while Chapter 4 will outline marketing strategies.

Let's get started by taking a look at what is going on, and the nature of the medium for marketing.

## What Is Working Out There Anyhow?

From a marketing perspective, there are some very successful sites that are providing value and, in some cases, a new revenue stream. There are marketing, informational, branding, and sales sites. What follows is a sampling to show some of the diversity.

### CDnow

*http://www.cdnow.com*

CDnow sells CDs—and lots of them: 165,000 products. This site is a great example of a sales site (Figure 2.1). It has the Internet Jukebox, us-

**Figure 2.1 CDnow (graphics interface).**

ing RealAudio. This facility lets you listen to music in six genres while you surf . . . it plays while you explore the Net.

It also has Music News for news, interviews, and information on the Net; JazzOnline, full of profiles, event information, concert schedules, and discussions; and The Concert Connection, for access to a large on-line database of concert information covering over 500 artists globally. Other features are Music of the World, the Magazine Warehouse, gift certificates, and job listings in the music business.

As a part of its search feature, CDnow provides access to the All-Music Guide discography, which includes titles not available for sale.

Some design niceties on the site include up-front choices for graphics or text, good navigation buttons, and search features. They have a consistent tool bar for finding music, classical music, games, movies, working with your account, going to "cool links," and getting help.

**Figure 2.2 The Cybergrrl Webstation (enhanced view).**

## Cybergrrl

*http://www.cybergrrl.com*

The Cybergrrl Webstation (Figure 2.2) is a site focused on reaching women on the Web. It has a variety of features, and also provides a marketing outlet for Cybergrrl creations—examples of Web site development and marketing. This site is targeted at a clear and growing segment of the Net market: women.

There are Cybergrrl columns to read, Sneakergrrl for sports and fitness, Cybergrrl travels, and modules on business, family life, health, and other information.

For creating community, Cybergrrl has created Webgrrls to network women on the Internet. This site also maintains a newsletter. And Cybergrrl offers a choice of no-frills viewing for low graphics browsing, or enhanced viewing for full graphics.

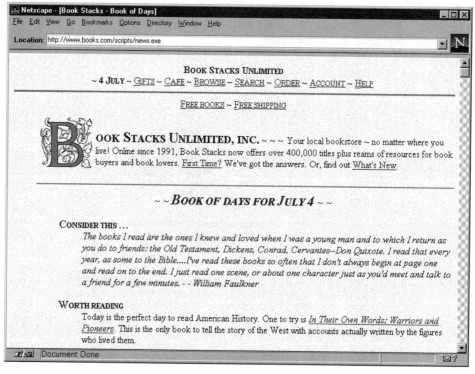

**Figure 2.3 The Book Stacks Unlimited page.**

## Book Stacks Unlimited

*http://www.books.com*

Book Stacks is a virtual bookstore on the Net. It is unusual in that it is a comprehensive bookstore selling all kinds of books, not just computer or Net books. This site has special sales, a cafe to chat and meet authors, gifts, and an excellent search facility (Figure 2.3).

Book Stacks is "your local bookstore ~ no matter where you live!" This site began life as a BBS (bulletin board) business that migrated to the Net first as a Telnet site, which is still maintained.

Book Stacks chooses books to feature under Worth Reading; the site also features audio files of authors and events with TrueSpeech or Real-Audio, community building reading groups, new arrivals, daily quotes, literary lore, special interest groups, events in history—and, of course, book sales.

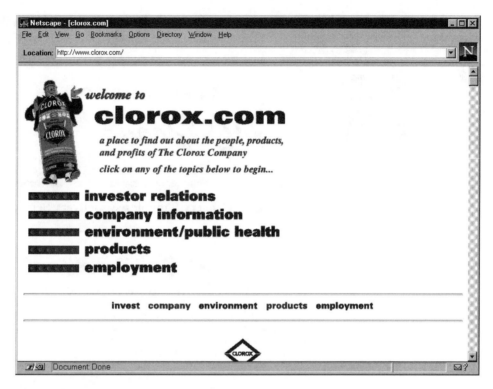

**Figure 2.4 The Clorox homepage.**

## Clorox

*http://www.clorox.com*

Now, this is not a jazzy site for hot sales. It is a corporate presence site. It maintains the brand image well. It covers investor information, the company and its history, products, employment opportunities, and environmental information. It is a good example of a solid company information site (Figure 2.4).

The link to "The Company" includes items such as a message from the CEO, access to press releases, a company profile, their history, and information about community affairs.

Under Investor Relations, for example, is a fairly standard set of documents including the 1995 Annual Report Highlights, Clorox Stock Price (CLX), 52-Week Price History Chart, Investor Information Package, Information on their transfer agent, First Chicago Trust Company of New York, and EDGAR-SEC Filings.

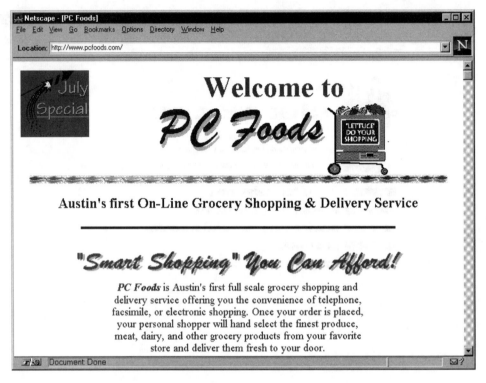

**Figure 2.5 The PC Foods homepage.**

## PC Foods

*http://www.pcfoods.com/*

PC Foods is a virtual business. It has no shelves of comestibles, paper towels, or dog food. No baskets, no aisles. It is a grocery shopping and delivery service. Orders can be placed via telephone, facsimile, Web page, or e-mail. The motto of PC Foods is: "Lettuce do your shopping" as seen in Figure 2.5.

Under About Our Service, they start with the hook "so what is the catch?" as a clever way of approaching the marketing issue of "why choose us." They provide a FAQ, and customer testimonials.

New customers can use a guest demo account to test out various options before you sign up. Accounts include access to the shopping page, bulletin boards, and your choices. Once you register, you are on your way.

## What Is the Nature of the Medium for Marketing?

Some people say that marketing is marketing regardless of the medium, and there is some truth to that. But on the Net, marketing *is* different. The online culture presents some expectations and challenges. It has some unique characteristics. The following themes will recur frequently throughout this book, since they are fundamental to understanding the Internet and the Web as media:

- It is *fast*—things happen quickly, and information flows like lightning.
- It *changes rapidly*—the Internet of yesterday is not the same as the Internet of today.
- *New tools* are coming along quickly—software and hardware development is incredibly nimble, and arises from nontraditional sources.
- *New users* of all kinds are coming online—the commercial services are bringing more users, and more diverse users, online, and Internet service providers are springing up everywhere.

The only constant? *Change.*

## Internet Culture: When in Rome, Do as the Romans Do

The Internet, like any place or community, has its own culture, and it behooves marketers to understand it and to become a part of that culture.

What are some of the hallmarks of this culture?

- Internauts expect information, and lots of it.
- Internauts expect to receive this information largely, or at least partially, for free.
- Internauts do not appreciate unsolicited commercial e-mail.
- Internauts expect good content at a site. They generally do not appreciate lots of flash and slogans with no substance.

This is not to say that creative marketers cannot push the envelope, but it does mean that being a member of the community is important. (In Chapter 5 you can find information on acceptable use policies.)

## What's the Buzz? Marketing Issues Raised by the Medium

Currently, the Internet and the Web area are characterized by some other key concepts regarding content and the character of the users:

- Everyone Can Be a Publisher

  Unlike offline marketing, the online medium permits everyone to be a publisher—anyone can put together a site, and can do so very economically. You can put massive quantities of information online, available to a large audience, quickly and relatively cheaply. This changes the nature of competition considerably.

- The Balance of Content and Design—Content, Content, Content

  The saying goes that in real estate, the key success is "location, location, location." The medium of the Web offers great interplay between spiffy design and solid content, and demands both: think content, content, content.

  Because of the expectation that sites will offer large quantities of information, paying attention to the site content is key.

- Is It Broadcasting or Is It Narrowcasting?

  Most business people think of marketing as a mass broadcast opportunity, but the Net is narrowcasting: you reach people one at a time through targeted messages. The Internet is for the most part a one-on-one medium, not a mass market.

  The audience can be one of qualified users, because they *choose* to visit your site. They are taking positive action.

- Push vs. Pull

  Marketing on the Internet is a "pull" activity. Mediums that can place the information "in your face" easily are "push" marketing mediums. As a marketer on the Internet, however, you must bring the audience to the site, and entice them to stay.

These characteristics help to make the Internet and the Web a unique marketing mileu, and challenges the marketer to think more creatively about the Net as a channel.

## Marketing *to* the Internet

The nature of the medium itself, the methods for access, and the people who use the medium, all suggest that on the Internet some kinds of products will sell better than others—with this caveat in mind: the range of successful activities in business, sales, and promotion is growing wider and deeper, not shrinking. The following characterizations of successful selling on the Internet represent a snapshot of current practices, and should not be viewed as constraints.

## Marketing Through Information

Items can be marketed through *information*. Items that sell well online can be described in depth; consumers are already accustomed to making purchases based on descriptions, from experience with mail-order catalogs. On the Net, as in a mail-order catalog, the consumer reads about the product, sees a picture, and uses that information to make a decision.

For example, consumers who come to the Virtual Vinyards page (*http://www.virtualvin.com*) come seeking particular items—say, a Chateau Montelena, 1993 "Calistoga Cuvee" Cabernet Sauvignon, Napa Valley. They are not coming to taste the wine! They either already know about a particular wine, or understand how to read the language of wine descriptions—they understand the terms *leggy, dry, acidity, tannin, oak,* and *complexity,* and they know what to expect from a Gewurztraminer or a Merlot.

In the business-to-business arena, Faucets Online (*http://www.faucet. com*) is another example. The company has moved its large catalog of faucets to the Web, and contractors purchase these via descriptions and stock numbers, not through browsing the shelves.

## Marketing to the Techno-Gadgeteer

One obvious group of products and services that are well-tuned to marketing on the Internet are those that are *technology related*. After all, just about every person that surfs the Net has a computer, software, and a modem, and is comfortable with that technology.

Other items that do well with Internet marketing are those items that appeal to the techno-savvy or the techno-gadgeteer. These consumers want the latest, most sophisticated hardware, gadgets, personal information managers, software, and satellite guidance system for their car. An example of a site that takes advantage of this is the Sharper Image site (*http://www.sharperimage.com*), which specializes in high-tech items (Figure 2.6).

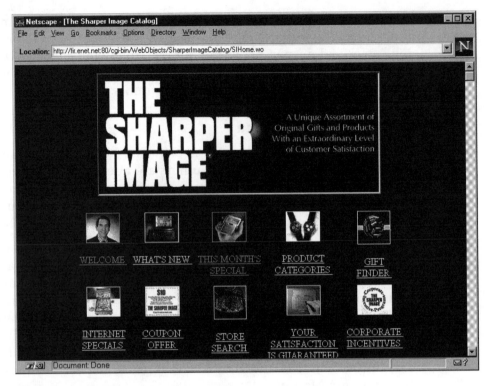

**Figure 2.6 The Sharper Image page.**

## Marketing to the Online Denizens

Products and services that appeal to the online demographic are naturals. The assessment of who is on the Net differs according to who is surveying, and the numbers change all the time, but an appeal to middle- and upper-income males under 40 is a good bet. According to recent studies, growth markets include women (part of the niche of Cybergrrl, mentioned above) and those over 60. Chapter 4 has more information on the demographics of the Web and Net.

## Marketing to the World

Products and services that appeal to a global market work well with Internet marketing efforts. Those that cross geographic and cultural boundaries are ideal for the global Internet.

For some businesses this market is an expansion of current core business functions, while for others it represents economically sound methods for reaching existing customers.

## Marketing to the Niche

Internet marketing can target users interested in unique items like crafts, collectibles such as antiques and baseball cards, and other very narrow, definable interests. Cliff Kurtzman, President of the Tenagra Corporation, calls this niche something that people have a passion for, such as golf or tennis. Sports fans are particularly representative of this niche marketing.

The iGolf site is a good example of this kind of niche market, covering all things golf (Figure 2.7).

**Figure 2.7 The iGolf page.**

## Internet Marketing Hazards

There are some potholes awaiting you as an Internet marketer. To avoid them, these strategies may prove useful:

- Before you commit to any Internet/Web strategy, do a thorough competitive and marketing assessment.
- Bring key management on board. Spend some time educating management about the Internet and its potential. Get substantial buy-in.
- Identify/hire a key manager. Don't try to do Internet marketing by committee.
- Prepare for the speed and reach of the Internet. It's blindingly fast (both good and bad news move quickly), and it's a global network.
- Be mindful of the medium—design for the Net and the Web rather than taking paper-based or television-based marketing and simply putting it up on the Net.
- Promote the Internet with your other media. Promote your Web site on and offline.

These concepts are further explored in Chapter 4 as well.

## New Technologies and How to Utilize Them

The Internet is still a train racing down the track. Time is very compressed, and traditional marketing professionals often do not account for this speed in their strategies.

One of the hallmarks of online marketing is that new tools sometimes present themselves overnight. Right now marketers need to think about such technologies as these examples:

- Java—provides for on-the-fly executable "applets" (mini-applications or programs) for motion, sound, calculation, and other functionality
- Shockwave—multimedia embedded movies
- RealAudio—audio in real time or via files
- New HTML/VRML tags—the new tags and 3D capabilities

- Internet Phones—the ability to use the Net as a full-duplex telephone
- Web chat—interactive group chats on Web sites

The bottom line, however, is that you must determine which of these tools your customer will have and use, and how you can use these tools to enhance the marketing message. If they are just for show, you may want to reconsider. The average surfer operates between 9600 baud and 14,400 baud (modem speed), and so would not be able to take advantage of the tools anyway, since most sophisticated tools operate at baud rates of 14,400 or more. Depending on the market you want to reach, the new technologies may or may not reinforce your marketing strategy. For more description of some new Internet technologies, see Chapter 7, where there is a discussion of adding animation, images, and sounds to your site in a realistic, customer-friendly manner.

## From Here . . .

Chapter 3 explains the Web and how to use it for business, and then Chapter 4 continues on to discuss successful Web marketing strategies.

# Successful Marketing on the Internet

# *The World Wide Web— Using It for Business*

The World Wide Web is a vast network of documents that are linked together; a set of protocols defining how the system works and transfers data; a set of conventions; and a body of software that make it work smoothly. The Web uses hypertext and multimedia techniques to make the Internet easy for anyone to use, browse, and contribute to.

The Web is nonlinear by nature and by design—you can jump from topic to topic, document to document, and site to site all over the Web. On the Web, any page is an entry point and can be used to navigate to others. Traditional written materials take a more linear approach to information, whereby one moves sequentially through a document. On the Web, individual readers will not be following the same structure of information in the same way.

The Web is a wide-area hypermedia system aimed at universal access. One of its key features is the ease with which an individual person or company can become part of the Web and contribute to the Web.

The World Wide Web began at the European Laboratory for Particle Physics (CERN) as a way of building a system of linked, distributed hypermedia—linked multimedia. Physicists were able to see models and images along with the text, and those files could reside anywhere on the Web.

The Web uses documents that have been created using HyperText Markup Language (HTML). HTML allows the creator of a document file to embed instructions for linking from specific points in that file to other files—images, sound files, movies, and more. When you activate one of these embedded links by selecting or clicking, you jump to the file it links to, whether it is at the local site or on another computer around the world. Just click on an item, and you move seamlessly through hyperspace to that item using a special Internet protocol called HTTP (HyperText Transfer Protocol).

When you create a Web page, you can link items on your page to other items at remote sites created by other Web authors. If this page were a hypertext document, I might embed a link to CERN to allow my readers to jump to the CERN site and then return here to keep reading.

To view the specially prepared documents, you use a browser—this is software that can read and interpret an HTML document and invoke the required transfer protocols. Some popular browsers are Microsoft Internet Explorer, Netscape, Mosaic, Cello, Lynx, and WebSurfer.

These browsers can access HTML files as well as other kinds of files using the File Transfer Protocol (FTP), Gopher, Net News Transfer Protocol (NNTP), Telnet, and other tools. A good Web browser can make navigating the Internet much easier. In addition, the browsers often make searching and downloading of documents easy. Appendix B describes some of the most popular graphical browsers, while Appendix C discusses Lynx, the most popular text-based browser.

When you look at a hypertext document using a browser, you will see the embedded pointers or links to other text—they appear simply as highlighted words, or images, or buttons that you can select or click on easily. HTTP hides the complexity of the technical side of the Web. When you select or click on a highlighted item, you quickly and seamlessly move around the vast Web, without having to enter a URL (address) like *http://www.oak-ridge.com*.

The Web links any file using:

- FTP
- WAIS
- Gopher
- Usenet

- Telnet
- Hytelnet
- Man pages
- Hypertext
- Hypermedia

## A Quick Web Tour

Suppose I wanted to locate information on marketing on the Web. My choice of starting place could be Thomas Ho's Favorite Electronic Commerce WWW Resources at URL *http://e-comm.iworld.com/*.

Using my browser, I enter the URL and arrive at the page. Ho arranges the information by topic:

- Introduction
- Background
- E.C [Electronic Commerce] Examples
- Visibility
- Information
- Related Areas

I'm a little unsure where advertising information might be, so I do a little exploring and find it under *Background:*

- General articles
- Advertising (Figure 3.1)

I have a look around at these items under Advertising:

- The Bottom 95%
- Internet Express
- QVC Local
- ReliefNet (EarthWeb)
- TechWeb Live
- Newspaper advertising
- "Interesting" niche marketing

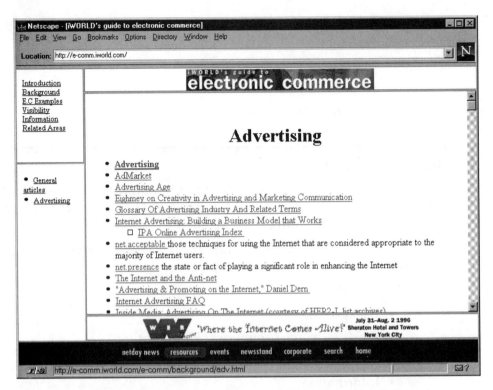

**Figure 3.1 The Advertising page of Thomas Ho's Favorite Electronic Commerce WWW Resources.**

Each of these items is linked to its own URL; if I click on an item, I will be taken to another page. For example, Internet Express is linked to *http://www.usa.net/* and The Bottom 95% is linked to *http://www.dartmouth.edu/~jaundice/bottom95/*. However, I don't have to know about these URLs; I can just click items of interest and surf the Net, never worrying about the URL or location of the pages I visit.

On this Advertising page, again there are a number of interesting choices, but at this point I move back up by just clicking, to *Information* (as shown in Figure 3.2) and choose *Print* and then *Print Publications Related to Business Use of the Internet*, which takes me out to Tenagra Corporation's page (*http://arganet.tenagra.com/books.html*), shown in Figure 3.3.

The link I select is to the Online Advertising Discussion List at *http://www.tenagra.com/online-ads/* (Figure 3.4).

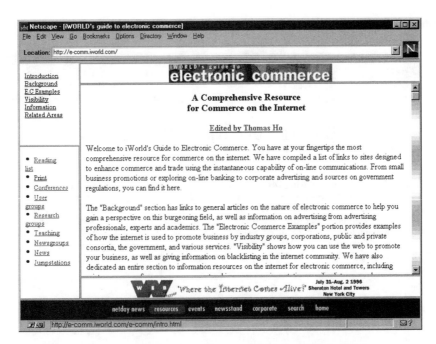

**Figure 3.2 The Information section of Thomas Ho's list.**

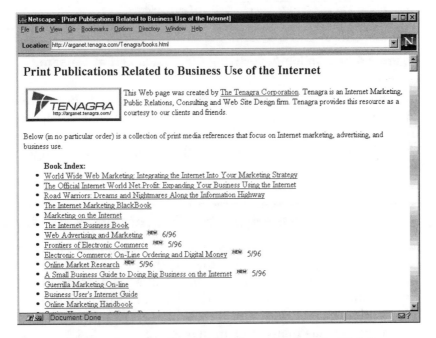

**Figure 3.3 The Tenagra Corporation's page showing Print Publications Related to Business Use of the Internet.**

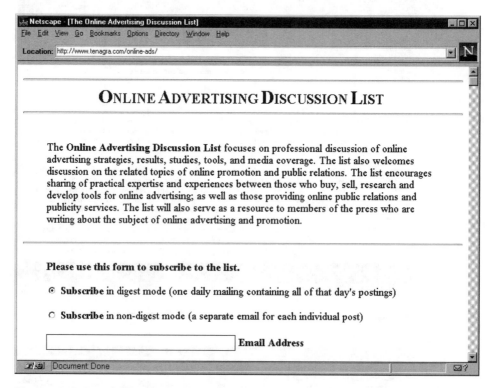

**Figure 3.4 The Online Advertising Discussion List at Tenagra.**

This journey is to illustrate the power of the Web—seamless movement from topic to topic—and to demonstrate that at each page, there are other branches to take. Visitors structure their own journey through the information, which is one of the significant challenges to online marketers.

## HTML, HTTP, and Multimedia—the Foundations of the Web

The crux of the excitement over the Web in support of commerce is in two main features: its multimedia capability, and its interactivity. Web pages can display full-color, animated images accompanied by sound using some of the more user-friendly point-and-click browsers. The powerful interactivity of the Web, which allows data entry and interactive response, has many uses in marketing.

## HyperText Markup Language (HTML)

HyperText Markup Language, or HTML, is the system used to create pages and documents for display on the Web. HTML documents can be prepared on any standard text editor, though the task is easier with an editor designed for HTML authoring such as HotDog, FrontPage, or GNNPress. Some HTML editors can convert plain text files to HTML documents, and some help you create more sophisticated documents with the use of templates. In either case, you need to learn the structure of HTML documents and how to use the individual components.

In the following example, the strange-looking character combinations are HTML tags that tell the browser program how the page is to be displayed (text size and location, which pictures to display, etc.). Chapter 6 will go into detail on how you can use these to write your own Web pages, but for now, this is just a quick peek under the hood.

```
<HTML>
<HEAD>
<!- HTML document prepared by Oak Ridge Research
oakridge@world.std.com  ->
<TITLE>Oak Ridge Research's Selected Internet Business
Resources</TITLE>
</HEAD>
<BODY bgcolor="#ffffff">
<CENTER>
<IMG ALIGN=bottom SRC="ibr.gif"><BR>
<B>There are tens of thousands of resources for businesses on
the Internet.</B><BR>
<B>Here are some good starting points for exploring
them:</B><P>
</CENTER>
<H5>Reminder: Add this page, or the <A HREF="orr.html">Oak
Ridge Research Home Page</A>, to your browser's bookmark file
before you link out to one of these sites. That way you'll
easily be able to find these resources on another day.</H5>
<H6>Updated 6/18/96</H6>
<IMG ALIGN=bottom SRC="starblbl.gif"><BR>
<IMG ALIGN=bottom SRC="rwb6line.gif"><BR>
<B>RESOURCES ABOUT, AND FOR, CONDUCTING BUSINESS ON THE
INTERNET</B><BR>
<IMG ALIGN=bottom SRC="rwb6line.gif"><P>
```

```
<a href="http://www.yahoo.com/Business/"><B>Yahoo's Business
Resources</B></a> provides a huge, well maintained, well
organized, and annotated list of Internet business resources
in categories such as:<BR>
Markets and Investments<BR>
Organizations<BR>
Electronic Commerce<BR>
Business Schools<BR>
Conventions and Conferences<BR>
Classifieds<BR>
Yahoo also lists in excess of 90,000 individual companies on
the Internet.<P>
<IMG ALIGN=bottom SRC="rwb6line.gif"><P>
<a href="http://galaxy.einet.net/galaxy.html"><B>EINet
Galaxy</B></a> provides many good starting points for Internet
searches. Their <A HREF="http://www.einet.net/galaxy/Business-
and-Commerce.html"><B>Business and Commerce</B></A> category
has business resources for business administration,
investment, marketing, sales, and organizations, and
directories of businesses and online product sources.<P>
<IMG ALIGN=bottom SRC="rwb6line.gif"><P>
The large collection of resources at Washington and Lee
University contains the category
<A HREF="http://honor.uc.wlu.edu:1020/%20%20%23hf/cl">
<B>Commerce, Business, and Accounting</B></A>which contains a
highly varied, searchable group of links to over 900 business
related resources.<P>
<IMG ALIGN=bottom SRC="rwb6line.gif"><P>
<B>LISTS OF BUSINESSES CONDUCTING BUSINESS ON THE
INTERNET</B><BR>
<IMG ALIGN=bottom SRC="rwb6line.gif"><P>
Search by keyword, or browse alphabetical lists of links to
business sites at Open Market's <a
href="http://www.directory.net/"><B>Commercial Sites
Index</B></a>. You can also register your business's Internet
site with them.<P>
<IMG ALIGN=bottom SRC="rwb6line.gif"><P>
The <a href="http://www.bbcnc.org.uk/babbage/market.html">
<B>BBC</B> </a>, source of radio and TV for Britian and
international shortwave, provides a list which includes
businesses and business resources world-wide in a searchable
database.
```

```
<IMG ALIGN=bottom SRC="rwb6line.gif"><P>
<A HREF="http://e-comm.iworld.com/"><B>iWorld's Guide to
Electronic Commerce</B></A> is a very high quality source of
business resources and resource links including conferences,
articles, small business information, advertising, government
regulations, and news. It's editor, Thomas Ho, provided one of
the earliest online commerce resource lists.
<IMG ALIGN=bottom SRC="rwb6line.gif"><P>
<a href="http://www.bizweb.com/"><B>BizWeb</B></a> provides
links to over 4500 companies in a list with approx. 120
categories. It also provides acess to the "Big Book" a
database of businesses nationwide, both on and off the Web,
including, among other information, maps showing the
business's location.<P>
<IMG ALIGN=bottom SRC="rwb6line.gif"><BR>
<a href="http://branch.com:1080/"><B>Branch Mall</B></a> is a
good example of a Web based virtual mall. They provide a site
for over 100 virtual stores..<P>
<IMG ALIGN=bottom SRC="starblbl.gif">
<P>
<IMG ALIGN=bottom SRC="rwb6line.gif"><BR>
<A HREF="topnib.html"><B>The New Internet Business Book main
page</B></A><BR>
<A HREF="orr.html"><B>Back to the Oak Ridge Research
homepage</B></A><BR>
<IMG ALIGN=bottom SRC="rwb6line.gif"><P>
</BODY>
</HTML>
```

Figure 3.5 shows the same file as displayed by the Microsoft Explorer browser. Quite a difference!

Once this screen is displayed, the mouse can be used to move the pointer to one of the highlighted words. When the mouse button is clicked, the browser checks the HTML document for the URL associated with the highlighted words. It then automatically retrieves the file indicated by the URL and displays it on the screen. This new page may also have highlighted items that can be selected in order to view more documents.

This is the basic manner in which you navigate through the World Wide Web—from page to page to page and site to site, each time making your selection to move forward, or backing up to a previous page and taking another path.

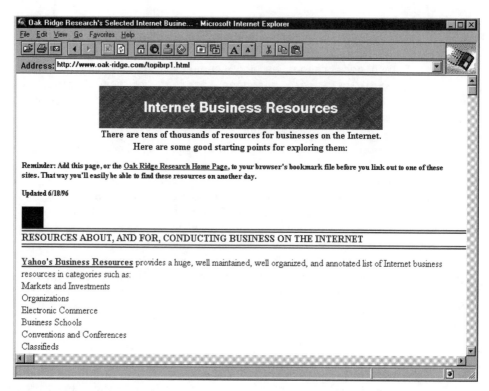

**Figure 3.5  Oak Ridge Research's Internet Business Resources page.**

## HyperText Transfer Protocol (HTTP)

The Internet operates using a suite of protocols that control and direct the passing of data across the network; collectively, these are called Transfer Control Protocol/Internet Protocol (TCP/IP). Some of these protocols are File Transfer Protocol (FTP), Simple Mail Transfer Protocol (SMTP), and HTTP. The HTTP protocol is used by the World Wide Web to transfer and process HTML files.

These protocols operate entirely behind the scenes; the average user has no need to know about TCP/IP in order to use the Internet or the Web.

## Uniform Resource Locators (URLs)

A URL is a standard way of specifying a site or page on the Internet. It is a remarkable thing—in one sense, it is the reason businesses can join the Internet so easily.

There are many different systems on the Internet for storing information and for making it available. Each system (such as Gopher, FTP, and Usenet) developed its own software and protocols. This meant that an individual had to learn the commands and characteristics of each system to use its resources. Recently, however, special programs called "browsers have been developed. These are programs that you run on your personal computer or on your Internet access provider's computer. You interact with the browser and the browser interprets your commands in a way the various systems on the Internet can understand.

The key to the browser's ability to work with so many different Internet systems is its use of URLs. URLs are a standardized way of presenting information about a file's content type and location: the file's name, the location of the computer on the Internet on which it is stored, where in that computer it is stored, and which Internet protocol is to be used to access that file. The Internet is a huge, interconnected, distributed, very un-uniform place, and the URLs bring a certain standardization to the chaos.

Here are some examples of URLs:

- *http://info.cern.ch:80/default.html*
- *gopher://gopher.std.com*
- *ftp://wuarchive.wustl.edu/mirrors*
- *news:alt.internet.services*
- *telnet://dra.com*

The first part of the URL identifies the method of access. After the colon, there are two slashes to indicate that what follows is a machine address. This can include a port specification, indicated by a colon and a number, as shown in the first example—*info.cern.ch:80*.

After the site address in the URL there is a slash and then a listing of the directory path to the file or other resource. (Notice that the slashes are *forward* slashes, not backslashes as used in DOS) In some cases the URL ends with the directory information; in others, such as HTTP URLs, a filename is often appended to the end of the URL, like *default.html* in the CERN example.

In effect, a URL pinpoints one single specific spot on the Internet—it specifies the transfer protocol, the exact location in the world of that machine, where on the machine to look, and what document to load. Browsers allow you to directly enter a URL to go to a specific document.

## Web Searching

The Web can be searched for information using any of the Web "search engines" such as Lycos (*http://www.lycos.com*), Alta Vista (*http://al-tavista.digital.com*), HotBot (*http://www.hotbot.com*), or WebCrawler (*http://www.webcrawler.com*). These and other searching programs are discussed in Chapter 9.

None of these search engines has cataloged anything close to all of the files on the Internet, but Alta Vista currently has the largest catalog.

## Getting More Information About the Web

There are numerous sources of information about the Web. The quickest introduction is a useful document called the WWW FAQ, located at *http://www.boutell.com/faq/*. A Guide to WWW Tutorials at *http://www.lib. flinders.edu.au/Guides/Web/Tutorials.html* is also helpful.

The following newsgroups have useful information:

- *news:comp.infosystems.www.users*
- *news:comp.infosystems.www.providers*
- *news:comp.infosystems.www.misc*
- *news:comp.infosystems.www.authoring.html*

## Using the Web for Business—Becoming Part of the Web

To become an information provider on the Web, you must have a Web page to start from—a "homepage." This page will have a unique URL in this form: *http://your.site.com/yourpage.html*. With this single page, you can become part of the Web and then promote your products and services, and provide information.

Businesses are using the World Wide Web with its multimedia capabilities for many of the usual business functions for developing new business, vendor contact, creating new revenue streams, brand building, communications, recruitment, information management and distribution, presenting a good public image, customer service and technical assistance, cost containment, and of course, marketing, sales, and promotion.

## Communication—Internal and External

Businesses are using HTML and the WWW for numerous communications tasks: to utilize the links, forms, and annotation features to build a set of documents, to get feedback and input on proposals, to solve problems, and to coordinate ongoing projects.

The hypertextual, multimedia characteristics of the Web are well suited to the creation of very complex linkages between documents, data, and sound files—an individual can annotate a document with a verbal comment, a picture, or a link to another document or supporting information.

Newsletters are often created using the multimedia features of HTTP, and are then made available internally (within the company's own network) and/or externally (publicly, on the Internet). Internally, they become employee communications tools. Externally, they can be for marketing and in support of other normal business communication.

Intranets—local area networks using the TCP/IP protocols for internal webs—are increasingly popular. These sites offer employees information, opportunities for collaboration, working group communication, personnel information, document development, and more.

## Information Management and Distribution

The amount of information on the Web is staggering. Business people can get everything from travel advisories and weather to stock market quotations and up-to-date news reports. They can search archives on thousands of subjects, obtain software, and much more. Chapters 9 and 10 outline some of these resources and access points.

Information is the forte of the Internet, and the Web browsers make hunting down information much easier. The browsers facilitate Gopher navigation, Gopher searches, FTP file retrieval, and Archie searches, making the locating and retrieval of information easier. The Web pages themselves, however, provide the most versatile way of offering information: with pictures, sounds, and one-click links to other documents and resources. This, combined with the ability to present documents with formatted text and layout, allows Web sites to offer information in an attractive, easy-to-understand manner.

In addition, because of the hypertext linking abilities of HTML/HTTP, any Web page author can create access to information supplied by others—databases, directories, files, images, sounds, and other resources.

Two interesting, and very different, examples of information sharing on the Internet are the Advertising Law Internet Site, and Mama's Cucina.

The Advertising Law Internet Site (Figure 3.6) was created by Lewis Rose, a partner with Arent Fox Kintner Plotkin & Kahn, who specialize

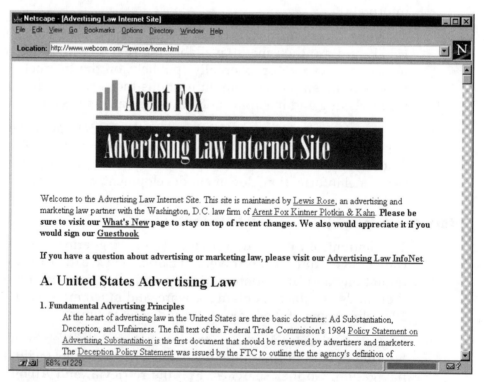

**Figure 3.6 The Advertising Law Internet page.**

in advertising, consumer protection, antitrust, and trade association law. Rose maintains a homepage (*http://www.webcom.com/~lewrose/home.html*) covering subjects related to his business, full of links to numerous kinds of information related to advertising law. For example, under United States Advertising Law you will find:

- Fundamental Advertising Principles
- Articles about Advertising Law
- FTC Advertising Guidelines and Enforcement Policy Statements
- FTC Trade Regulation Rules
- FTC Consumer Brochures
- FTC Business Compliance Manuals
- Testimony and Speeches

The site offers links to other Internet advertising, marketing, and consumer law sites:

- Federal Trade Commission
- Council of Better Business Bureaus
- European Commission on Advertising and Consumer Law

Rose also offers information about the Advertising Law Internet Site itself, a chance to join the mailing list, and an online fill-out form for e-mailing comments, accessed by clicking on his address.

The Ragu folks have a page called Mama's Cucina—Mama's Kitchen (Figure 3.7). This site (*http://www.ragu.com*) is full of information, and of course serves as a place to establish brand recognition, and to advertise and market Ragu products.

You can visit Mama's kitchen and living room, have a look at Mama's cookbook, find goodies, enter a contest to win a home theater, learn Italian, find out Mama's favorite places, read the latest installment in the Ragu soap opera, enter the Mama's Look-alike Contest, get a guided tour of Italian art and architecture, learn how to make pizza like Mama makes, take a tour of Little Italy, get the Italian desserts guide, find coupons and offers under Presents From Mama, and tell Mama what you think under "Mama Wants to Know. "

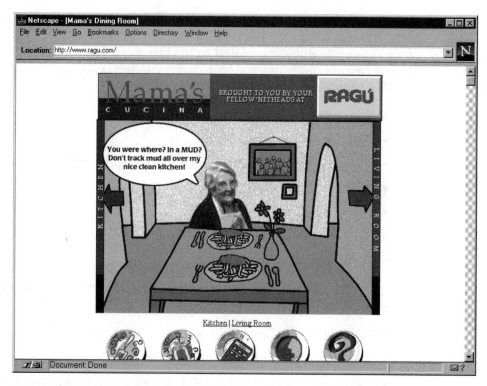

**Figure 3.7 Mama's Cucina.**

## Customer Service and Technical Assistance

Customer support and technical assistance are often provided using the WWW. Customer feedback can be sought by the use of online, on-screen forms and the "mail to" feature of Web documents.

### Technical Support

Many companies are using the Web to provide technical support to customers. The Dell Computer Corporation offers a Technical Support page at *http://www.dell.com/techinfo/* (Figure 3.8). This page offers options for Web or e-mail support, a link to Dell's newsgroup, and an opportunity to search its vendor list. In addition, Dell is offering an AutoTech system, with a branching troubleshooting guide online.

Dell's online form for requesting technical support for its products is quite extensive (Figure 3.9). You can reach it through the Technical Support page or directly at the URL *http://www.dell.com/techinfo/tsform html*.

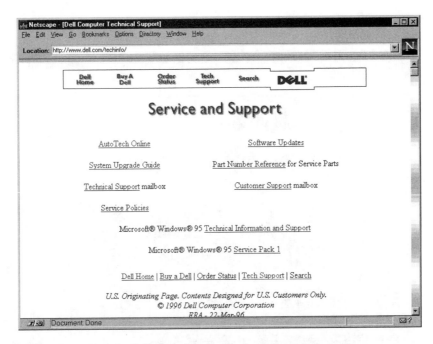

**Figure 3.8 The Dell Computer Technical Support page.**

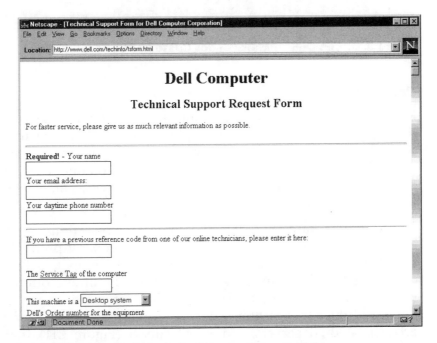

**Figure 3.9 The Dell Technical Support request form.**

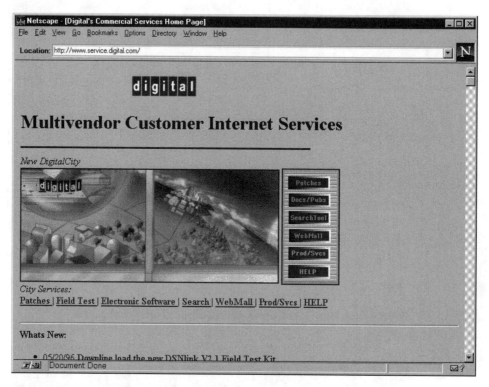

**Figure 3.10 The Digital Multivendor Customer Services page.**

### Customer Services

Many companies are offering a full range of customer services online through their Web page. For example, the Digital Equipment Corporation's Multivendor Customer Services page (*http://www.service.digital. com/*), shown in Figure 3.10, offers: information on field tests, electronic software, patches, a search feature, product services, an extensive help feature, and the WebMall.

Hewlett Packard offers the HP SupportLine page (*http://support. mayfield.hp.com*), where customers can look at company products, obtain newsletters, search the problem-solving database, look at information contributed by other users, get information about site offerings, read news about new and existing products, find information on patches and download them, get technical tips, read digests of related information, access related HP servers, and offer feedback (Figure 3.11). It also has a feature for learning to navigate HP's Web databases and information.

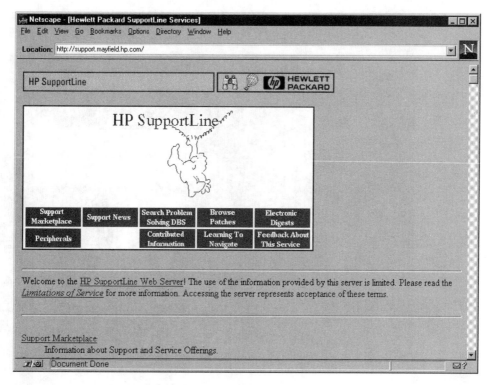

**Figure 3.11 The HP SupportLine page.**

## Presenting a Good Public Image

The Web has the ability to level the playing field for businesses dramatically. For people who encounter your business through your Web page, that page provides the image of your company. They won't necessarily know what your physical location is: whether you have offices in Trump Tower or in Yellowknife, the Northwest Territories. It may also mean that your company can move from a local into a global market, where you can gain considerable competitive advantage.

Your corporate headquarters on the Net—your homepage on the Web—can be professional, eye-catching, and functional. You gain the ability to go toe to toe on the Internet with larger and more established companies. On the Web, your business looks good if its site does.

Instead of setting up a separate site, some businesses present their pages through Internet access providers that have groups of businesses at one site. These "cybermalls," or virtual storefronts, provide a very

**Figure 3.12  iMall.**

easy way for a business to present a page; the malls also usually provide services such as online order taking, statistics about visitors to the page, and aid in developing pages.

The iMall, at *http://www.imall.com*, is one such cybermall (Figure 3.12). There you will find businesses under categories like:

- Art & Collectibles
- Automotive
- Books & Media
- Business
- Clothing
- Computers
- Electronics
- Food Court

- Gifts
- Health & Fitness
- Housewares
- Money & Finances
- Professional Services
- Real Estate
- Specialty Shops
- Sports & Recreation
- Toys & Games
- Travel

Becoming part of a cybermall means that you can fit your business into an existing "place" on the Internet. This solution is useful for some businesses; but in general, having your own site and domain will tend to make it easier for you to carry out your marketing plans.

## Cost Containment

In many cases, building and maintaining a Web presence is considerably cheaper in terms of per person contact than mass media. (The Web is not a mass medium, but rather is a one-on-one activity.) Depending on volume and your choice of access provider, the cost per visitor to your page may be less than one quarter the cost of an equivalent size mailing—and your Web page can change quickly and frequently, unlike paper-based flyers, catalogs, and other media, which change seldom and expensively.

In addition, having customers use your Web site for certain functions can create enormous savings in personnel and equipment. According to recent accounts, FedEx saves nearly $7.00 each time a customer tracks a package through its Web site form (seen in Figure 3.13) instead of calling its 800 customer support line.

## Using the Web for Marketing and Sales

Like all other activities on the Internet, Web-based marketing and sales cannot take the form of in-your-face advertising or unsolicited e-mail advertising. Your marketing and sales activities on the Web must take

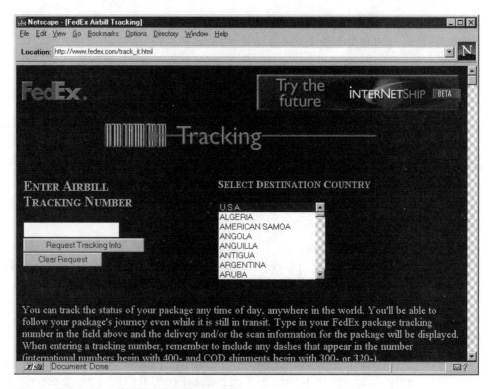

**Figure 3.13 The FedEx Tracking page.**

place in reaction to interest from customers and other site visitors. You must first attract customers to your page by providing services and information that will be useful to them. (See Chapter 4 for details on how this is done.)

One very strong marketing strategy on the Web is to offer good information and support that demonstrates the quality and expertise of your company; this will improve your business and credibility.

The Web can be used for many aspects of your marketing and sales program:

- Customer opinion surveys and feedback
- Cybermalls and virtual storefronts
- Direct sales
- Marketing research
- Public relations

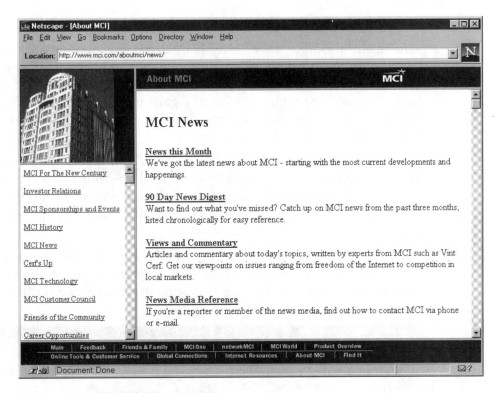

**Figure 3.14 The MCI News page.**

# Public Relations

There are numerous public relations activities that are possible on the Internet and the Web. One can cautiously distribute news releases, and sponsor events, pages, and publications.

## Press Releases

It is increasingly common to do short informational press releases of new products and services online, giving your page's URL for those seeking more information. These releases are typically posted to appropriate Usenet newsgroups, and to a few mailing lists such as *net-happenings*. One good resource is *Publicty on the Internet*, by Steve O'Keefe, published by John Wiley & Sons.

Most companies then archive their releases and informational items on the Web server for ongoing user access, as shown in the Web page of MCI (*http://www.mci.com/aboutmci/news/*) in Figure 3.14.

## Corporate Sponsorship

One useful promotional activity is that of page sponsorship for conferences, public information, government, or nonprofits. As when sponsoring a public television show, you can support useful and important activities, and through your efforts, gain visibility for your  company, products, or services. When you do this, establish a hypertext link to your page from the sponsored page.

Xerox was a major sponsor of the Olympic Games in Atlanta (*http://www.xerox.com/olympics.html*), and the Sprint Corporation sponsored the World Cup Soccer page, to the enjoyment of sports fans. In each case, a link was provided from the corporation's page—the Xerox link is seen in Figure 3.15.

Many conferences are creating homepages for conference updates, maps, room descriptions, and access to conference proceedings and papers after the conference. The sponsorship of such pages offers oppor-

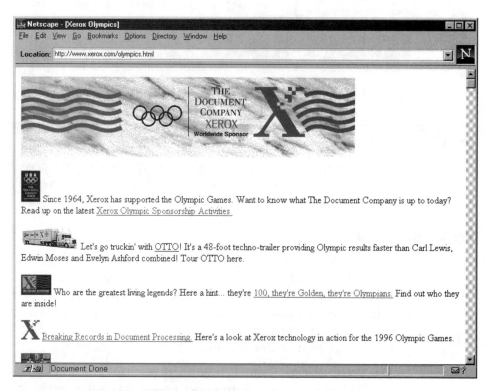

**Figure 3.15 The Xerox Olympics page.**

tunities for visibility. In addition, some companies provide listserver and archiving support to popular discussion lists, as in *com-priv* at psi.net and *online-ads* at tenagra.com.

Companies that sponsor a Web page of nonprofit activities often ask for an acknowledgment on the page in return. Figure 3.16 shows The Davis Community Network, Davis, California (*http://www.dcn.davis.ca.us/*), with its nod to its sponsors, including the California State Department of Transportation, the University of California at Davis, American Cabling and Communication, Sun Microsystems, and QUALCOMM, Inc.

## Direct Sales

The Web has opened up the entire Internet for sales activities. Your Web page can accept data entry, and can allow for direct, secure sales, either through your own site or in a cybermall or virtual storefront.

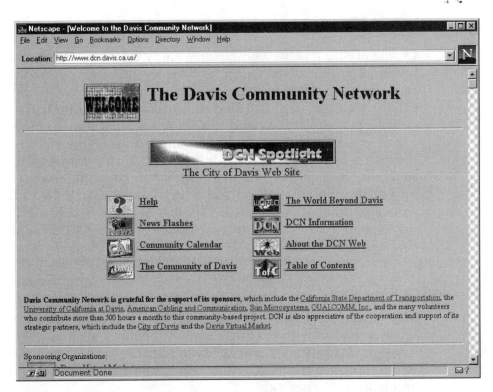

**Figure 3.16 The Davis Community Network homepage.**

### *Product Information and Flyers*

Most companies with Web pages offer a large assortment of information-rich files about their products, their industry, and related subjects. On your business Web site, you can place short flyers, teasers, and full product descriptions, pricing, and purchase information. As an example, the catalog from the Faucet Outlet Online (*http://www.faucet.com/*) is shown in Figure 3.17.

The multimedia nature of the Web makes this more interesting than it can be on the text-based online systems such as Gopher and FTP. A Web site can shine with movies, animation, colorful logos, fonts and formatting, even real-time sound. A Web site permits the Internet equivalent of a television commercial.

It is important to make your Web site interactive and interesting and provide reasons for it to be visited repeatedly. See Chapter 4 for a discussion of interactivity in Web pages.

## Online Ordering

Online ordering is becoming increasingly common. Often this involves an initial setting up of an account for an individual by sending credit card or other sensitive information via fax, telephone, or postal mail. (There are more sophisticated and more secure transaction schemes coming online, as discussed in Chapter 5.) Once an account is established, ordering proceeds through online forms on the Web site itself, or through e-mail. Book Stacks Unlimited (*http://www.books.com*) is a virtual business that has online ordering. You begin the purchase process by establishing an account, and then you can search the online bookstore and order as you browse. Another business that has online ordering is Land's End—a traditional clothier gone to the Web at *http://www.landsend.com* (Figure 3.18).

## Marketing Research

This function is just developing, but already you can use your Web site to carry out some marketing research functions such as customer surveys, product interest and reaction surveys, and some experimental real-time focus group activities using some of the Web chat software and Internet Relay Chat.

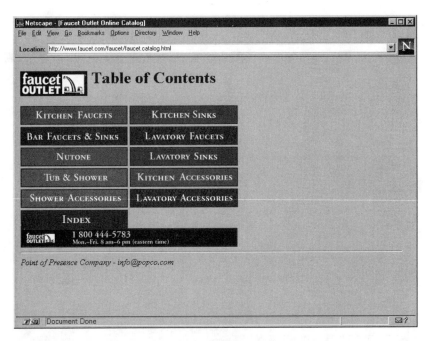

**Figure 3.17  The Faucet Outlet Online Catalog page.**

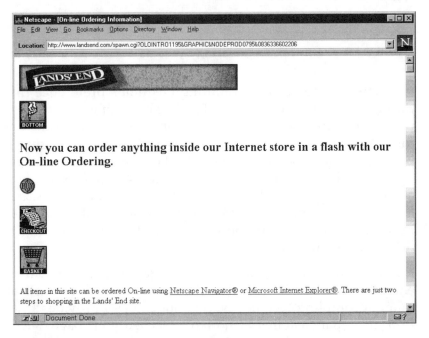

**Figure 3.18  The Lands' End Ordering Information page.**

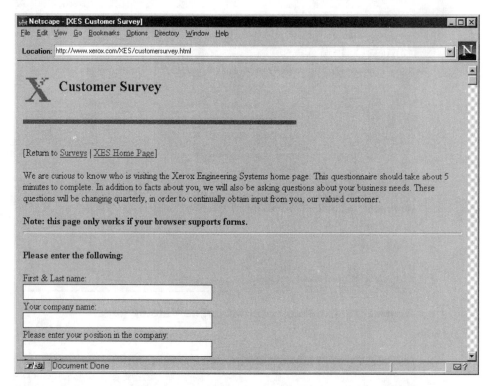

**Figure 3.19 The Xerox Engineering Systems survey data entry form.**

Some businesses are obtaining customer preference information through surveys and reviews. The Xerox Engineering Systems survey page (*http://www.xerox.com/XES/customersurvey.html*) seeks detailed information about its customers and their businesses (Figure 3.19). The page tells you how long it should take to answer the survey—5 minutes—and that the questions are changed quarterly to encourage you to come back again. The Brew Guys at *http://www.brewguys.com/survnew.htm*, who sell products to home brewmeisters, ask new customers for information about their computers, what kind of brewing they have done before, clubs, and interests.

For product development, a Web page can offer interactive database entry and reaction forms online. While not based on statistically sound random sampling techniques, this nonetheless provides fast feedback from potential customers who have reached your page. Such feedback can assist with product development and niche information for product

```
Netscape - [Netsurfer Digest Reader Demographics]                              _ □ ×
File  Edit  View  Go  Bookmarks  Options  Directory  Window  Help

Location: http://www.netsurf.com/surveys.html                                  ▼  N

Services where you maintain accounts:
    America Online               1182   17%
    Compuserve                   1687   24%
    Delphi                        133    2%
    Prodigy                       315    4%
    GEnie                         103    1%
    eWorld                        234    3%
    BBS's                        2415   34%   86%

Interests:
    Mail/Mailing Lists           5698   81%
    Usenet News                  5638   80%
    Chat/social                  1677   24%
    Education                       8    0%
    Erotica                      1555   22%
    Files/Shareware              5331   76%
    Games/Entertainment          2580   37%
    Investment/Money Management  1292   18%
    News/Information             5864   83%  420%

Internet services used:
    World Wide Web               6560   93%
    FTP                          6334   90%
    Gopher                       5242   74%
    Archie                       3963   56%  313%

Time online (hr/wk):
    1-5                          1711   24%
    6-10                         2125   30%
    11-15                         994   14%

Document: Done
```

**Figure 3.20 The Netsurfer Digest Reader Demographics page.**

placement. For example, Netsurfer Communications provides information on Netsurfer Digest reader demographics through its page at *http://www.netsurf.com/surveys.html* (Figure 3.20).

In addition, a well-constructed Web site can track the number of visitors, and the number of times your page has been accessed or "hit." Logging of page activity can include the e-mail address of the people visiting, their domain type such as *.com* or *.org*, how frequently they have visited, how long they spent, and which pages were hit the most often. This offers the marketer an idea of the popularity of a site, and can be used to track visits after a PR or advertising event.

Here are some of the Web tracking tools available now:

- NetCount (*http://www.netcount.com/*), from Price Waterhouse, offers a number of services and products, including the NetCount basic service, which is a summary of weekly activity; NetCount

Plus, which offers daily and weekly reports of traffic; and the Net-Count transfer agent. The NetCount AdCount includes counts of Exposures, Inquiries, and Click-throughs.

- I/PRO (*http://www.ipro.com/*), in partnership with Nielsen Media Research, provides services and software for independent measurement and analysis of Web sites, for site owners, advertisers, and media buyers. Products include I/COUNT for Web site usage, I/AUDIT for third-party audit reporting of Web site activity, and I/CODE Universal Registration System, which allows site owners to learn more about the demographics of visitors.

- Intersé (*http://www.interse.com/*) offers *market focus 2*, Web analysis software that includes predefined reports to analyze site activity.

- Web Reporter (*http://www.openmarket.com/reporter/*), from Open Market, is designed to track site activity and conduct visit analysis, including data filtering for log files, and cross-tab bivariate analysis for data relationships.

- Getstats (*http://www.eit.com/goodies/software/getstats/*), by Kevin Hughes, is a Web server log analyzer available for free.

## From Here . . .

Chapter 4 details strategies for Web marketing, and ways to support that marketing through collateral media and Internet tools.

# *Effective WWW Marketing— An Integrated Approach*

Getting someone's attention on the Internet is a subtle process that takes some significant time and effort.

Until 1993 the Internet was largely a text-based medium—there was no GUI for the Internet. How times have changed! The rise of multimedia on the Internet has been mirrored to a large extent by a rise in commercial interest and activity on the Internet. The multimedia Web has thus become the most popular Internet tool for marketing, advertising, and sales, allowing businesses to communicate directly with the customer (or potential customer). When the marketing on the Internet is discourse-based, businesses can expect the market to reward them.

Marketing on the Web is not like marketing using any other media. Here are some of the important differences:

- Market aggregation is somewhat different on the Internet than in offline marketing. The Web in particular is not generally considered a mass market (in spite of its numbers); rather it involves one-on-one promotion. It is a "pull"—rather than "push"—marketing environment, as discussed in Chapter 2.

- The Internet via the Web supports both vertical and horizontal markets, depending upon your product and the particular slant that you wish to give to your WWW activities. Mecklermedia started its MecklerWeb as horizontal marketing, but in its infancy changed over to a vertical market.

- Environmental scanning on the Web and the Internet generally involves a narrower look, including competitive, technological, and cultural scanning.

- Market segmentation and demographic research are very new on the Web. Reliable and valid surveys of Web demographics are just starting to be available.

## Internet and Web Demographics

There have been a number of recent studies about the Internet that attempt to describe the people who are on the Net. Some of these are discussed below; here is an interpolation of their findings.

On the Internet at large it appears that these characteristics generally hold:

- gender: 65% male [Quarterman survey 3:1, O'Reilly, 66%]
- age range: two peaks at 20-24 and 35-45
- occupation: technical, computer, academic, professional
- income: two peaks in the data, at 21K-24K and 40K-45K
- education level: highly educated

On the World Wide Web the statistics look a little different:

- gender: 68% male [new estimate: 64% male]
- age range: 20-24 [new average: 35]
- occupation: computer, technical, education
- income: 21K-25K and 35K-40K, with some estimates as high as $65,000 as an average
- education level: highly educated [67% have a college degree]

Now, time for a caution light. The Internet and the Web are moving targets—as soon as we measure them, they have changed. The studies do not have good validity and reliability, and are thus necessarily imperfect. This in no way makes them worthless; it just means that for the most part the specific numbers need to be taken with a grain of salt. The online marketer will still find it useful to compare them and observe the trends.

Dr. K's page of Internet Demographics (*http://www.bgsu.edu/depart ments/tcom/survey.html*) offers access to most of the major surveys, along with other Net measurement information. These are the major studies:

- Matrix (*http://www1.mids.org/ids2/.index.html*)
- CommerceNet/Nielsen (*http://www.commerce.net/work/pilot/ nielson_96/index.html*)
- Find/SVP (*http://etrg.findsvp.com/features/internet_demo.html*)
- GVU (*http://www.cc.gatech.edu/gvu/user_surveys*)
- Vals (*http://future.sri.com/vals/ivals.html*)

# Web Marketing—Getting Them Hooked

First you have to get someone who is on the Internet to visit your homepage—the section on registration below about making your site visible will offer ideas about this. Then you have to keep your Web site visible, on the Internet and in your print media. And once you get Web users to visit your site, it is important to supply activity and interactivity, to keep them coming back.

What can encourage a visitor to return to your site?

- *Curiosity*—If it is a large site, and there is too much to see in one online session, visitors will come back. The information and activities must not be confusing, but visitors should feel that there is a nugget just around the next corner, and that this is a valuable site, worth returning to for more exploration.

- *Item turnover*—Provide at least one item that changes frequently—even every time someone visits. This may be a "what's new" feature, but often it can be something as simple as a daily aphorism, or coverage of a current event broadly related to your industry. It can also be something like a random URL each time someone arrives at the site, or a new audio file.

- *Indispensable tool or resource*—Your page can offer links to existing databases, collections of Internet and Web guides, search tools, or a repository of images and files. While any such resources are worthwhile, your site is more likely to bring people back if the collection of links is unusually complete or high in quality. The links can be on any subject, but it makes sense to have them relate in some way to your business. Make it easier to come to your page for the set of the tools and resources than to go elsewhere.

- *Personalization*—You can let the visitor make the site "my site," customizing the environment, making the page a *home* page for the user. A good example of this is at *http://my.yahoo.com,* where the visitor creates a personal version.

- *Unique event or resource*—The page can provide contests or give-aways—some sites have given away gold coins, a house, a car, conference registrations, and other items. Or you might be able to offer first-person coverage of events such as business conferences or trade shows to increase interest in your business activities and products. Or offer an "ask the expert" feature—invite Web users to type in or e-mail questions, and then place your answers on the page. There are lots of possibilities for making your site unique and worth returning to regularly.

## Levels of Web Marketing Engagement

Much of the appeal of the Internet is its interactivity. People use the Internet because they can give and get information and services. If you use the Web solely for the static provision of information, without allowing the interactivity, your marketing will be less successful.

A successful site will allow for at least some interactivity—a place for people to post information, put their own URL by category, and so on. It is crucial to ask yourself frequently, "What can I do to bring customers to the site?" and equally important, "How can I get them to return?" Currently, there are three levels of interactivity for Web homepages:

*Level 1. Visiting the page*—The Web user navigates to the page and just views and reads it. This is the level of simple presentation of information and data: getting foot traffic.

*Level 2. Activity*—The potential customer visits the page, and can click on buttons, search for information, follow threads of interest. This is the level of nurturing more interest in the product, company, or service: getting the visitor to linger awhile.

*Level 3. Interactivity*—The page visitor can leave feedback, send e-mail, leave comments, order, chat, exchange or post messages, and in general feel some personal engagement with the page. Some of the best marketing pages, such as those offered by *Time* magazine, the Woodstock page, and HotWired, have BBS-like forums where page users can interact with each other and with people from the site. This is the level where you can actually close sales or form some kind of relationship with the potential customer: repeat business. The new Web chat and virtual worlds interfaces like The Palace are particularly good for this level.

Your site should move quickly from reactive to proactive, engaging the potential customer in an activity, and better, interactivity. The prize will go to the pages or sites that engage people. The static page will be ignored.

Some sites are currently offering a great deal of interactivity. To illustrate this point we will look at HotWired and Time Inc.'s Pathfinder.

## HotWired

HotWired, at *http://www.hotwired.com*, is an online "e-zine" (electronic magazine), sponsored by *Wired* magazine (Figure 4.1). *Wired* magazine subscriber services are offered online. HotWired's very colorful multi-faceted Web pages are designed to get the reader engaged. HotWired is having readers "join" in order to use its pages, playing on one of the fundamental needs of people, called by psychologist Abraham Maslow the need to belong.

In the site's Piazza, members can participate together in discussions in various message "areas":

- Club Wired —- real-time interactive chat
- Threads
- Forums—HeadSpace, Feedback, Electric Frontier, WireSide Chats, Wired Arena
- Rants and Raves

Members interact in the Piazza with one another, with guests, and with authors and other net.glitterati. HotWired has made extensive use of "hot" colors and abstract Picasso-esque images and icons. Figure 4.2 shows the Piazza page.

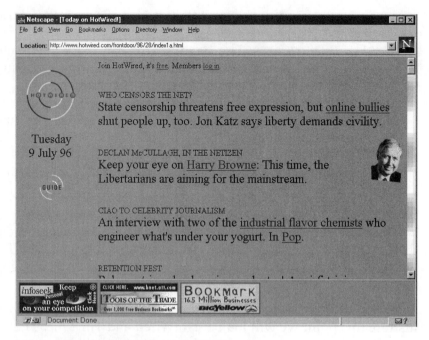

**Figure 4.1 The HotWired homepage.**

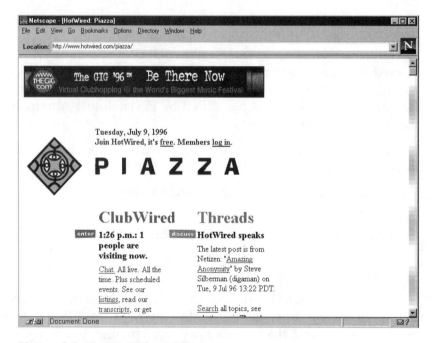

**Figure 4.2 The HotWired Piazza.**

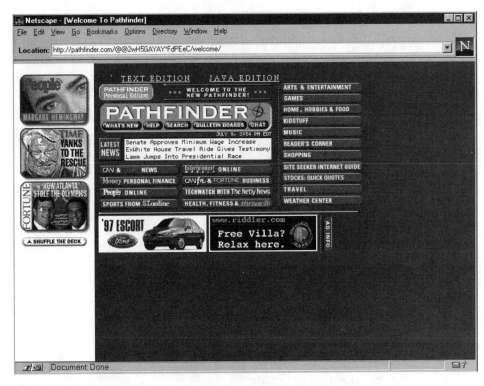

**Figure 4.3  The Time Inc. Pathfinder homepage.**

## Time Inc.'s Pathfinder

Time Inc. offers its online Pathfinder at *http://www.pathfinder.com*. Through this site, users have online access to some of Time's print materials, available to the editors and reporters at *Time* magazine and to other readers. The site has a very eye-catching homepage, as seen in Figure 4.3, but the user is offered alternative views which include pages with high graphics, pages which are mostly text and pages which use Java.

Time Worldwide offers the opportunity for users who visit its page to read articles and participate in "threaded" (topical) discussions as well as real-time interactive chats. Individuals can dialog with one another, and with *Time* editors and reporters, about content and issues.

The Pathfinder covers these topics, and includes a search feature, bulletin boards and chat:

- Pathfinder Personal Edition
- CNN & *Time* News
- *Money* Personal Finance
- CNNfn & *Fortune* Business
- *People* Online
- Sports From SIonline
- Entertainment Weekly Online
- Techwatch with The Netly News
- Health, Fitness & thrive@
- Arts & Entertainment
- Games
- Home, Hobbies & Food
- Kidstuff
- Music
- Reader's Corner
- Shopping
- Site Seeker Internet Guide
- Stocks: Quick Quotes
- Travel
- Weather Center
- Ad Info

In addition to offering a vast amount of information to readers in the form of online articles and written materials, Pathfinder offers a What's New area, interesting search services, chat areas, and message boards arranged by subject to break down "walls between readers and editors" (Figure 4.4). You can introduce yourself, and see who else has checked in to participate.

Currently, a sample of the message boards include (in Time's own words):

- Washington: How good a political analyst are you? Here's a chance to make election predictions.
- Society: People are discussing religion, racism, and they're writing great original poetry.

**Figure 4.4 The Time Pathfinder page with access to the message boards.**

- Asia/Pacific: Do you think there will ever be "Democracy in China?"

- Europe: History has a list of great statesman in Europe, but where are the Giants of Today and Tomorrow?

- Middle East/Africa: Out with the old and in with the new. Discuss the impact of the Israeli Elections on The Palestinian People.

- The Americas: Pat Buchanan is against immigration but is it really bad for the U.S.?

- The Sexes: They're still debating the idea of a cure for homosexuality while the rest of us...

- Science & Technology: Are there Alien Ruins on the Moon?

- Health & Medicine: It's the bane of people like us who are always on the keyboard...Carpal Tunnel Syndrome.

- Digital Issues: This is the place to talk about the philosophy of cyberspace as well as the "nuts and bolts" issues of hardware and software and, of course, the Communications Decency Act comes under discussion.

- Crime: Tell us how you feel about Guns, The Unabomber, and The U.S. Prison System.

- Movies, Music, Arts and Entertainment: You've always wanted to be a movie and book reviewer, right?

# Value-Added Web Sites

Web-based marketing is an opportunity to be a good Net citizen by participating in the tradition on the Internet called "giving back to the Net" or, as an Internet founder Vinton Cerf and others call it, the "gift economy" of the Internet. This activity can also make a Web-based marketing strategy work better. In planning a Web site, include consideration of what value to add. The tradition of giving back, or the gift economy, is very strong, and any business using the Web for marketing would be well advised to heed that expectation.

The range of services, products, and information used to add value to a Web site is almost limitless. Some companies offer links to related sites, some maintain directories of businesses or resources, some offer free copies of their software, or news feeds.

The homepages of Downtown Anywhere, EUnet, and Quadralay are examples of this value-added activity.

## Downtown Anywhere

Downtown Anywhere (*http://www.awa.com/*) has a Main Street for shopping, a library and newsstand, museums, galleries, a financial district, a travel center, and areas for education and sports.

Main Street, part of Downtown Anywhere, is a set of storefronts selling books, videos, financial services, CDs, encryption services, oriental rugs, computer supplies, secretarial services, and more. The site designers have structured the page to emulate a town (Figure 4.5).

In addition to the commercial vendors, Downtown Anywhere sponsors a very useful and well-structured virtual library:

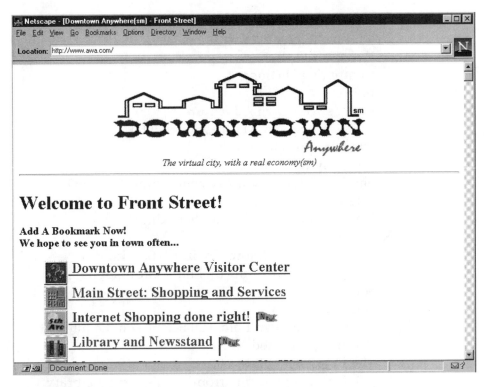

**Figure 4.5 The Downtown Anywhere homepage.**

News
    Time Magazine Online
    The Nando Times
    San Jose Mercury
    Create your own Newspaper!
    Net-Happenings Gleason Sackman's Announcements
        (Recent)
        (Searchable Archives)
    Usenet Newsgroups (with search!)
Reference Section
    Bill of Rights Status Report
    U.S. Constitution
    California Legal Codes
    Reference Desk
    Reference Shelf

Encyclopedia Britannica
On-line Reference Works
Webster's Dictionary
Computing Dictionary
Fiction
Choose Your Own Adventure
Cool Darkness by Matthew Carpenter
Dracula by Bram Stoker
The Jayhawk series by Mary K. Kuhner
Sherlock Holmes stories by Sir Arthur Conan Doyle
Tarzan of the Apes
Umney's Last Case by Stephen King
Non-Fiction
The Hacker Crackdown by Bruce Sterling
Travels with Samantha by Philip Greenspun
Science
Science Books
Cognitive and Psychological Science on the Internet
Psychology-related Newsgroups
The PSYCGRAD Project
The Psychology listing from Cern's Virtual Library
Poetry
Internet Poetry Archive
English server's Poetry Archive
Periodicals
National Computer Tectonics
Webster's Weekly
Time Magazine Online
Wired Magazine, hip &cool on the 'Net
Verbiage Magazine, short fiction
E-zine list
Other Libraries
Books On-line
Project Gutenberg Master Index
Miscellaneous
UNIX
UNIXhelp for users
the UNIX Reference Desk

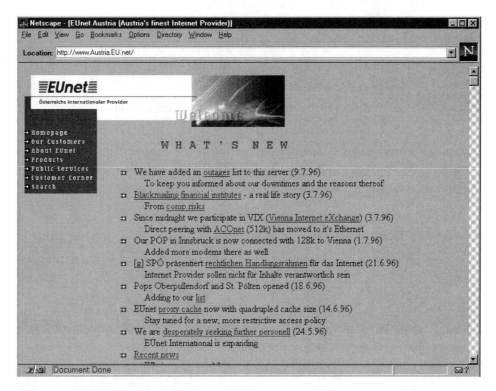

**Figure 4.6 The EUnet Austria homepage.**

In addition to the full-text books and other documents, the library section of Downtown Anywhere has links to other commercial sites such as Gadgetboy, National Computer Tectonics, OmniMedia Books, IntelProp Central, and Webster's Weekly.

## EUnet

EUnet Austria (*http://www.Austria.EU.net/*) is part of a large ISP (Eunet) serving Austria, Europe, and parts of the Middle East and Africa. Its homepage (Figure 4.6) has links to:

- EUnet services
- Information on customers and customer services
- Opportunities for feedback
- Search

All of this would be pretty well expected; but the site has value-added features including:

- HALSoft HTML Validation Service
- WWW Security FAQ
- Austria Information Systems (Sponsored)
- Domain Administration
- Online Manuals
- Archie (File Locator)
- Infotainment

## Quadralay Corporation

The Quadralay Corporation has created some Web-related commercial products, including Web Works Publisher, HTML Lite, and Web Works Search. On its homepage, seen in Figure 4.7 (*http://www.quadralay.com/*), there is a guest book, and links to product information, information on the company, an FTP server for the downloading of evaluation copies of their software, and other customer services.

Quadralay gives back to the Net by offering these free services:

- Austin City Links—Everything you ever wanted to know (and more) about Austin, Texas
- Favorite Places—links covering animals, Austin on the Web, computers, financial information, food and drink, government, HTML creation and maintenance, Internet resources, language and culture, music, news, science, sports, and travel
- C++ Archive—C++ programming-related information
- Crypto Archive—Archive of cryptography-related information
- CyberPotpourri—A miscellaneous collection of goodies
- Fuzzy Space—Archive of Fuzzy Logic information

The Austin City Links page (*http://www.quadralay.com/Austin/austin .html*), seen in Figure 4.8, provides information on Austin, the University of Texas, government, local computer people, local user groups, local restaurants, press contacts, local writers, movies, online services, local organizations, pictures of the area, recreation, services, and local Internet service providers.

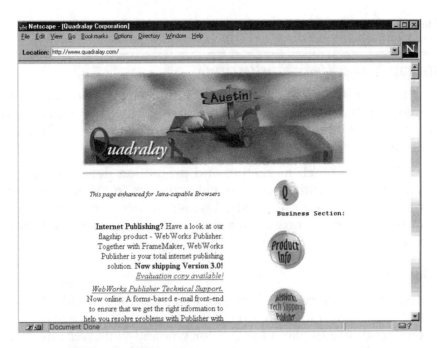

**Figure 4.7 The Quadralay homepage.**

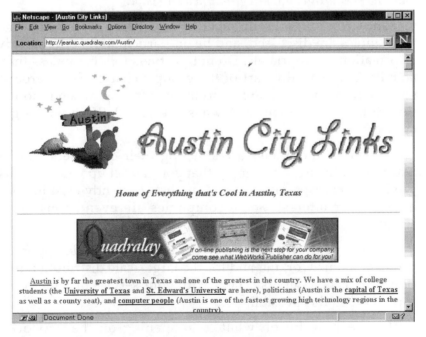

**Figure 4.8 The Austin City Limits homepage.**

# Integrating Your Web Marketing

Ultimately, the key to online marketing success using the WWW is to integrate the Web presence with other online activities, and with your existing traditional advertising and marketing efforts. It is one channel among many.

Successful Web marketing and promotion depends on supporting Web activities with other Internet activities to bring Internauts to the page. Using discussion lists, Usenet newsgroups, your e-mail, and other Internet resources to make your Web page visible can bring many new visitors to your business's page.

## Discussion Lists

The Internet discussion lists are a method for individuals to network with others on a focused topic. Joining appropriate discussion groups is one good way to gain visibility for you and your Web site. You can locate appropriate groups by using Inter-Links, a Web site designed to search for discussion lists and Usenet newsgroups by keyword—*http://www.nova.edu/Inter-Links/cgi-bin/news-lists.pl*.

Once you join a group, spend some time "reading the mail." See what topics are discussed, and begin participating, offering advice and information appropriately. Do not post ads to a list unless that kind of activity is specifically part of the group's charter. Some groups permit short, information-rich announcements offering to send more information to those who inquire. Always use your URL in your sig file (discussed below).

Most ISPs these days are assisting their customers with access to listserver software. This means that you can set up your own discussion group. This is especially useful if no lists currently exist in your area of expertise or interest. Some companies are even sponsoring groups specifically to discuss their products.

Having your own discussion list will also provide opportunities for professional networking and for the large-scale distribution of information such as newsletters. Check with your service provider for more information on this possibility.

For keeping up on what is happening on the network, joining *net-happenings* is one of the best things you can do. It is a list that broadcasts network announcements—new Web pages are announced, new sources of software and resources are mentioned. Join the list by sending the message "subscribe net-happenings" to *listserv@lists.internic.net*. *Net-happenings* can also be read as the newsgroup *comp.internet.net-happenings*.

## Usenet Newsgroups

Usenet newsgroups are another way to gain visibility. There are an estimated 15,000-20,000 groups covering almost every topic. The best approach is to locate groups to investigate by getting their FAQs (Frequently Asked Questions) and reading their charters. This will tell you more about the groups, including whether advertisements or product announcements are permitted. Many groups permit a once-a-month factual posting with pointers to your other information. The FAQ "How to find the right place to post" is invaluable in hunting down elusive groups. You can find it at *http://www.cis.ohio-state.edu/hypertext/faq/usenet/finding-groups/top.html.*

After you locate some group prospects, begin to read them regularly to see what kinds of message traffic each group has, the types of people posting, and what the norms are. Once you have done this research, you are then ready to participate. Remember to put your homepage URL in your signature when you post to the group.

In addition to participating in existing newsgroups, you can create your own group at will under the *alt.* and *biz.* hierarchies, or undertake to create a group under the existing traditional Usenet hierarchies. The FAQ called "Creating a Usenet Group" outlines the rather complex creation process. It can be located by going to URL *http://www.cis.ohio-state.edu/hypertext/faq/usenet/usenet/creating-newsgroups/top.html* (Figure 4.9) and looking under "FAQs—Creating a Usenet Group." This site will also let you access all of the Usenet FAQs, the Internet Requests For Comments (RFC), and Internet Engineering Notes (IEN).

## Mail Servers and E-mail

Many businesses have an automated mail reply feature called a mailbot or mail server that can automatically return a message to someone requesting information. Available from some ISPs, it is an easy way to support your Web site. Have the server send out the information requested, but be sure to include the URL to your Web site and informa-

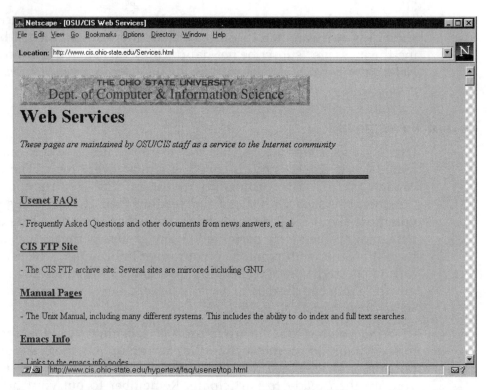

**Figure 4.9 FAQ menu of the Ohio State University CIS Department Staff Services page.**

tion about your business. Because the e-mail message is being requested, you're free to respond with less subtle advertising—as long as it is related to the topic the user was led to expect. Addresses to mail-bots usually look like this: *info@oak-ridge.com*.

## Sig Files

Signature blocks at the end of e-mail, list, and newsgroup postings are called signature (.sig) files or sigs. Most Net entrepreneurs maintain several signature files to use for different purposes. Sig files are short, 5–6 lines maximum, and generally give your name, your company, e-mail addresses, phone numbers, fax numbers, and most importantly, your homepage URL. Some people put some kind of funny or interesting saying in their sig, but be cautious about this—there is always someone who will not understand it, or possibly take offense. Here is an example of a sig file:

```
+----------------------------------------------------------+
Harrison A. Binford            Binford Internet Marketing
harrison@binford.com        http://www.binford/binford.html
1.555.555.5555 (voice)              1.555.555.5555 (FAX)

==========================================================
```
                    Internet Presence Marketing

Use your sig file as a small discreet ad for your Web site and business. Advice on using signature files and "finger" (discussed below) can be found in the FAQ "Signature and Finger Frequently Asked Questions," which can be reached on the Web page *http://www.cis.ohio-state. edu/hypertext/faq/usenet/signature_finger_faq/faq.html*.

## Announcements

Many companies make monthly announcements to various newsgroups regarding the availability of product information. Certain book publishers, for example, announce their new books all in one list (not an ad!) on the *technical.books* groups. At the top of the file they usually show their URL so that someone can visit their sales sites for more complete information.

There are public relations firms and announcement services that can assist you with this; see Chapters 10 and 11 for more information.

## FAQs

Documents that present a compilation of commonly asked questions and answers to these questions are called FAQs (Frequently Asked Questions). These were developed so that regular readers of the postings to a Usenet group or discussion list would not have to see the same questions and the same answers month after month. Now it is expected that people new to the group will read the FAQ when it is periodically re-posted to the group or list, or get it from one of the archives that store FAQs. Many of these are also posted periodically to *news.answers*.

Take a look at several FAQs to understand the usual style, and read the postings to a group for a while to gauge the type and level of the questions. Then select a subject area that is appropriate to your business and create a FAQ. This can then help establish your business's expertise, build confidence in your business, and give your business a sense of increased approachability. Updating the file frequently will help send the message that your company is active and, by attracting more attention, get wider coverage for your Web site's URL.

The FAQ is definitely not an advertisement, though you can mention your company if, for example, it is the only producer of widgets, and the subject of the FAQ is "Sources of Hard-to-Find Products."

## FTP and Gopher

While FTP and Gopher sites are being overshadowed by Web installations, FTP sites in particular can be quite useful for certain large document files, binary files, and so on. In addition, Gopher menus and FTP directories can be displayed by most Web browsers.

Gopher sites are not terribly popular anymore, but some companies choose to maintain them because their customers (often those from educational institutions) still depend on them.

## Plan or Profile Files—Using Finger

Plan (.plan) files are similar to sigs: they are files in which you can place your URL, or any information about yourself or your business which you wish people to see. Your plan file is displayed whenever your account is "fingered." "Finger" is a utility that.... To finger my account, for example, use your browser's finger utility if it has one, or, at your system prompt, type `finger je@world.std.com`, and you will automatically receive my plan file of information I want to share with others.

Check to see if your ISP allows the display of a plan file. Plan files can be several pages long, but some providers allow only a shorter "address book" listing.

Be sure to put your URL in the plan file along with some information on what can be found at your site. A plan file might look like this:

```
             Presence Industries
Are you looking for a company to help you get on the Web?
Presence Industries can assist you with:
    *   Custom homepages
    *   Web site design and maintenance
    *   Your machine or ours
```

```
Call or e-mail Jeff Marcos    Have a look at our homepage
http://www.p-i.com         info@p-i.com         jeff@p-i.com
1.555.555.5555                            FAX 1.555.555.5555
```

Plan (.plan) files are becoming very much less popular as PPP accounts grow.

## World Wide Web Service Providers

Many businesses find that they need assistance in locating Web services, or in getting on the Web with a marketing presence.

One result of the enormous growth of the Internet is seen in the swelling number of businesses that offer Web-related services. They come in a number of flavors, but many offer services such as:

- General advice on using the WWW as a marketing tool
- Assistance in Web services purchase
- Market research
- Document writing
- Document conversion
- Image manipulation
- Script creation

There are sites where you can place your own Web materials. At one end of the scale are the providers that just offer disk space where you can put materials you yourself have prepared. Plain vanilla, nothing fancy. At the other end, there are sites that offer a full range of Web services, including customized Web sites, document writing, market research—the full nine yards. And there is everything in between.

In addition, there are companies offering consulting on creating a Web presence, some of whom are in the Web site business, some of whom will help you contract for Web site services. These Web presence, Internet presence, and consulting firms are springing up quickly. Even the oldest firms have not been in business all that long, so it is imperative to evaluate your choice of consultant and/or provider carefully. (See Chapters 10 and 11 for more resources.)

The first rule of acquisition is: Get references from current customers.

And the second rule of acquisition is: See it for yourself—be sure to have a look at the company's own page and the pages of customers so you can see the quality and functionality of their work firsthand.

Here is a checklist for assessing and comparing the services of a WWW services/presence consultant and/or provider:

- Services provided—compare oranges with oranges
  - Initial and on-going marketing research/assessment
  - Integration of Web site into Internet presence and corporate image
  - Tracking and analysis of site traffic
  - Defining page content, format, and function
  - Defining input forms
  - Image processing
  - Site selection advice—if site is not provided
- Site characteristics—Web-associated FTP, Gopher, mailbot capabilities
- Charges/costs
  - Fees for consultation and advisement
  - Setup fees
  - Monthly fees
  - InterNic domain registration services and fees
  - Page creation fees—authoring per page/per job
  - Maintenance/update fees
  - Page registration services and fees
  - Image preparation and transformation
  - Disk storage costs per unit
  - Minimum sign-up requirements
  - Other additional charges—per access or hit, etc.
- Equipment and capabilities
  - Type of Internet connection (T1, 56K, etc.)
  - Security precautions

- Type of equipment and software used by server
- Number and kind of lines in and out
- Number of businesses hosted on the site
- Speed and size of storage
- Power source and battery backup—emergency plans
- Background on the business and its principals
  - Key personnel—qualifications and experience
  - Location—physical and address, telephone, fax, etc.
  - Length of time in business
  - Client base
  - Professional/business references
  - Ownership
  - Financial stability—annual report

## Making Your Page Visible on the Web

Registering or listing your homepage's URL for inclusion in directories and with the search engines is an important part of making sure that potential customers visit your homepage. These directories are maintained by a variety of groups, at various sites, through the Web. Often they are organized by topic or kind of business. Registering or listing your page places a link to your page with a variety of kinds of resources, and can build traffic to your site.

EPages maintains a FAQ regarding How to Announce Your New Web Site at *http://ep.com/faq/webannounce.html* that is very useful in figuring out where to make your site visible.

### Directories

Directories are usually large listings of resources, often organized by hierarchy or category. The more places that have a cross-link with your page, the greater your chances are that someone will see your page's link and visit. Keep a careful listing of the sites where you have listed your information—if your URL changes for any reason, you have an obligation to inform each of those sources of the change so that their own pages are not afflicted with a dead link.

There are numerous places to list and register, and more coming on the Web all the time. Here are some examples of places to notify about your page to gain visibility.

BizWeb encourages Web and Gopher entries via a form on its homepage. The data entry page URL is *http://www.bizweb.com/InfoForm/infoform.html*.

Open Market encourages businesses to list their pages in the Commercial Sites Index through their online submission form (Figure 4.10). It lists companies, institutions, and organizations with a presence on the World Wide Web, not individual products or services. The URL for submission is *http://www.directory.net/dir/submit.cgi*. Use the site's online search facility to be sure that your page has not already been listed in Open Market's database.

To add your site to the Yahoo listing, an online fill-in form (*http://www.yahoo.com/bin/add*) is provided via Yahoo's homepage. You are

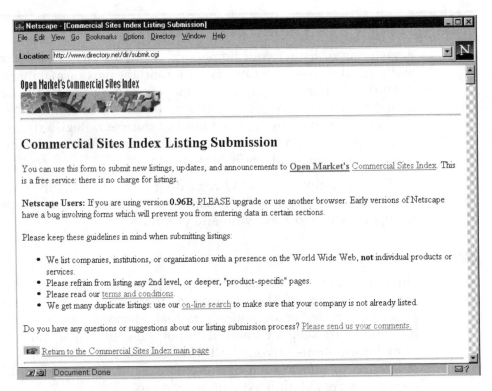

**Figure 4.10 The Commercial Sites Index listing form.**

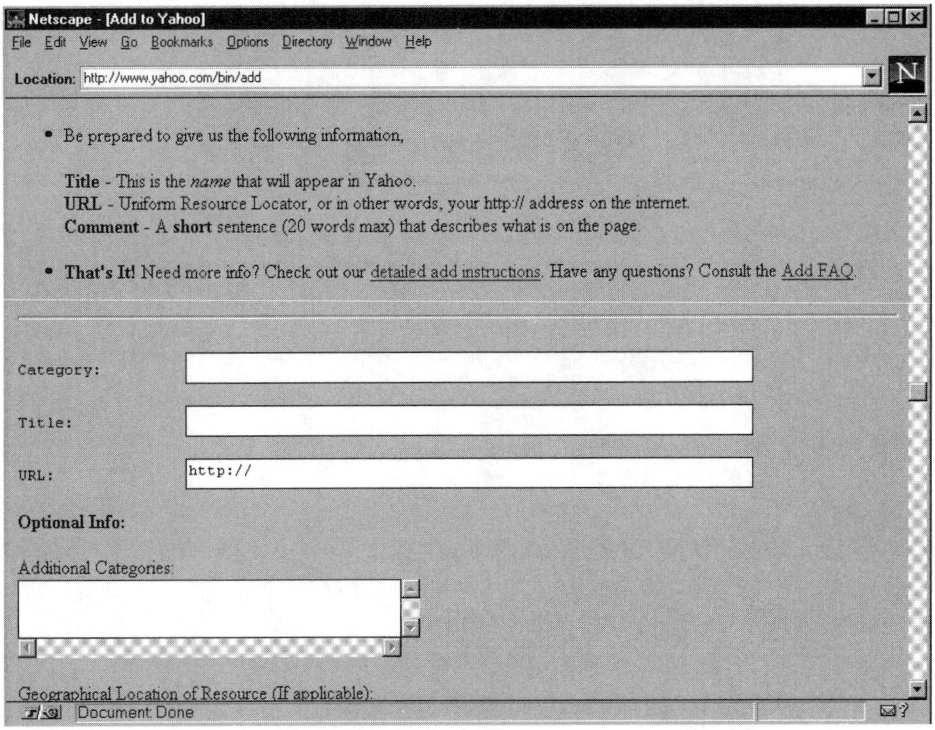

**Figure 4.11 The Yahoo Listing entry form.**

asked to supply your page's title and URL and to choose the category in which your site will be listed. The Yahoo page is shown in Figure 4.11.

## Search Engine Registrations

There are a number of Web search engines that seek out new pages using search algorithms, and then create an index of sites. Most of these also accept (welcome!) page registrations for inclusion in their indexing process. Here are just a couple of examples; have a look at Chapter 9 for more ideas.

The Lycos database is described in Chapter 9 in detail. To register with Lycos, fill in the form at *http://www.lycos.com/addasite.html*.

Also described in Chapter 9 is the WebCrawler database of Web sites (Figure 4.12). To register with the WebCrawler, fill in the form at *http://www.webcrawler.com/WebCrawler/SubmitURLS.html*.

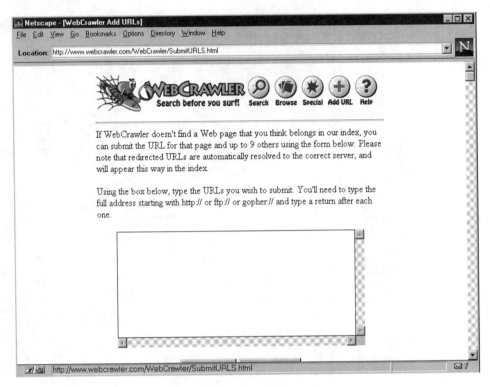

**Figure 4.12 The WebCrawler Index URL entry page.**

Because the Web is growing so rapidly, it is important to watch for new places to list your pages. One of the best ways to do this is to do some Web cruising to look for new sites. Also subscribe to the *net-happenings* list or read the *comp.internet.net-happenings* newsgroup and some of the *www.\** news hierarchy for opportunities.

## Other Traffic and Visibility Builders

While the registration process is critical to visibility, other kinds of activities can be undertaken that will help you build traffic to your site:

- *Local pages and industry pages*—register and cross-link with local and regional sites, and make sure that you are linked with industry pages

- *What's New pages*—there are numerous sites that maintain What's New or What's Hot listings

- *Newsletters and mailing lists*—site and business-related newsletters and discussion/distribution lists are very useful for building loyalty and a sense of community and for offering specials, hints, and tips to customers and potential customers
- *Non-Web search tools*—be sure to register your Gopher with Veronica, and your FTP site with Archie
- *Cross-links*—"put me on yours and I'll put you on mine"—carefully chosen cross-links with sites sharing similar niches can increase your traffic flow as well. Do affinity marketing.

## Advertising on the Net

Part of getting your site noticed on the Net is online advertising. The most common commercial forms are banners, sponsorships, and click-through ads.

*Banners* are small graphic buttons or images containing tempting information, inviting users to click for more information. Companies are paying $15-250 per thousand (CPM) for banners. At the low end are those placed on very general pages or search engines. At the high end are the most narrowly targeted, delivering the "best" audience. The Excite search page, shown in Figure 4.13, has a banner that indicates sponsorship, which changes according to the kind of search performed; in this case the sponsor is Toshiba.

*Click-through* pricing results when a user actually presses the button and retrieves the advertised information. Pricing for click-throughs is in the $200-800 range CPM, but your mileage may vary.

*Sponsorships* can be found on Web pages and on discussion lists; for example, this was found on the Online Advertising Discussion list:

---

```
This week's Online Advertising Discussion List sponsor:
The Internet Developers Association, http://www.association.org/
The professional trade association for Internet content developers.
Join through June 30, 1996 and the annual membership fee is waived.
```

---

The prices for these are usually based on traffic, narrowness of focus, and quality of the list.

**Figure 4.13 The Excite Lycos page with a Toshiba ad.**

Here are just a few good resources for finding places to advertise on the Internet:

- Interactive Publishing Alert (*http://www.netcreations.com/ipa/ adindex/index.html*)—a nifty site with an Advertising Index that is searchable
- Web Track's Adspace Locator (http://www.webtrack.com/ sponsors/sponsors.html)
- Abbott Wool's Market Segment Resource Locator! (*http://www. amic.com/awool/*)
- Internet Advertising Resource Guide (http://pilot.msu.edu/unit/ adv/internet-advertising-guide.htm)

In addition, Chapter 11 discusses advertising resources including online advertising agencies.

# Promoting Web Sites with Other Media

The cross-fertilization between your Web site and your traditional marketing media is very important to the success of the Web site. Your URL and e-mail address should be placed somewhere in every print-media advertisement that you do—magazine, newspaper, newsletter. The Internet provides an exciting and enjoyable experience for most users—those that might ignore the information in your more traditional print ads may be intrigued with seeing your Web site. Also, the presence of Internet addresses on your printed materials projects a modern, up-to-date image for your company, even to those who don't use the Internet. Other media you can use to promote your Web site include the following:

- Your business card—Putting your URL on all of your office stationery and on your business card can stimulate interest and conversation. If recipients are Web-wise, they will appreciate it; if they are not, they just might ask about it, opening the door for dialog.

- Radio spots—More problematic is the issue of how to handle an unpronounceable URL in audio situations. Most businesses just give their relatively short e-mail address instead. Who wants to explain and pronounce *http://www.BinFord/cgi-bin/Binford/binford.html*? (Imagine the daunting task of trying to say "capital B-small i-n-capital F-small o-r-d stroke . . ."—well, you get the idea.) You may be able to say *Bob@binford.com* easily enough, however, or mention that you have a Web page without mentioning the specific address.

- TV commercials—Television advertising is starting to show URLs and e-mail addresses. Be sure they are displayed long enough for the viewer to write them down correctly.

# Corporate Identity and Your Web Site

The need for the establishment of a consistent corporate identity is well documented. The importance of creating an appropriate eye-catching logo and putting it on every piece of stationery, on business cards, and so on is also taken for granted these days. Continue this practice of consistency on your Web site where possible with logos and layout.

To promote the online part of your corporate identity, you should consider putting your URL and e-mail address on just about every piece of corporate literature:

- Letterhead
- All stationery—large and small
- Business cards
- Flyers
- Brochures
- Fax cover sheets
- Press packets
- Press releases
- Notebooks
- Folders
- Report covers
- Mouse pads (or other promotional give-aways)
- Magazine bingo cards
- Newsletters—both internal and external
- Bulk mailing items

And so on.

## How Do We Know It's Working? Measuring Success

One of the ongoing challenges for Internet marketers is figuring out what is working. The time-tested methods such as focus groups can be useful, as is a traditional (and nontraditional) return on investment calculations.

### Return on Investment

Most companies use some form of these methods to estimate ROI for their Internet enterprise:

- Overall business growth—has the business grown overall, in what department, and in what product lines?

- Overall business profitability—has the business returned a profit, which departments, which divisions?
- Actual ROI, if involved with sales—this is a simple calculation
- Customer responses—formal and informal; market research
- Use of site logging data (see below)

Oak Ridge's recent study of over 450 Internet businesses shows that overall, 69.8% were satisfied with their return on investment, while 30.2% were to some degree unsatisfied. Those with marketing-only sites were more satisfied than those with sales sites. The time for the ROI varied widely. For sales-only sites, the average was 6.5 months, with a range from half a month up to 17 months. For Marketing/Advertising/Visibility sites, the average was higher at 8 months, with a range of 3 months to 24 months.

## Indicators of Marketing Success

While return on investment is very important in evaluating marketing, there are some other useful Net-centric measures available to the Web marketer:

- *access*—who is visiting, how long they are staying, what domains they are coming in from—an analysis of hits, hosts and sessions, identification of sites that refer the most traffic
- *activity*—guest book signings, survey takers—an analysis of what visitors are doing, what actions are taken
- *becoming part of the community*—mailing list sign-ups, traffic and volume of the lists, Web chat participation, message board participation
- *sales/transactions*—how much they are purchasing—item analysis, which items
- *advertising volume and revenues*—who is buying advertising on your site, what kinds, and how much they are paying; retention of advertisers
- *media attention*—online and offline, stories, citings, features
- *awards and hot sites*—whether the site is a featured site at "hot" pages or in top 10 listings; ratings from engines; awards
- *cross-link requests*—how many and from whom, quality

**Note:**

In Chapter 3, you'll find a quick guide to some software and services for tracking Web site traffic and demographics. And Chapter 8 has tips for good page design.

## From Here . . .

Web marketing is just beginning, and can be expected to evolve and grow. Go on to Chapter 5 for information about security.

# *Caution, Security, and Customs of the Natives—A Cautionary Tale*

The Internet and the Web are still so new to many companies that they have only a vague idea of good practices, and how to stay out of trouble on the Internet. Some have even heard that "you can't advertise on the Internet." Of course you can, but what is required is some caution and knowledge of the online culture of the Internet and the Web.

Caution is needed in several areas:

- Operating within the rules of the Internet—acceptable use policies
- Advertising—avoiding intrusive practices
- Communication
- Copyrights
- Security and authentication of sites, pages, and transactions

## Acceptable Use

Most of the networks connected to the Internet have what are called "Acceptable Use Policies" (AUPs) or Terms of Service contracts. These policies are the written rules of engagement for working on the Internet. Users large and small must abide by these policies, whether they have access through a provider or become a part of the Internet with their own site. The most well-known AUP was that of the National Science Foundation (NSF), which no longer applies to business on the Net.

All of the National Access providers (NAPs) have AUPs, as do the smaller mid-level networks. Most ISPs also have their own AUPs or rules of the road. These AUPs are varied, ranging from fairly complex contracts to less formal codes of behavior.

Virtually all of the AUPs of NAPs and mid-level networks prohibit unsolicited advertising and spamming. Note the modifier—"unsolicited." This means never sending bulk e-mail to people who are not expecting it. This does not say that you cannot advertise, it just says you cannot do "in-your-face" advertising. As an example, here is what PSINet says, "PSINet does not condone and will not permit abusive behavior by its users. . . . PSINet considers net-abuse an action that undermines the ability of a newsgroup, mailing list or IRC to serve as a discussion forum. In addition, net-abuse may be a violation of state or federal law, or the laws of other countries." PSINet's policies can be found at *http://www.interramp.com/support/net-abuse-policy.html* and *http://www.mindspring.com/aboutms/policy.html*.

This prohibition of unsolicited advertising is why Web pages are ideal for advertising—each visit to your business page is "solicited" by the visitor.

When selecting an Internet access provider or network, ask about the provider's acceptable use policies—make sure they support the kind of business activities you would like to pursue.

## Advertising vs. Marketing on the Web

In traditional media, advertising is everywhere—on TV, in the newspaper, on the sides of buses, on motorcycles, through direct telephone marketing, and so on. On the Internet, intrusive or proactive advertising is not permitted by AUPs and is strongly disliked by the citizens of the network—your potential customers.

Marketing, on the other hand, can be accomplished by gaining visibility. A Web site is your virtual corporate headquarters, where you can market and sell products and services. The trick is to get Internauts to visit the page. Making your page a good place to visit is the best Internet advertisement. Techniques for gaining this visibility are discussed in Chapters 3 and 4.

While the Internet has great power for marketing and spreading the good word about your business, it also has the power to damage your business's reputation. Sending unsolicited e-mail or posting inappropriate ads to newsgroups or mailing lists can result in swift, angry responses from those on the Net. Negative postings about your company to key discussion lists and groups can reach millions within hours. Use the Internet long enough that you have an understanding of the prevailing attitudes of those on the Net before you conduct any business.

# Security

There are some security issues that are important to consider as you develop your Web presence. This is an area of considerable interest currently, and there are numerous groups, organizations, and businesses working on security issues such as:

- Authentication and secure transactions
- Site security
- Privacy
- Encryption
- Identity verification

## Authentication and Secure Transactions

Doing business and marketing with a Web page brings numerous authentication issues to the forefront, involving authentication of:

- Data
- People
- Products
- Transactions

Just as with transactions involving the postal system and the phone system, and in-person transactions, Internet transactions will never be perfectly safe, but taking a few precautions can reduce risks to a reasonable level.

Remember, though, that both your business, in its role of consumer of goods and services purchased via the Web, and you as an individual, should exercise caution when substantial amounts of money are involved. Traditional business practices of checking on the claims and representations should be pursued to determine what kind of company lies behind the homepage.

In order to make purchasing from a Web page attractive to consumers, there are several companies and organizations working on techniques for secure transactions. Because communication on the Internet is not wholly private, consumers are reasonably shy about sending their credit card number to a vendor via the Internet. Public concerns about these issues are lessening: several companies offering online sales report that more than 90 percent of their customers are now using secure forms to order and transmit payment information.

Secure transactions—through credit cards, the purchase of virtual money tokens, the establishment of accounts, and more—is a growth area for business on the Web.

Here are some current solutions to the security problem:

- *Creating an account*—In this case, the consumer or business makes offline arrangements (by phone, mail, fax, etc.) for payments through a credit card or the establishment of a line of credit. Orders can then be made using input forms on the Web page or though e-mail.

- *Purchase orders*—in business-to-business commerce, the use of existing purchase order "technology" is popular.

- *Buying virtual bucks*—This system involves purchasing tokens, or virtual money, to be used with a variety of vendors who accept this kind of payment. While more flexible than creating an account, there is still the matter of security of the codes transmitted across the Internet, and the limited number of vendors using these systems.

- *Encrypted e-mail and page entry*—In this case encryption is offered in an e-mail message, through Secure MIME mail, PGP encryption, or the use of secure HTTP, or Secure Sockets Layer (SSL) so that you can transmit credit card or other data directly to each vendor.

- *Cyber credit cards or checks*—Here, the use of special electronic versions of cash, credit cards, and checks are used to make purchases.

The following are some examples of companies offering secure electronic transaction plans for use over the Web.

### Secure HTTP

Secure HTTP was developed by Enterprise Integration Technologies (EIT), the National Center for Supercomputing Applications (NCSA), and RSA Data Security. This is a HyperText Transfer Protocol that offers secure transactions between user and server using a data entry form. The user can click on a secure submission button, and the client program will generate a secure key for that session using the form. Currently, they are releasing the software to CommerceNet members (Figure 5.1), and they are planning to let NCSA distribute it as they currently do with Mosaic. More information is available at *http://www. commerce.net/work/sects/index.html*, or send e-mail to *shttp-info@eit.com.*

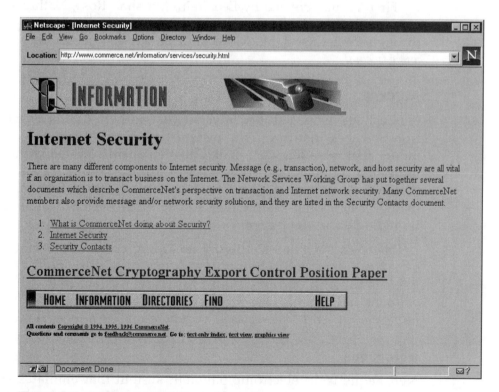

**Figure 5.1 CommerceNet Security page.**

### Secure Sockets Layer (SSL)

Secure Sockets Layer is another Internet security protocol that provides privacy. SSL allows client/server applications to communicate in a way that prevents "eavesdropping," keeping the channel secure end to end. Using SSL, servers are always authenticated, while clients may be authenticated optionally. More information can be obtained from *http:// search.netscape.com/misc/developer/conference/proceedings/cs2/*.

### First Virtual Holdings

The First Virtual Payment system, created by First Virtual Holdings Incorporated, is a system that offers linkages between banks, credit card companies, companies doing business on the Internet, and Internet customers. The system verifies transactions, and has built-in monitoring systems to spot problems. Information technology equipment and services are provided by Electronic Data Systems (EDS).

First Virtual, created by Lee Stein, Marshall Rose, Nathaniel Borenstein, and Einar Stefferud, has its credit card transactions processed through First USA Bank. More information can be obtained at *http:// www.fv.com/*.

### NetCash

NetCash, developed at the University of Southern California's Information Sciences Institute, is a system based on "coupons" or virtual money that is traded via e-mail. The NetBank associated with NetCash issues the coupons, and converts NetCash U.S. funds for a 2% charge. NetCash concentrates on micropayments—small transaction charges made for accessing information and services—usually under $100, although often just a few cents.

NetCash is traded simply by including coupon information in an e-mail message, and sending it from one person to another. The NetBank is the online transaction processing system that validates the coupons and provides the currency exchange. Check out the Web site at *http://www.teleport.com/~netcash/* or send e-mail to *help@agents.com*.

### NetCheque

NetCheque is an electronic payment system that emulates standard checks. Like NetCash, it was developed for the Internet by the Information Sciences Institute of the University of Southern California.

Users who register through prearrangement with NetCheque accounting servers are able to write electronic checks to other users. These checks can be transmitted using e-mail or other network protocols. Like conventional checks, when it is deposited, a NetCheque check authorizes the transfer of funds from the buyer to the seller. The signatures on the checks are authenticated using Kerberos. More information can be obtained through the Web page at *http://nii-server.isi.edu/ info/NetCheque/*.

### Net Bill

NetBill is another system that allows micropayments on the Internet. Created by researchers at Carnegie Mellon University, it offers a method for making money "a little at a time" based on a high volume of payments.

The secure transactions work this way: the buyer creates a NetBill account, the "goods" (information) are transferred from a seller to a buyer, the buyer's NetBill account is debited, the seller's account is credited. More information can be obtained at the NetBill Web page: *http://www.ini.cmu.edu/netbill/*.

### DigiCash

Electronic cash by DigiCash, created by David Chaum, combines computerized monetary exchange with security and privacy. DigiCash relies on an encryption system for the identification of the purchaser. E-cash is a software approach to funds transfer, where the user's equipment generates a random number that serves as the electronic note. This note is bound to a random factor that transmits it to a bank, where the bank's system verifies the debiting of the encoded amount from the user's account. The system relies on signature verification and fund verification for every purchase. Information on Digicash may be found at *http://www.digicash.com/* or *http://digicash.support.nl/publish/digibro. html*.

### Netscape

In addition to creating a Web browser called Netscape, Netscape Communications has created a number of products for secure Web commerce, including the Enterprise Server, LivePayment, and the Commerce Platform (Figure 5.2). When using Netscape for browsing, you can connect to a secure server and transact business. The Netscape

**Figure 5.2 The Netscape Commerce Products page.**

browser will display a color bar when you connect to a site—red means not secure, and green means secure.

Netscape supports both Secure HTTP and SSL. You will find Netscape secure servers associated with Web site providers, individual businesses, cybermalls, virtual storefronts, and corporate Web pages. Netscape's Commerce Products may be found at *http://www.netscape. com/comprod/business_solutions/commerce/index.html* and *http://www. netscape.com/comprod/products/iapps/index.html*.

### Other Secure Transaction Systems

There are numerous other transaction and authentication projects under way which will facilitate the development of secure commerce on the Web.

- Premenos Corporation and Cisco Systems are using the RSA Data Securities public key system to support electronic commerce.

- CyberCash, Inc. is working on a system to make online credit card verification for cyber-retailers, for transactions involving debit cards, credit cards, and forms of digital cash.
- Terisa Systems, in a joint venture with Enterprise Integration Technologies and RSA Data Security, is producing a secure Mosaic product for commercial transactions.

Further evidence that the cyberbucks business is booming is that Microsoft, Netscape, MasterCard, and Visa International have teamed together to make online electronic bank card transactions more readily available.

## Site Security

Most businesses have some concern about their Web site—can someone obtain transaction information, break in and change data, or destroy data? For the most part, these concerns can be handled through existing methods.

### Firewalls

A firewall is usually a combination of hardware and software that insures that only authorized entry into a system is permitted. It creates a virtual "Checkpoint Charlie" where only those packets that meet certain criteria are permitted entry. In some cases this is just a filtering function on e-mail; in others it is as sophisticated as separate hardware with only outward connectivity.

Firewalls that work very well are difficult to create, and require consistent monitoring for effectiveness. None are foolproof. The creation of a firewall is a highly sophisticated process, usually undertaken only by large companies with dedicated lines and computers. Most companies do not need the ultra-high security provided by firewalls.

### Computer Emergency Response Team (CERT)

The Computer Emergency Response Team has a key role in Internet security. It was created after a major attack on the Internet that made it very clear how vulnerable the Net was, and more particularly, that there was no way to deal with a large-scale problem.

CERT provides around-the-clock technical assistance for responding to security incidents, as well as information, discussion lists, documents,

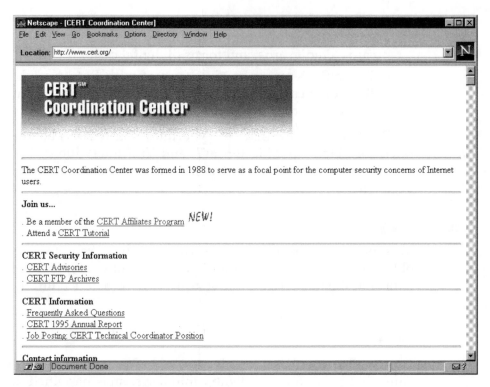

**Figure 5.3 The CERT page.**

and training sessions. CERT posts its advisories to *com.security.announce* and through mailing lists. Some of the documentation can be accessed through its page at *http://www.cert.org/* (Figure 5.3).

CERT can be reached by e-mail (*cert@cert.org*), on a 24-hour telephone hotline ((412) 268-7090), or via fax ((412) 268-6989).

### A Word or Two about Passwords

One of the simplest protections that you can invoke is keeping your personal and system passwords private. Here are a few quick ways to safeguard your passwords:

- Don't put them on a Post-it on your monitor.
- Change your passwords frequently.
- Mix upper- and lowercase letters (if your system is case-sensitive).

- Do not use plain words as passwords—combine words and numbers, or use odd spellings.
- Do not use names or other things associated with you—hobbies, spouse's name, birthdays, etc.—for passwords.

A password like *B-3mike* is better than just *mike,* and *B-3m_K* is even better—but be sure that you can remember it, too. Some companies use a security algorithm to create good passwords. Some people find it useful to use the letters from a memorable phrase—for example, *idrarm:* "I dig rock-and-roll music."

### File Protection

Because electronic files can so easily be altered without leaving much of a trace, it is important to spend the time to learn your system's protection methods for files and directories. If your pages are being maintained by an Internet access provider, find out specifically how they protect your files from being altered by others, and how they protect your customers' purchase information from being read by others. This has not been a serious problem on the Web, but there are dangers here.

### Secure E-mail

There are existing ways to have secure e-mail. The most well-known is a new secure extension to MIME called Secure Multipurpose Internet Mail Extensions (S/MIME). This can provide security for messages and other files sent between S/MIME-compatible mail programs. Several leading software companies, including Microsoft, Netscape, Lotus, Banyan, VeriSign, ConnectSoft, QUALCOMM, Frontier Technologies, Network Computing Devices, FTP Software, Wollongong, SecureWare, RSA Data Security, and IBM, are supporting the S/MIME specification developed by RSA Data Security. This means that e-mail and attached files can be securely transmitted over the Internet and cannot be "opened" or read in transit. S/MIME is based on the popular Internet MIME standard (RFC 1521). More information on S/MIME can be obtained at *http://www.rsa.com/.*

### Encryption

Encryption involves the encoding of material so that the information is relatively inaccessible. Encryption methods called "strong encryption" are now available that would take more than 100 years of computer time to break.

The process begins by encrypting the out-going message or file with encryption software, using a unique "key" or algorithm (this is your secret decoder ring). The encrypted, unreadable message is then transmitted across the Internet. The recipient then uses decryption software compatible with the sender's encryption software, using the message's key. The material is then reprocessed back into its original form.

A single key that both encrypts and decrypts is called a one-key algorithm or system. A system that requires two keys typically uses a public key to encrypt the message, and a private key to decrypt the message. Anyone can use your public key to encrypt a message to you, but then only you can decrypt it with your private key. A good example of a two-key system is the program Pretty Good Privacy, developed by Phil Zimmerman. This is currently available from *ftp://net-dist.mit.edu/pub/PGP*. It is legal to distribute PGP in the United States and Canada but not elsewhere.

This double key kind of encryption is good for sensitive data and messages.

Kerberos (named for the dog in mythology who guarded Hades) is a complex authentication system that can be used to identify users and systems and determine their permission to use files and systems. Kerberos is being used on secure Web sites to allow only authorized access. In addition, it can be used to prevent the unauthorized modification of files. More information on Kerberos is available in the Usenet newsgroup *comp.protocols.kerberos* and from the Web site *http://www-cis.usc.edu/~laura/kerb_refs.html*.

An excellent source for more information is the Cryptography page at the WWW Virtual Library, *http://world.std.com/~franl/crypto.html* (Figure 5.4).

---

**Note:**

Just as with transactions involving the postal system, the telephone system and in person transactions, Internet transactions will never be perfectly safe, but taking a few precautions can greatly reduce risk to a reasonable level. Nothing can safeguard all of your pages and data, but the careful management of passwords and the use of encryption can minimize the risks.

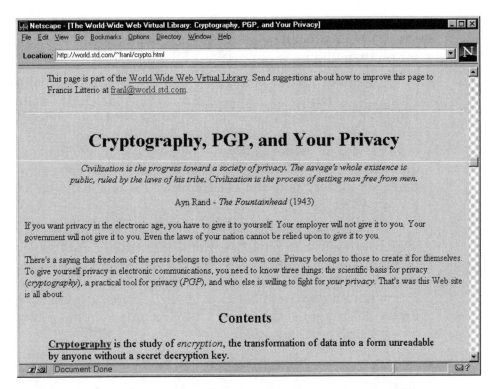

**Figure 5.4 The WWW Virtual Library page for Cryptography, PGP, and Privacy.**

---

# Legal Issues

There are a variety of legal issues concerning intellectual property that are of importance for Web and Internet marketing, which include:

- copyrights
- trademarks
- globalization and contests
- advertising practices

## Copyrights

Everything online on the Internet is copyrighted, including all art and text associated with a Web site. The only material that is not will be clearly labeled "in the public domain." This means that text, image, and sound files and homepages cannot be used in certain ways, particularly for profit, without the permission of the copyright holder.

This covers Usenet newsgroup and discussion list postings, e-mail, Web sites, FTP files, and so on. Since 1978 in the United States, a copyright is created the moment you write original copy, create an image, write a song, or create an audio file. This material cannot be used without permission, except as defined by fair use—in attributed excerpts, in quotations, and in reviews. The Berne Convention copyright treaty extends similar rights to the 114 countries (as of 1995) who have signed the agreement.

Marking your material with the copyright notice is not required, nor is registering it with the Library of Congress, but doing so entitles you to additional legal protections. The U.S. Copyright Office General Information and Publications at the Library of Congress has a wealth of information on copyright basics and registration, copyright application forms and circulars, Copyright Office records, and more at *http://lcweb. loc.gov/copyright/* (Figure 5.5).

## Trademarks

A trademark is some sort of clearly distinguishable word, logo, symbol, design, or phrase that identifies the source of goods or services. Domain names (registered by InterNic) are *not* trademarks. However, many companies are now trademarking their domain name—bigbiz. com ®—to protect it from use by someone else. The use of the ® is restricted to trademarks registered with the Patent and Trademark Office. Reach the Patent and Trademark office at *http://www.uspto.gov/*.

## Globalization and Contests

Many online businesses are marketing utilizing various forms of contests. Because of the global nature of the Net, this entails adhering to the law that governs contests in a great number of countries in the world. Take some time to check out the legal implications of contests and fulfillment in other countries.

## Advertising

Many entrepreneurs assume that the Internet operates under a different set of advertising laws than offline businesses, but thus far, that is not

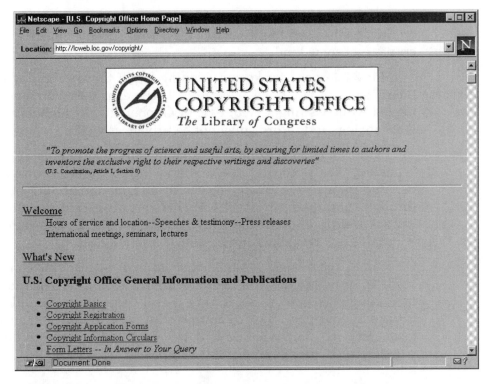

**Figure 5.5 The Library of Congress Copyright Office page.**

true. There are numerous laws, policies, and rules that pertain to the advertising of products and services, and they apply for the most part to your business online. This is especially important for businesses advertising products for sale on Web pages, or actually selling directly from a Web page.

## Privacy Issues

Internet traffic in general offers a modicum of privacy, but there are some general privacy issues that need to be considered.

E-mail is fairly private, but just how private depends upon the system administrator's behavior and ethics. Messages can be trapped if someone wants to do it. The legalities are especially muddy about this where an employer is involved in providing access. The privacy of postal mail is clear under law; the privacy of e-mail is not. As a practical matter, for day-to-day traffic this has not been a problem, but if you are involved in sending sensitive data, you should consider using encryption of some kind.

Many Internet sites keep a running log of those people who access the system and what files they used. This means that your activities are logged while visiting a Web, FTP, or Gopher site. Remember that some Web site logs and records may not be private as well.

There is a capability built into many sites for creating and reading "cookies" files. A cookies file is a tracking file (created on your hard drive) designed to provide sites with information about your travels through cyberspace. In effect what this means is that you are leaving virtual footprints of all the sites you have visited. More information about this is a available from *http://help.netscape.com*.

Many page owners log the access to their pages. This can even include information about a visitor's login site and user name. From a marketing perspective, this is very useful data—you can find out who is visiting your page, how often they visit, what domains they are from (*.edu*, *.com*, etc.), and what time of day they hit the page—or how many people visited after your big "ad" campaign.

## Resources

There are a number of online resources for finding more information about security, secure transactions, authentication, legal matters, and related issues.

### The Internet Engineering Task Force (IETF)

The IETF currently has a number of security-related projects underway, including a number focused on secure transactions. These are long-term projects aimed at examining and creating several standards that will affect many phases of online commerce and business. IETF's Security Working Group has some draft standards under development, including:

- Authorization and Access Control
- Authenticated Firewall Traversal
- Commercial Internet Protocol Security Option

- Common Authentication Technology
- Internet Protocol Security Protocol
- Network Access Server Requirements
- Privacy Enhanced Mail

These topics can be tracked on the homepage of the IETF at *http://www.ietf.cnri.reston.va.us/*.

## The Security for Businesses on the Internet Site

Here is a site that has a lot of information about business and security on the Internet: *http://www.catalog.com/mrm/security.html* (Figure 5.6). This page has an organized set of links to resources covering tools and practical examples for securing your business on the Internet. In addition, it provides access to sites on encryption and authentication.

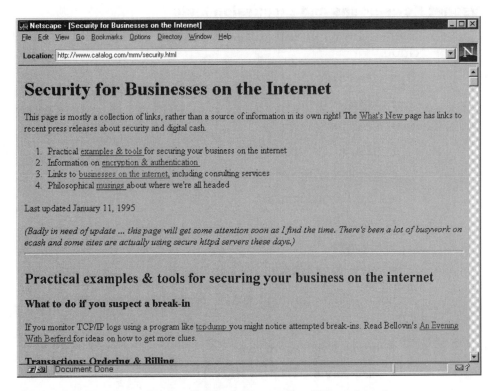

**Figure 5.6 The Security for Businesses on the Internet page.**

## The GNN Personal Finance Center

The GNN Personal Finance Center maintains a number of interesting pages, including a page on E-Money and Network Money Sites at *http://gnn.com/meta/finance/feat/links.html*. This has lots of information on electronic monetary systems, plus links to information on encryption and other forms of secure electronic commerce.

## The Advertising Law Internet Site

The Advertising Law Internet Site at *http://www.webcom.com/~lewrose/ home.html* contains information on advertising, marketing, and related law. The site is maintained by Lewis Rose, an advertising and marketing law partner with the law firm of Arent Fox Kintner Plotkin & Kahn. This site also contains a wealth of information on United States advertising law, and FTC information.

## Usenet Newsgroups and Discussion Lists

Usenet newsgroups that discuss online security and related topics include:

- *alt.security*
- *alt.security.index*
- *alt.security.keydist*
- *alt.security.pgp*
- *comp.security.announce*
- *compt.security.misc*
- *comp.risks*
- *sci.crypt*
- *talk.politics.crypto*

Some discussion lists related to electronic commerce are:

- *com-priv@psi.com*
- *online-ads@tenagra.com*
- *www-buyinfo@allegra.att.com*

## From Here . . .

These security measures are good to keep in mind as you move into marketing on the Web. Chapters 3 and 4 provided a guide to integrating your Web marketing strategies into a larger Internet and traditional media plan. Now it's time to move to Chapter 6, where you will learn how to prepare HTML documents.

# PART III

# Constructing Effective Web Sites

# *Preparing HTML Documents for the World Wide Web*

A wise marketer understands the marketing medium, and in this case that medium is the Internet and the Web. Even if you decide to have someone else professionally prepare your business's Web pages, it will be helpful to at least have some understanding of what HTML is, and what can be done with it. It is easy to learn to write a simple HTML document The elements of the syntax and "directives" used in HTML are rather limited in scope and easy to understand; the challenge, however, comes in using them in complex and creative combinations.

## Preparing a Very Simple Document

Web browsers will display any plain ASCII text file. About the only "formatting" of the words done by the browser when displaying a plain text file is the proper display of any spaces or carriage returns/line feeds. The only additional feature the browsers usually add to the display is word-wrap.

HTML files are also ASCII text files, but with commands embedded in the text which direct any browser that displays it, how to display it, and how to use information about embedded links to other documents. HTML documents are named using the letters "html" as the filename extension: for example, *texas-homepage.html* or *catalog.html* (documents written on Windows machines and other systems limited to a three-letter filename extension use "htm").

Any ordinary text editor or word processor can be used to author HTML documents as long as it can save the text as pure ASCII characters with no unseen formatting information. Plain text editors usually don't offer or add any formatting, and so work well for HTML. Word processors do add their own hidden codes, but you can usually choose to "Save as ASCII" or "Save as Text" to create a plain text file. (It is usually best not to use the similarly named "Save as Formatted Text" function, since it adds line-feed/carriage return characters to the document.)

---

**Tip:**

If you are not sure whether your word processor is saving in pure ASCII, boldface or underline some portion of the text. Now "Save as Text." Close the current document and re-load the newly saved text file. If the boldfacing or underlining is gone, that word processor will probably work well for creating HTML documents.

---

There are specialized word processors available to help create HTML documents. They greatly speed up the preparation of documents, especially complex documents with many links. These word processors will be discussed later in this chapter.

Even with the most sophisticated of these programs, your success in creating Web pages will be much greater and more predictable if you understand the fundamentals of HTML.

HTML documents give directions to the browsers displaying them by use of "tags." Tags are made up of a < (left arrow—the mathematical "less than" symbol), some letter(s) or symbols, which are called the directive, and then a > (right arrow—the mathematical "more than" symbol)—for example, <H2> or <B>. These tags are usually used in pairs:

```
<H2>Texas-West Electronics Distributors</H2>
```

The beginning tag, <H2>, tells the browser when to start formatting the text as a size 2 headline, and the ending tag, </H2>, tells the browser when to stop this text style and return to normal text. Notice the slash that is used to indicate an ending tag. The text between the tags will be displayed in upper- and lowercase characters, just as it is written. But it makes no difference to the browser whether the letters *within* the tags are upper- or lowercase.

Here's an example of a very simple HTML document:

```
<HTML>

<HEAD>

<TITLE>The Texas-West Electronics Supply HomePage</TITLE>

</HEAD>

<BODY>

<H3>West-Texas Electronics Supply -- Welcome!</H3>

West-Texas supply can supply OEM parts from all areas of the
world.<P>
We specialize in fast shipment of parts made here in Austin's
own Silicon Gulch.<P>

</BODY>

</HTML>
```

Well, not a stunning example of a homepage, but it's a start. After typing it, save this file (in ASCII text) as, for example, *tex-west.htm*. This file can then be viewed by a browser on your own computer. Figure 6.1 shows how it would appear displayed with the Microsoft Explorer browser.

Let's take a look at what the tags used in this HTML document do, and how they are generally used.

First, note the pairs of tags used to organize the HTML document:

```
<HTML> </HTML>
```

The HTML tags tell the browser when the HTML document starts and when it ends—when to start interpreting the tags and text as part of a Web page.

```
<HEAD> </HEAD>
```

The HEAD tags enclose the "header" portion of the document, where general commands about the whole document are given, the

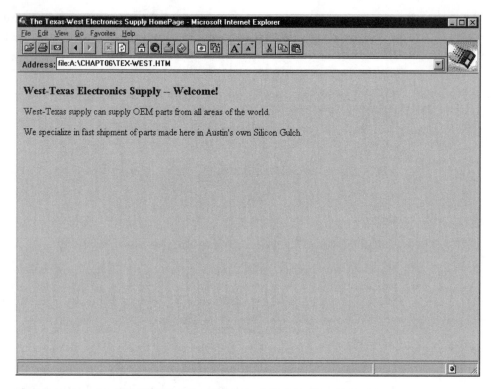

**Figure 6.1 A simple HTML file displayed by the Microsoft Explorer browser.**

document title is presented, and various messages about the document itself are stored (such as owner, modification dates, etc.).

```
<BODY> </BODY>
```

The BODY tags surround the portion of the document where the bulk of the active document is stored. This is where the text, links, and formatting commands are placed.

```
<TITLE> </TITLE>
```

A title is not required in an HTML document, but it does increase the effectiveness of the document. Some browsers display the title in a separate box somewhere on the screen. The title is also used by various Web search programs as a way of identifying the contents of the document. A title with several well-chosen words will improve the chances someone will find your page.

> **Note:**
>
> Web browsers generally ignore any tags that they cannot use. If you include more advanced features in your Web document, older, less sophisticated browsers will generally be able to read the document, but the particular layout and formatting of the document may be unpredictable, and some text and display features may be lost.

```
<H3> </H3>
```

There are six levels of headline, with <H1> being the largest and <H6> the smallest. Browsers interpret these in different ways, using size, boldfacing, linespacing, and alignment to indicate different levels of heads. (Do not confuse headlines, also called heads or headings, with headers.) The exact size, color, and boldness of each of these depends on how a particular graphical browser has been configured; it is not in your control.

```
<P>
```

The paragraph tag is one of the few tags that doesn't have to be used in pairs. The <P> tag is placed at the end of the paragraph. When the browser displays the HTML document, it reduces indents, blank lines, and extra spaces to just one space. It then word-wraps the words on the screen until the <P> tag is encountered. The <P> tag creates paragraphing by adding a line space and starting a new line.

The following two HTML documents would result in identical screen displays, despite differences in the way the words are laid out on the page.

```
Document A.htm

<HTML>

<HEAD>

</HEAD>

<BODY>
Texas-West supplies:
```

```
transistors,

integrated          circuits,
precision resistors,
and                              surface mount capacitors.<P>

</BODY>

</HTML>

Document B.htm

<HTML>

<HEAD>
</HEAD>

<BODY>
Texas-West supplies: transistors, integrated circuits,
precision resistors, and surface mount capacitors.<P>

</BODY>

</HTML>
```

The resulting display would be the same in each case:

```
Texas-West supplies: transistors, integrated circuits,
precision resistors, and surface mount capacitors.
```

When the <P> tag is encountered most browsers add a blank line. If you want to start a new line of text, but not an intervening blank line, insert the <BR> break tag at the point in the text where you want the break.

---

**Note:**

A way to preserve the formatting so that it will be displayed exactly as entered into the HTML document will be mentioned later in this chapter.

---

Because browsers vary greatly in the number of characters they can display across the width of the screen, and because the person using a browser can usually resize the window and change the screen width, you can't predict where a browser will make a word-wrap break. To prevent words from being broken apart, place the tag <NBSP> between the words with no spaces. In the example:

```
Our business opened its first store in 1948 in
Broken<NBSP>Chair, Texas and is now located in 14 Texas cities.<P>
```

the words "Broken Chair" will be treated as one word for word-wrap purposes.

---

**Tip:**

Most browsers offer a way to view the unprocessed HTML file that they are currently displaying (look for "View Source," "View Document," or a similar command in the browser's menus). If possible, while reading this chapter, go online with a Web browser. View a Web page as normal and then view it in its unprocessed state to see how the Web page authors accomplish various aspects of formatting and linking. After you've seen several such pages, these HTML documents will start to make more sense.

---

## Adding HTML Features for New and Legacy Browsers

While use of the latest Web page techniques and functions can create an impressive Web site, practical business considerations should make you check the impulse to always go with the newest. The majority of those on the Web are using previous generation (legacy) browsers. If reaching more customers is your prime motive, be sure to test your Web page designs on several popular browsers.

Here are some basic HTML features that are displayed and used well by graphics-oriented browsers and even by Pleistocene-era text-oriented browsers. Authoring HTML documents with both of these types of browsers in mind will maximize the number of people who can successfully use your business's pages.

### Lists

HTML provides several ways to present formatted text and lists that work with most existing browsers.

**Numbered Lists**

A numbered ("ordered") list can be displayed using the tags <OL>, </OL>, and <LI> in this manner:

```
<OL>
<LI>Transistors
<LI>Power Supplies
<LI>RAM
<LI>Resistors
<LI>Cadmium Cells
</OL>
```

This would be displayed by a browser as this numbered list:

1. Transistors
2. Power Supplies
3. RAM
4. Resistors
5. Cadmium Cells

HTML tags are easy to remember because they are generally simple abbreviations. Here, <LI> stands for "list item."

**Unnumbered Lists**

An unnumbered, bulleted list can be created using the tags <UL>, </UL>, and <LI> in this manner:

```
<UL>
<LI>Transistors
<LI>Power Supplies
<LI>RAM
<LI>Resistors
<LI>Cadmium Cells
</UL>
```

This would be displayed by a browser as a bulleted list:

• Transistors
• Power Supplies
• RAM

- Resistors
- Cadmium Cells

The shape and size of the bullet is determined by the particular browser being used by each reader.

### Definition Lists

HTML's definition list format provides for a short phrase or "definition term" (which is boldfaced and/or set on a separate line, depending on the browser) and a paragraph of text (the "definition"). The tags <DL>, </DL>, <DT>, and <DD> are used in this manner:

```
<DL>
<DT>Power Transistors
<DD>These are a special purchase lot of RF transistors. All are
25 watt, rated to 200 Megahertz. Call for specs and prices.
<DT>RAM
<DD>We specialize in keeping ALL kind of Random Access Memory
in stock AT ALL TIMES -- If you need it, we have it NOW.
</DL>
```

Figure 6.2 shows Microsoft Explorer displaying the three kinds of lists covered so far.

### Nested Lists

Any of these three list types can be inserted within any of the other lists or within a paragraph. For example, a numbered list can be used within an unnumbered, bulleted list:

```
<UL>
<LI>RAM
<LI>Precision Resistors
<LI>Transistors
<OL>
<LI>Audio Frequency Transistors
<LI>Radio Frequency Transistors
<LI>Switching Transistors
</OL>
</UL>
```

The manner in which nested lists are displayed varies from browser to browser. Netscape's display of this nested list is shown in Figure 6.3.

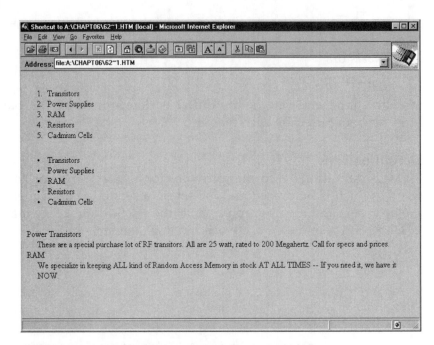

**Figure 6.2 Numbered, bulleted, and definition lists.**

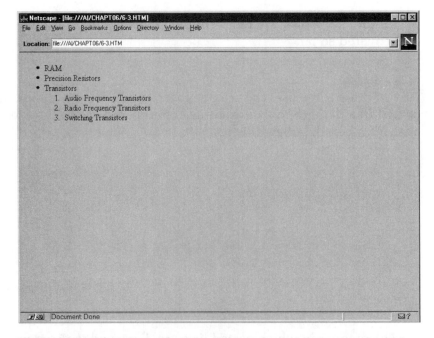

**Figure 6.3 Netscape's display of a numbered list nested within a bulleted list.**

## Preformatted Text

In addition to the list formatting options, You can use the <PRE> and </PRE> tags. HTML browsers will follow your formatting of spaces, indents, and extra lines for any text enclosed by these tags.

```
<PRE>
             At West-Texas Distributors

Transistor
          Prices
                Are
                   Dropping
                          F
                          a
                          s
                          t
                          !
</PRE>
```

This will be displayed just as it is appears above (minus the tags, of course); without the <PRE> tags, there would be no line breaks other than those that might be caused by word-wrap.

> **Tip:**
>
> When doing preformatting, keep in mind the fact that some browsers may be configured with larger fonts than yours, thus they may not display as many characters per line. Generally, try to keep preformatted text lines under 50 characters—additional characters will just disappear off the right side of the screen, beyond notice or beyond the capability of the browser. Users control many of the features in the browser, which means they will render the HTML quite differently as to width and font.

## Arrow and Ampersand Characters

Occasionally you may want to use the less than (<) and greater than (>) signs in the text of your document. Web browsers do not, however, interpret these as normal characters, but rather as belonging to command tags. Consequently, a way was developed to indicate to the browser that you want the < or > character displayed on the screen.

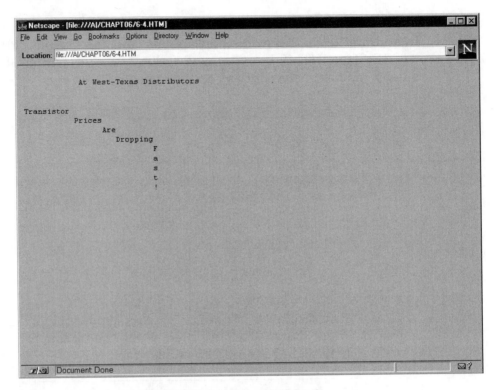

**Figure 6.4 Browser display of preformatted text.**

If you want a "<" enter this instead: `&lt;`
If you want a ">" enter this instead: `&gt;`

And because the browsers are therefore also looking at the ampersand (&) as a control character, you must use `&amp;` to direct the browsers to display the ampersand.

For example:

```
&lt; W. W. Smith &amp Sons &gt;
```

would be displayed as

```
< W. W. Smith & Sons >
```

### Horizontal Line

A horizontal line can be draw across the screen by using the <HR> (horizontal rule) tag. There is no ending tag to go with <HR>, so the line will be displayed by the browser with just this tag entered in this manner:

```
<HR>
```

### *Block Quotation*

To have a section of text offset as in a block quotation, use <BLOCK-QUOTE> and </BLOCKQUOTE> in this manner:

```
<blockquote>
Industry analysts are predicting steadily increasing costs
for power supplies, due to exceptionally high demand. You can
pre-purchase power supplies at current prices from Texas-West
now and have them shipped at your convenience.
</blockquote>
```

The way blockquotes are displayed varies greatly from browser to browser, but the displayed text would generally be indented from both left and right, appearing something like this:

```
           Industry analysts are predicting
           steadily increasing costs for power
           supplies, due to exceptionally high
           demand. You can pre-purchase power
           supplies at current prices from Texas-
           West now and have them shipped at your
           convenience.
```

### E-Mail Address

An e-mail address can be typed in as normal text in a paragraph, headline, list, and so on. But you can also use HTML to make your address an active "mailto" link. It will appear highlighted as a link, and when a visitor to your page clicks on it, a window will be displayed by the browser which allows the visitor to send an e-mail message to you. In the following example the label "Oak Ridge Research" has been used with the address "oakridge@world.std.com":

```
<A HREF="mailto:oakridge@world.std.com">Oak Ridge Research</A>
```

This will be displayed as:

```
Oak Ridge Research
```

### *Comments in an HTML Document*

To insert information in an HTML document for your own future information, or for others who may need to read your HTML source document, a pair of comment tags, <!— and —>, can be used:

```
<!--Reminder: Change prices listed in this chart early
January-->
```

Because comments are not displayed by the browser, you can insert them at any point and they will not interrupt the flow of text and pictures. Comments are especially helpful when constructing long or complex documents. They can be used as outlines, reminders to add information later, or to note, for example, which price list the displayed prices came from. Comments can be as long as you want; the only requirement is that they are enclosed in the tags shown. Remember that comments are viewable by anyone using the browser's "View Source" menu command; do not use them for information you would not wish others to see.

## Combining Formatting Features

These formatting elements can be combined in hundreds of ways to make an interesting and useful homepage or other Web page. Here is an one example combining the elements discussed so far to make a homepage for a mythical company:

```
<HTML>
<HEAD>
<TITLE>The Texas-West Electronics Supply HomePage</TITLE>
<BODY>
<H6>Welcome to:</H6>
<H2>Texas-West Electronics Supply</H2>
<H6>Retail Throughout Texas -- Wholesale Throughout the
West</H6>
<HR>
Texas-West maintains in stock, at all times, in OEM quantities,
these electronic components:<P>
<UL>
<LI>RAM
<LI>Precision Resistors
<LI>Transistors
<OL>
<LI>Audio Frequency Transistors
```

```
<LI>Radio Frequency Transistors
<LI>Switching Transistors
</OL>
</UL>
Specials this week -- &gt; <P>
<DT>RF Transistors
<DD>Over 2 dozen types of 12 watt transistors have currently
become available for 60 % off of list price. All these units are
rated above 200 Megahertz. Give us a call for specifications.
<DT>Power Supplies
<DD>OEM type internal units, 5 and 12 volts, 20 watts. Call us
-- Let's make a deal.
<P>
<blockquote>Industry analysts are predicting steadily increasing
costs for power supplies, due to exceptionally high demand. You
can pre-purchase power supplies at current prices from Texas-
West now and have them shipped at your convenience.
</blockquote>
<HR>
<PRE>
                Drop by our page often --
                        DAILY Specials beginning next week.
</PRE>
<HR>

<A HREF="mailto:texas-west@xxx.yyy.com">Click here to send
e-mail to Texas-West Electronics Supply</A>
<!--This document prepared by Oak Ridge Research.-->
</BODY>
</HTML>
```

Figures 6.5 and 6.6 show this page from top to bottom.

# Linking Documents

At this point the page is written and formatted, but one of the most important elements that makes the Web so valuable—links to other documents—has not been added. Fortunately this is a relatively easy process with HTML.

Any text or pictures can be used as a link (or "anchor"). If you used items in a simple list as individual links, they might be called menu choices; HTML documents allow words or phrases in lists, paragraphs,

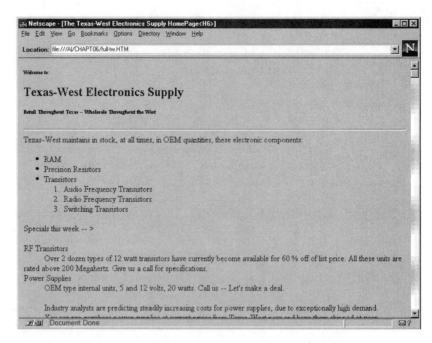

**Figure 6.5 Screen 1 of 2 of the Texas-West basic page.**

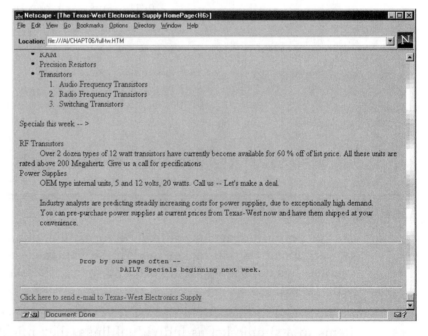

**Figure 6.6 Screen 2 of 2 of the Texas-West basic page.**

and headlines, as well as pictures, to become active links to other documents. Depending on the browser, links may be displayed as boldfaced, colored, or underlined text, graphic links are usually highlighted with an outline.

## Local Links

The procedures for linking to local documents (files stored in the same computer and subdirectory as the homepage document itself) will be discussed first; then the additional procedures for linking to documents in computers throughout the Internet will be covered.

### Links to the Top of Other Documents

It's possible to create links from any parts of the document shown in Figures 6.5 and 6.6: the headlines, the paragraphs, or (as will be shown here) the lists. Here is the list section from that document:

```
<UL>
<LI>RAM
<LI>Precision Resistors
<LI>Transistors
<OL>
<LI>Audio Frequency Transistors
<LI>Radio Frequency Transistors
<LI>Switching Transistors
</OL>
</UL>
```

Suppose Texas-West decided to write an HTML page with prices and descriptions of their RAM products. If this new page was named *"ram-list.htm"* it could be linked to the word "RAM" on the Texas-West homepage product list by modifying the HTML line from the original document:

```
<LI>RAM
```

by adding `<A href=""> </A>` in this manner:

```
<LI><A href="ram-list.htm">RAM</A>
```

On the browser display the word "RAM" will now be underlined or highlighted to indicate that it is a link. If a visitor to the Texas-West homepage site clicks on it, the Web page called *"ram-list.htm"* will be downloaded and displayed.

This procedure is used for each link you want to add to the document. Multiple links to one document are common: for instance, each occurrence of "Texas-West" on the homepage might be linked to the file describing Texas-West.

> **Note:**
>
> HTML documents are often prepared and tested using DOS, Windows, or other operating systems that only allow eight-character names with three-character extensions. Most browsers accept the three-letter extension *.htm* to identify HTML files. But when these files are copied to your ISP's computer for public use, the filename extension should be changed to the four-letter .html extension, and local links in each document should usually be changed to *.html* as well.

### *Links to Specific Locations Within Documents*

The linking procedure just described directs the browser to download a particular HTML document and to display the top of the file. You can, however, link to any part of that document that you want. For instance, suppose Texas-West's marketing department turned out one long document of transistor prices, instead of one each for audiotransistors, RF transistors, and switching transistors. No matter which of the three kinds of transistors the customer activated, the same full transistor document would be downloaded, but you could indicate to the browser that the document should be displayed starting at a particular relevant point. This is done by a special kind of anchor code.

To add this kind of link, both the file you are linking from, and the file you are linking to, will need to be modified. First use a text editor to edit the document that is the full list of transistors (we'll call it *transist.html*). At the point in the document where the list for each type of transistor starts, insert a "named anchor"—for example:

```
<A NAME="switching">Switching Transistor Prices</A>
```

The name "switching" was just chosen as an easy-to-remember name for this location in the document. You can assign any name or number you wish, as long as it is unique in the NAME tags for that document.

Let's assume that "Switching Transistor Prices" is text that already existed in the transist.html document as a subhead. `<A NAME="switching">` is inserted before this text and `</A>` is inserted after it. This makes it the destination or target of the link you are creating.

This procedure is done for each of the locations in the document that you will be linking *to*.

In the document you will be linking *from*, a link is installed in much the same manner as was previous explained for linking to the top of a Web page. The link *to* the switching transistor section would be entered this way:

```
<A HREF="transist.html#switching">Switching Transistors</A>
```

This is like a normal link to the top of *"transist.html"* but with the addition of the pound sign (#) followed by the *named anchor* in the document being linked to. With this addition, a click on the link will bring the user directly to that section of the target Web page.

Links can also be made to other parts within the *current* HTML document. This allows for very fast movement within the document because it has already been read into memory by the user's browser. A document can have a table of contents, for example, with each item linked to the appropriate section of the document.

For marketing this feature can be important—many people visit a homepage and either just look at the first screen, or scroll aimlessly down a few screens and then leave. Links from the top of the page to other parts of the document will more quickly sort out customers with different interests and bring them to sections that interest them.

To make links within a document, install named anchors at points you will want to link to, exactly as was explained before. To install the links at the points you will be linking *from*, use the same procedures previously described for linking to other documents with one exception: leave out the document's filename.

**Tip:**

Some of those visiting your homepage may have relatively slow links to the Internet—many of your potential customers are using dial-up Internet access providers currently with 9600 or 14,400

baud modems. Putting too much in one document will cause delays—and irritation with your Web site. A rule of thumb under
current conditions is to keep documents under 100 kilobytes when
possible.

## Remote Links

The links shown so far have only been to files on one computer, in one
subdirectory. But you aren't restricted to links to your own pages. There
are around 50 million Web pages on the Internet, and any of these can
also be linked to your Web pages. In addition, most Web browsers can
deal directly with other kinds of remote servers, including handling
Gopher, FTP, WAIS, and NNTP protocols.

Many browsers have been programmed to connect with these various servers and interact with them using the remote server's own protocol. The information the browser needs to do this is in the URL. A
URL contains information about the remote server's protocol, address,
directory structure, and the filename. For example, Oak Ridge Research's homepage has this URL:

*http://www.oak-ridge.com/orr.html.*

The URL can be broken up into these parts:

- Server's protocol: *http*
- Server's address: *www.oak-ridge.com*
- Subdirectory path to a particular file on the server's computer: (In
  this case no subdirectory was needed. If needed it would be in the
  form of directory/directory/directory)
- Filename of document being sought: *orr.html*

Let's say you want to link to this page on Oak Ridge's site by
adding the <A HREF> tag to some appropriate anchor words, such as
"Oak Ridge's Homepage." Here's how it would look:

```
<A HREF="http://www.oak-ridge.com/orr.html">Oak Ridge's
Homepage</A>
```

When your page is read in a browser, the words "Oak Ridge's
Homepage" would now appear highlighted as a link, and clicking on
the words would immediately bring the reader to the Oak Ridge page.

Following are some of the URL protocol types most often used in links. While the Web HTTP protocol is by far the major protocol on the Internet, several older Internet systems still contain substantial information that you may want to provide links to from your Web pages; these are discussed in the following sections.

### HTTP

This is the Web's native protocol. HTTP links allow the best use of the browser's full abilities. The preceding example uses an HTTP link to the URL *http://www.oak-ridge.com/orr.html.*

### Gopher

Gopher is a menu-based Internet client-server system. Many ISPs, organizations, businesses, and others with nodes on the Internet run Gopher servers. Each server has a top menu that branches extensively through layer after layer of menus. Menu items lead to other servers throughout the world and to files that can be text documents, images, sound files, or any other kind of binary or text files. Some GUI interfaces are available for Gopher, but it is primarily used in text mode. Web browsers have made Gopher, which was itself a major improvement in user-friendliness, even easier to use.

A URL such as this leads to the top-level menu of a particular Gopher: *gopher://gopher.std.com.*

If the Gopher you are linking to has a port number listed with it, the number must be included in the URL (as it is very occasionally done for http addresses as well) in this manner: *gopher://gopher.std.com:70.*

When linking to a particular Gopher menu, the path from the top of the Gopher down through each menu must be indicated in this manner using the URL displayed by your browser when you visit the site:

*gopher://gopher.tc.umn.edu/11/Other%20Gopher%20and%20
Information%20Servers/all*

### FTP

FTP sites have been the traditional mass storage area of Internet files. Access to these sites in the past has been through command-line style FTP programs. That means that if you didn't learn to type in an ordered series of commands, the program would pretty much just sit there with a blinking cursor. Web browsers now make access to FTP directories and files very easy.

Web browsers display FTP sites' directories as if they were HTML documents, with each directory listing displayed as a link. To go to the next directory, just click on it. The selected directory will then be displayed. To go up the directory tree, use the usual procedure in your browser for going back to a previous document. Most of the browser's usual downloading and viewing options can be used with the FTP files as they are with HTML documents.

A URL for the top public directory at an FTP site takes this form:

*ftp://wuarchive.wustl.edu/.*

If a specific directory is wanted, add the directory path such as this one:

*ftp://wuarchive.wustl.edu/pub/MSDOS_UPLOADS/*

If a specific file is to be linked, use this form:

*ftp://wuarchive.wustl.edu/pub/MSDOS_UPLOADS/READ.ME*

Most browsers will, when connected with FTP sites, recognize the ".html" extension, and display any such document with full formatting and links. Thus, a single HTML file or a group of interlinked files can be stored in an FTP directory at your ISP's site, and therefore offer a useful, though not full-featured, "Web site."

### Usenet (NNTP)

Many of the approximately 20,000 Usenet news discussion groups can be viewed using some Web browsers (and with some browsers, the messages can be responded to). There are probably groups that directly or indirectly discuss issues related to your area of business. Links to these groups can be offered from your business's homepage to increase interest in your products and services, and to bring individuals back to your homepage later as a convenient route to the newsgroup.

The URLs for newsgroups have a special syntax. For example, the URL for the group alt.business.misc is *news:alt.business.misc.*

The particular collection of newsgroups available at your site depends on which locally defined news server your ISP defines. Be sure to check the availability of a group before linking it to your document, and read the group's postings for a while to determine its suitability.

## Adding HTML Style and Appearance Features

Most of the HTML functions and elements so far have to do with the basic workings of a Web page, and in fact, would be displayed on a text-only Web browser in much the same way as on full-featured graphics-oriented browsers such as Netscape or Microsoft Explorer. For a business, a Web page's appearance, in this era of widespread online competition, is very important. Following are some of the basic style and appearance elements that should be part of any basic Web page. (See Chapter 7 for existing and developing multimedia elements for further enhancing Web pages.)

### Font Sizes and Styles

The headings installed in the example of Texas-West's homepage used tags with numbers from 1 to 6, indicating the size of the heading. There are several other ways to alter the appearance of displayed words.

```
<EM>text you want to emphasize</EM>
```

The emphasis tag, depending on the browser your visitor is using, will cause some noticeable change in the words' appearance. Sometimes this will be a color change or use of italics.

```
<STRONG>text you want to emphasize more dramatically</STRONG>
```

The strong emphasis tag will, depending on the browser, cause some more noticeable changes in the words' appearance. Sometimes this will be a color change or the use of boldfacing.

```
<I>text you want to italicize</I>
```

The italics tag will, on most GUI browsers, display the text between the tags in italics.

```
<B>text you want to be bolded</B>
```

The bold tag, on most GUI browsers, displays the text in bold type.

```
<CODE>text you want displayed in a fixed width font</CODE>
```

On many browsers CODE will produce a typewriter-like font for the text between the start and end tags.

```
<U>text you want underlined</U>
```

Many, but not all, browsers support the underline feature.

---

**Note:**

Underlining on a Web page may look like the link highlighting on some browsers and may lead your site's visitors to think you have links that don't work.

---

**Tip:**

Because each browser interprets formatting commands a bit differently, and because individuals may have configured their headline size and other characteristics differently, HTML formatting is not an exact science. If possible, get a hold of several browsers, and check how each displays your documents.

---

## Inline Images

Inline images are those which are automatically displayed by browsers within an HTML page (unless this function has been turned off in the browser to save time). They are usually kept small to speed up the acquisition, and display, of a page. They are excellent for marketing because they can quickly give a page a much more memorable identity than even the best text-only displays. They can be used for company logos, menus of product types, and for making all of your business's documents quickly recognizable with common style elements.

Each time someone visits your page, a separate call goes to your ISP's server to load each of the image files (which are usually in either GIF or JPEG format, as indicated by the filename extension). Image files can be a lot bulkier than text files, and it can take a while for them to reach the visitor's browser, and then for the browser to display them. However, subsequent displays of the same image take very little extra time, since once they are loaded, the images stay in computer memory for some time. This means that it doesn't hurt to use logos, buttons, and other images on every page of your site.

Inserting an image only requires one tag (there is no paired ending tag). In this example, Texas-West's logo, the butterfly image, is stored in a graphics file named *butterfly.gif*. At the point in the document where you want the picture displayed, type the HTML tag for inline images:

```
<IMG SRC="">
```

Then insert the image's filename between the quotation marks:

```
<IMG SRC="buterfly.gif">
```

Have the graphics file stored in the same subdirectory at your ISP's site as your other Web documents. That's all there is to it!

> **Note:**
>
> Currently, most browsers only have built-in capability to display GIF and JPEG types of graphics files. Therefore, to insure that everyone can see your inline images, it is best to convert all graphics files to one of these two types. (Chapter 7 explains how to get, make, and convert graphics files.)

Inline pictures can also work as anchors for links to other files. Instead of clicking on highlighted word(s), the visitor to your page just clicks on the picture. The link can be to any kind of resource, document, sound, or picture that a text anchor could link to. Often the small inline picture is linked to a larger version of the same picture, allowing the visitor to your page the chance to choose which images are worth the download time.

A picture link anchor is constructed just like a text anchor, except that the inline image's <IMG SRC> tag, instead of text, is between the anchor's starting and ending tags.

In this example, Texas-West's company logo inline image is used as an anchor to link to its HTML document *"about-tw.html"* (a Web page describing Texas-West). A normally constructed pair of link tags are written to enable the browser to link to the document *"about-tw.html"*:

```
<A HREF="about-tw.html"> </A>
```

Then the inline image tag is inserted between the tags:

```
<A HREF="about-tw.html"><IMG SRC="buterfly.gif"></A>
```

## External Images

Large images are usually best as external pictures that don't show at the time the homepage is first displayed, but can be viewed when an anchor is clicked on. The anchor for linking to an external picture can be text or a small inline miniature of the external picture.

When you are visiting a Web page and click on a link to an external picture, the browser on your personal computer doesn't always use its own built-in graphics viewer, but may instead load another image viewer as a window over part of the browser. The viewer program can then be closed and the browser will function again. Most browsers come with some external viewers, but you can also use others as long as you reconfigure your browser with the new program name and directory path to it. (This is something only the visitor, not the Web page designer, has control of.)

External graphics files should be stored with their normal graphics file extension (.gif, .jpg, etc.) so that viewer programs can recognize them and display them appropriately.

To provide a link to a picture, use the standard link tags:

```
<A HREF=""> </A>
```

Insert the graphic file's name between the quotation marks in the beginning tag:

```
<A HREF="our-logo.gif"> </A>
```

Then insert the tag somewhere appropriate in the document's text, surrounding an appropriate anchor word, phrase, or <IMG SRC> tag with the beginning and ending tags:

```
Our newly designed <A HREF="our-logo.gif">company logo.</A>
```

> **Tip:**
>
> While some individuals may have a dozen different image viewers linked to their browser, most don't. Your pictures are more likely to be viewed if you make them in, or convert them to, one of the popular image types such as GIF or JPEG (extensions .gif, .jpg).

When images are used as anchors for links to other documents, or when they convey some instructions or other information, some provision should be made for text-mode browsers and browsers that have display problems. One approach to this is to use an HTML feature that allows you to offer text in place of graphics automatically when the graphics file isn't displayed. In this example the text sentence: "Give us a call for specifications." has the word "call" marked as an anchor linked to the graphics file "phones.gif" (this is a picture of Texas-West's offices, with the company phone numbers in the corner).

```
Give us a <A HREF="phones.gif">call</A> for specifications.
```

Text browser users wouldn't have direct access to this picture (they would have to download the GIF file and then load a GIF viewer to get the phone number—not exactly great PR). HTML, however, allows you to insert some alternative (ALT) text in place of the picture by adding

ALT="" (with the text of your choice between the quotation marks). Assembled, the link looks like this:

```
Give us a <A HREF="phones.gif" ALT="Texas-West 1 800 555-
1212">call </A> for specifications.
```

---

**Tip:**

A large percentage of those browsing the Web view pages on standard VGA screens. Therefore, for good screen layout check your HTML documents by viewing them on a browser using the 640x480 VGA mode. Layout usually suffers less from being displayed on a screen with higher resolution than yours than on one with lower resolution.

---

# A Look at a Finished Homepage

This document provides examples of most of the HTML commands and features mentioned in this chapter, and shows how they might be used together to make a homepage. Figures 6.7 through 6.9 show the results as displayed by the Netscape browser.

```
<HTML>

<HEAD>
<TITLE>The Texas-West Electronics Supply HomePage</TITLE>
</HEAD>

<BODY>
<CENTER> <IMG SRC="buterfly.gif"> </CENTER>
<H4>Welcome to:</H4>
<H2>Texas-West Electronics Supply</H2>
<H4>Retail Throughout Texas -- Wholesale Throughout the
West</H4>
<HR>
Texas-West offers deep discount <A HREF="#specialoffers">
specials</A> and maintains in stock, <U>at all times</U>, in OEM
quantities,<BR>these electronic components:<P>
<UL>
<LI><A HREF="ram-list.html">RAM</A>
<LI><A HREF="resistor.html">Precision Resistors</A>
<LI>Transistors
<OL>
<LI><A HREF="transist.html#audiotransistors">Audio Frequency
Transistors</A>
<LI><A HREF="transist.html#rf-transistors">Radio Frequency
Transistors</A>
<LI><A HREF="transist.html#switching">Switching Transistors</A>
</OL>
</UL>
<P>
<IMG ALIGN=bottom SRC="buterfly.gif">
<A NAME="specialoffers"><B>&lt; SPECIALS THIS WEEK
&gt;</B></A><P>
<DT>RF Transistors
<DD>Over 2 dozen types of 12 watt transistors have currently
become available for 60% off of list price. All these units are
rated above 200 Megahertz.<BR>Give us a <A HREF="phones.gif "
ALT="Texas-West 1 800 555-1212>call </A> for specifications.
<DT>Power Supplies
<DD>OEM type internal units, 5 and 12 volts, 20 watts. <A
HREF="phones.gif " ALT="Texas-West 1 800 555-1212>Call</A>us --
Let's make a deal.
<P><P>
<blockquote>Industry analysts are predicting steadily increasing
costs for power supplies, due to exceptionally high demand.<I>
```

```
You can pre-purchase power supplies at current prices from
Texas-West now and have them shipped at your convenience.</I>
</blockquote>
<HR>
<PRE>
Drop by our page often --
              <B>DAILY SPECIALS</B> beginning next week.
</PRE>
<HR>
<A HREF="mailto:texas-west@xxx.yyy.com">Click here to send
e-mail to Texas-West Electronics Supply</A><BR>
<A HREF="about-tw.html"><IMG ALIGN=bottom
SRC="buterfly.gif"></A>
<B>Learn more about the Southwest's top parts supplier, click
on this Texas- West "BubbaFly"</B>
<!--This document prepared by Oak Ridge Research.-->
</BODY>
</HTML>
```

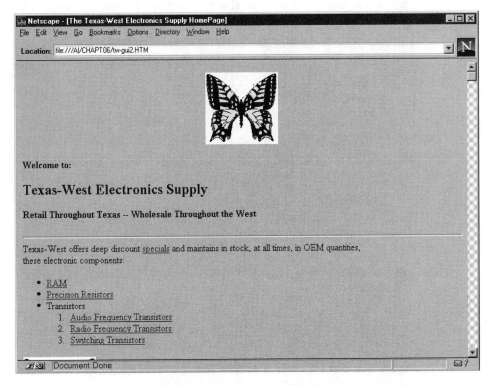

**Figure 6.7  Screen 1 of 3 of the Texas-West Homepage example.**

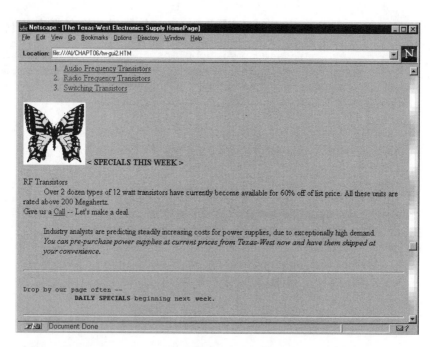

**Figure 6.8  Screen 2 of 3 of the Texas-West Homepage example.**

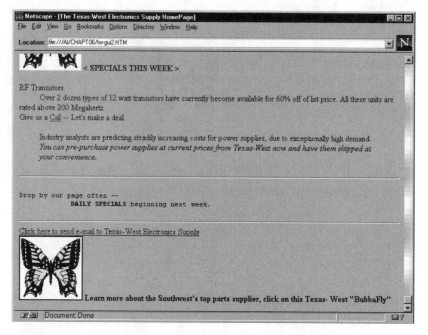

**Figure 6.9  Screen 3 of 3 of the Texas-West Homepage example.**

# Online Resources for Learning HTML

At this point you have the basics you need for understanding the whys and hows of HTML. If you decide to pursue Web page design yourself, you can get books that cover nothing but HTML writing. You can also keep very up-to-date with online resources. Here are some of the best:

- *Netscape* provides a site with information for beginning and advanced HTML authors: *http//home.netscape.com/assist/net_sites/index.html*.

- *The Web/HTML Documentation and Developer's Resource* site at the University of Toronto provides well-organized and well-written documents to help in learning and writing HTML: *http://www.utoronto.ca/webdocs/webinfo.html*.

- *The Web Developer's Virtual Library* is a huge collection of information on writing HTML and many other aspects of creating a Web site. For a quick overview of what is available, check the Table of Contents page: *http://www.stars.com*.

- *The World Wide Web Consortium* provides a very up-to-date site for system administrators, webmasters, and HTML authors. The information for HTML authors includes several well-written beginner's guides. This site can also help give insights into the problems and challenges faced by system administrators and webmasters that you'll be dealing with as your Web site becomes more sophisticated. Look for the page "Putting Information onto the Web" at *http://www.w3.org/hypertext/WWW/Provider/Overview.html*.

## Software Assistance in HTML Authoring

While you can get started writing HTML documents with a simple word processor, that will become tedious in very short order. There are three basic types of HTML editors:

- *HTML Editors.* These programs provide an assortment of features that speed up document writing and provide ways to avoid having to remember the exact syntax of HTML. These editors usually provide a way to automatically link the document you are writing to your Web browser so you can periodically examine your progress.

- *Word Processor Macros and Overlays.* These are files that work with particular word processors. They bring the power of some of the more advanced word processors to HTML editing.

- *WYSIWYG HTML Authoring Programs (WYSIWYG stands for "What You See Is What You Get.").* This category of authoring program presents the Web author with a screen that looks much like a Web page. Text is typed on this virtual page, formatted, and moved much like text in a word processor. Images are moved and resized with the mouse. The authoring program then processes this virtual page into an HTML file that can be displayed as normal by Web browsers.

While the WYSIWYG programs seem like the obvious choice, they handle only the HTML functions they were initially designed to handle. Even if you use a WYSIWYG program for designing the initial page, you may also want to be comfortable with an HTML editor so you can go beyond the capabilities of the WYSIWYG program and incorporate new techniques and tags as they develop.

HTML Assistant is a free-standing HTML editor that has buttons to click on for various HTML functions as well as aids to getting a Web page started. This program is available online from *ftp://ftp.cs.dal.ca/htmlasst/*. Click on the file *"htmlasst.zip"* to download it to your computer.

Numerous macros and overlays for several popular word processors are listed at *http://www.unimelb.edu.au/html-info/dev-page2.html*.

Here are some additional products to explore:

- The free 2.0 version of HoTMetaL can be downloaded at *http://www.sq.com/products/hotmetal/hm-feat.htm*. A commercial version (HoTMetaL 3.0) is also available.

- FrontPage from Microsoft is another full-feature editor. Find out more at *http://www.microsoft.com/frontpage/*.

- HotDog and HotDog Pro are available from *http://www.sausage.com/download.htm*.

## From Here . . .

While HTML documents as discussed in this chapter can be written in many creative and interesting ways, pages can be made much more attractive, useful, and easy to use by adding pictures, movies, sounds, input forms, and databases.

Chapter 7 discusses multimedia additions that can make your Web pages stand out from the crowd—a real competitive advantage in Internet marketing.

# Adding Graphics, Sound, Databases, Action, and Interactivity to a Web Site

Web browsers are designed with the ability to take on the display and processing of a great variety of file types—even file types not yet invented. This is possible because browsers can use helper programs to process and display files retrieved from the Web. These helper programs can be the picture viewers mentioned in Chapter 6, movie viewers, sound file players, PostScript and other formatted file viewers, databases, word processors, or just about any program that can be opened as a window over the browser program. Commands are added to the HTML documents that direct the browser to download a particular file, open the appropriate program, and process the file. If the browser version being used doesn't recognize the file type, it will either ignore the file, or open a window allowing you to download and store the file for later processing or display.

In order to experience the page the way you intended, the visitor to your page must therefore have the appropriate viewer (sometimes called plug-in or add-on) for the type of external file you have offered a link to, and it must be appropriately added to that visitor's browser configuration files. In Mosaic, for example, you can configure these options under the Preferences item, and then under .gifs and Data Engines. In Netscape these are also found under Options, Preferences, and

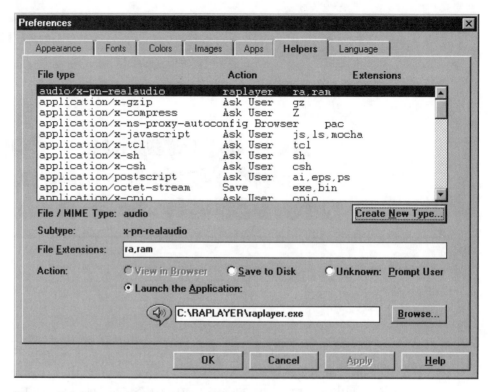

**Figure 7.1 The Netscape Helpers pane.**

then Helpers, as seen in Figure 7.1. In Microsoft Explorer, these can be found under the View, Options menu with the File Types tab.

Keep in mind that from a business standpoint, it does no good to have pages that can glow, rotate, and beam down space aliens, if most of your potential customers are using last year's garden variety browser—in fact, pages that are too cutting edge to display well on popular browsers may alienate potential customers.

## Graphics

Pictures and other graphics files can provide a much more memorable visit to your pages than text files alone. And, of course, pictures can include text—with total control over the formatting, color, and layout, just as on a magazine page.

Graphics can provide an easy and accurate way to present your products and company. They are also useful for entertainment and to provide additional information to attract visitors to your pages.

> **Note:**
>
> While there are dozens of graphics formats that can be used for digitally stored pictures, one is by far the most widely supported by browsers for inline images (images that are displayed when the page is initially downloaded): GIF (use filename extension .gif). JPEG (use filename extension .jpg), which can store pictures with fewer bytes, is now being accepted by an increasing number of browsers.

## Making Picture and Graphics Files

Original graphics and picture files can be made using computer screen captures, scanned hardcopy images, video frame grabbers, digital cameras, and computer-generated graphics (such as PaintShop Pro and Photoshop for example).

### *Screen Capture*

There are many programs that will "capture" your personal computer's screen image. A capture program makes a file on your disk that, when displayed by a viewer, will look exactly as your computer screen did at the time you requested the capture.

Captured images can come from anything that you can get on your computer's screen, such as: a portion of a spreadsheet, graphs and charts displayed by a spreadsheet, graphics from drawing programs, and for software sales, screens showing the software running.

To do a capture, start the capture program. After you choose the configuration settings for the format the file is to be saved in, name the image you will be saving, and so on, the program disappears, but continues to run in the background. Now open the program or file that you are interested in capturing. When everything on the screen looks as you want it, just press a previously defined key or combination of keys. The image on the screen is then captured as a graphics file.

### Scanned Images

If you have photographs, or graphics on paper, you can use a scanner to copy them as digital graphics files. Scanners vary in the resolution they can scan (usually measured in dpi—dots per inch), and the number of colors (if any) they can detect. As the number of colors and resolution increase, the graphics file size increases dramatically. While your may wish to do the original scan at the highest settings, the files will probably have to be reduced in size and resolution by some of the techniques mentioned later in this chapter.

Hand scanners are the least expensive scanners ($100+). They are available in models with moderately high resolution levels and numbers of colors. Most hand scanners cover a strip approximately four inches wide each time they are rolled over the picture. These strips of graphics can then be assembled in the computer into one whole image. For good results, you must take care to make a straight, smooth pass over the picture.

Page (or "flat bed") scanners ($400+) can usually scan a picture the size of a sheet of typing paper in one pass. There are an increasing number of businesses (such as photocopy centers) that offer page scan services. These could be a good choice if you need a relatively small number of graphics files.

### Video Frame Grabbers

Video frame grabbers are used with video cameras, camcorders, and videocassette recorders to capture still pictures. They use a combination hardware and software to capture one of the still pictures (frames) that make up a moving video picture. This picture is then uploaded to a computer as a normal graphics file.

While not nearly as high in resolution as a page scanner, video frame grabbers do have advantages for some applications. One obvious use is for taking pictures at regular intervals to assemble into a digital movie (see the Movies section below).

The frame grabber can also be used to offer picture files that are updated on a regular basis. Many companies are now showing frequently updated pictures of their offices, pets, and mascots—any view that might attract some attention to their site and business. There are many marketing possibilities with this technique. For example, a mall developer could show daily updated pictures of the mall being built, in order to keep it on the minds of vendors who might rent space, as well as to build customer attention and anticipation.

### Digital Cameras

Digital cameras use electronics systems similar to those in video cameras, but store still pictures, or short sequences of pictures. These cameras use a variety of storage systems, usually computer memory–type chips that allow a limited number of images (most often, several dozen) to be stored. The images then can be displayed on TV screens or printed (with some systems), and with most digital cameras, the pictures can be uploaded to a computer (and the memory in the camera then erased, awaiting new pictures). Most such systems come with at least basic image processing and file type conversion software—making them easy to use for quick Web page images.

### Computer-Generated Graphics

Graphics programs are useful not only for developing graphics images, but for modifying pictures originally created and stored electronically by any other of the techniques described. You can use these programs to add frames and text, to combine several picture and graphics files into one composite picture, or to do photo retouching and other alterations.

The graphics being displayed on the Web are, in many cases, very well done. Therefore, it is worthwhile to get a graphics program that is as sophisticated as possible.

## Processing Files

Basic drawing programs allow one to work on small parts of a photo; graphics viewing/photo processing programs, on the other hand, often offer a collection of processes that can be applied to the whole picture to affect size, color, and special effects.

### Changing the Image Size to Reduce File Size

The limits on file transfer speed on the Internet, especially at the user end, where many are still using 14,400 baud modems, puts a premium on carefully planned graphics that provide the most punch with the least load on the system. One good direct approach to reducing the number of kilobytes in a graphics file is to reduce the size of the picture. This can be done in several ways.

If there are any edges of the picture that are not needed (too much sky? too much grass?), the picture can be "cropped" (the unneeded edges removed). Image-viewing or drawing programs that do this usually place a vertical and a horizontal line on the screen. You then move them with the mouse to indicate at what point the picture is to be cut off.

If the picture looks fine as it is, but is still too large, it can be squeezed. Graphics programs do this by removing pixels within the image according to some predetermined calculation. If, for instance, you ask the program to reduce the height and width by 50%, it might remove every second row and column of pixels—resulting in a file approximately 25% the size of the original. If the size reduction is to something like 57%, the program can't remove lines at a regular interval (as it did reducing the size by 50%). It must therefore do some calculations, and by considering the color of surrounding pixels, decide what color each pixel should be. Graphics programs vary quite a bit in how successful they are at this. Some offer several techniques which you can experiment with.

Usually pictures are squeezed or expanded by the same percentage both horizontally and vertically, maintaining the "aspect ratio" of the original. Changing the aspect ratio can be helpful when working on the separate elements to be included in a composite picture. When working with pictures of people, though, you will probably need to maintain the aspect ratio (even if you find it tempting to take 20 pounds off and add 2 inches to the height of everyone in your staff picture).

### Reducing the File Size Without Shrinking the Image

Another good way to reduce the number of kilobytes required to store the image is to reduce the number of colors. Some images are stored with colors represented by 24 bits. Reducing these files to 8-bit colors reduces file size dramatically. While 24-bit colors do show more subtle differences, 8-bit colors work well for most pictures and other graphics files on the Web. Also note, many computers currently on the Web are equipped for a maximum of 256 colors, and while the files with more colors will be displayed, the extra color information will be lost to the end user.

When you tell a graphics program to reduce the number of colors in an image file, the program puts the file through a process called dithering in which it is decided which color should replace the original pixel color. The results of dithering vary widely from one method to another. If you aren't satisfied with the results of a color reduction, see if your program has alternate dithering algorithms that can be used.

### Color Balance and Special Effects

Image-processing programs are often used to improve pictures (especially scanned-in photos) that may be off in color balance or contrast. Sometimes these functions are also used in the extreme to make unusual, interesting graphics. These photo adjustment functions usually include:

- Color balance (control of red, green, and blue components)
- Saturation
- Contrast
- Brightness
- Sharpness

Many programs also include special effects functions that can be used alone, or combined with other special effects and adjustments:

- Posterizing (makes color change boundaries more noticeable)
- Reversing (swap left and right sides of picture)
- Rotating (usually only in 90-degree increments)
- Grayscale (convert color to shades of gray picture)
- Embossing (simulated embossing of image or texture overlays)
- Negative image
- Warping (various kinds of image distortion)
- Copy/Paste/Move portions of the picture

As an example, an embossed image is used as a background for the Oak Ridge Research Web page shown in Figure 7.2.

## Converting Files

You can work on your graphics files in any format that is convenient, but at the end of your work you will have to convert them into the pop-

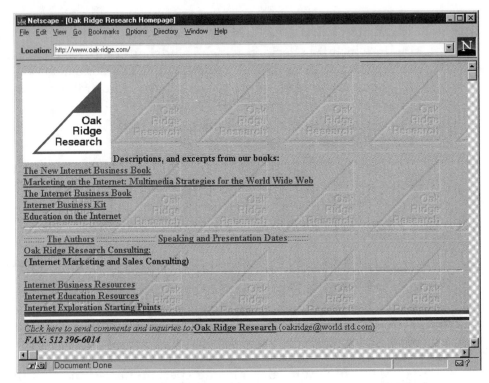

**Figure 7.2 The Oak Ridge Research page showing embossed images as background.**

ular GIF or JPEG file formats, for use on the Web. You may have to convert a file several times: if, for example, the scanner puts out a TIFF file and the drawing program you want to modify it with needs PCX files, and then the photo processor may require another format, and so on.

## Presentation Variations

There are many ways to create variations in image presentation; these include interlacing, sizing, and transparency.

### Interlaced Images

Standard GIF images can be converted to "interlaced" images. Browsers with this capability will load an interlaced image by drawing the image to the screen as a series of lines and spaces which initially look a bit like a view of the image through a set of venetian blinds, until all of the horizontal lines are filled in and the full image is displayed. (Otherwise, while a large image is loading, the viewer is likely to see an unreadable blur, or perhaps nothing at all.) This method allows the person viewing the image to get an idea of what the image is, and decide whether to wait and view the full image, or to move on down the Web page to other sections and pictures.

### Image Sizing

Some browsers allows the horizontal and vertical image size to be defined in the HTML tag that calls for the image, allowing the browsers to automatically re-size the image to match the defined size. This makes accurate page layout easier for the HTML author. It also makes viewing the Web page easier, since the browser will know how much space to leave for images as they are loading, and will lay out other elements accordingly.

### Background Transparency

Image files are defined as rectangular. This means that if you are using an image that is not rectangular, it will be surrounded by a background, so that the full image lies within a rectangle. Non-photographic images are usually prepared with some uniform background color. It is possible to define the background color to match the Web page color used by the browser; in that case, the image appears much more as if it were printed right on the page, and gives more room for creative design and layout. In the past this was fairly easy to accomplish, since most Web browsers used a standard shade of gray. Now, however, Web authors and browser users have some control over background colors. To re-accomplish the goal of making images "float" on the page, you can instead process your image designating one color as a transparent color, and use that for the background. The Web page background will then show right through the image background on browsers that support image transparency. Figure 7.3 shows how this process affects a GIF image.

Links to instructions and software for adding transparency to GIF files for UNIX, DOS/Windows, and Mac computer systems is available from:

- Adam Bernstein's "The Transparent/Interlaced GIF Resource Page" (*http://dragon.jpl.nasa.gov/~adam/transparent.html*)

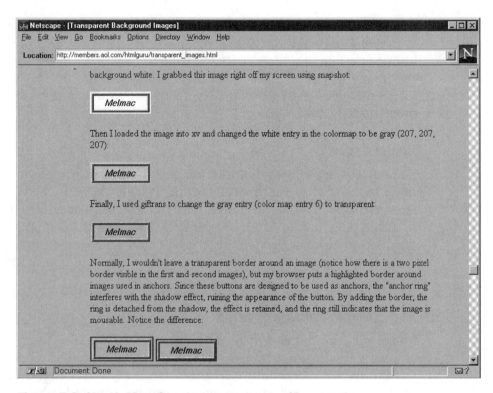

**Figure 7.3  Chuck Musciano's transparent .gif example.**

- Chuck Musciano's "Transparent Background Images" (*http://members.aol.com/htmlguru/transparent_images.html*)

## Creating Multiple Links from One Image

In Chapter 6, instructions were given for using a picture or other graphic as a link to another URL or image. One image can also be used to provide many different links at the same time. If you've explored the Web at all you have by now encountered single images that contain assortments of buttons, labels, pictures, and boxes. By clicking on portions of this larger image, you are taken to the appropriate Web pages. This kind of image is known as an imagemap.

This linking is accomplished by first making the large image using any of the techniques described above. Then, the individual portions of the image that you wish to link are mapped out based on the horizontal and vertical coordinates relative to the large image. Each of the smaller active parts of the image can be defined as a point, rectangle, circle, or regular polygon.

You must insert an ISMAP code within your IMG tag to tell the browser that an imagemap is associated with the graphic. At the same time, you must specify what URL each defined area of the image is linked to. Usually, this mapping information is provided to the ISP that handles your Web site. This information is then processed via a CGI (common gateway interface) file to deliver the appropriate Web page when it receives the coordinates of the area clicked on by the user.

Another system is currently supported by Netscape and may become a new standard—this is to do all of the processing within the browser itself. In this scenario, using the USEMAP code instead of ISMAP, you store the image-mapping information within the document itself. Then, when the user clicks on a portion of the larger image, the browser compares that portion of the image to the associated URL and directly requests that URL instead of first asking the Web server site for the URL.

Figure 7.4 shows the Time Warner Pathfinder homepage.

Programs to help you turn an image into an imagemap for use with either browser (USEMAP) or server-based (ISMAP) methods include:

- Mapedit for Windows 3.1, NT, 95, and UNIX (software and instructions available at *http://www.boutell.com/mapedit/*)
- The Absolute Resource table of contents page offers access to information and programs (select IMAGEMAPS from the topics list at *http://www2.southwind.net/~miked/ar_toc.html*).

## Sound

Links to sound files, whether inline or external, are written in HTML documents in the same way picture and HTML document links are. The sound file's filename extension indicates to the browser what the appropriate sound player program is. (Commonly used extensions are .au, .wav, .snd.)

For visitors to your page to hear an audio clip, they must have the appropriate hardware (usually a "sound card") and software drivers in-

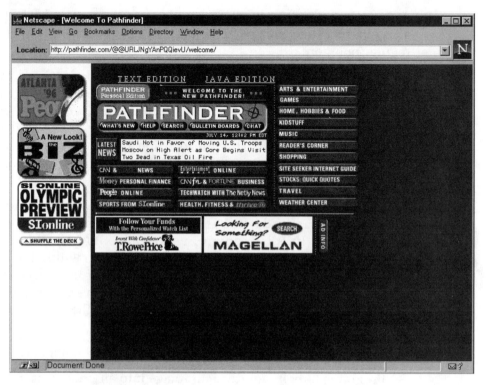

**Figure 7.4 ISMAP from Pathfinder.**

stalled in their computers. This is becoming increasingly common due to the rise in the number of multimedia-equipped computers that contain CD-ROM drives and sound cards.

## Creating Sound Files

Most multimedia computers are equipped with recording capabilities. They can be used with microphones or other external audio sources such as tape recorders. Most also have at least some minimal audio editing capabilities: sounds can be strung together, shortened, overlapped, faded, and echoed—after, or while, they are being recorded.

The best way to keep file size reasonable is to determine the lowest sampling rate (the sound capture programs provide a way to set this) that gives acceptable-sounding results. Once this sampling rate is set, you can determine how many seconds of audio you can fit into a file of reasonable size (e.g., 10 kilobytes for an inline sound, or 100 kilobytes for an external sound file).

## Continuous Feed Sound

Another approach to delivering sound is to use a bitstream delivery system. With this kind of system, after a small initial set of data is sent, the user's software starts playing the sound recording, such that while the user listens, the sound data continues to feed. With such a system, a visitor to your site can listen to sound of unlimited duration. Bitstream delivery systems are being used to, among other things, offer real-time transmissions of some radio station and network audio feeds. For examples, visit the RealAudio Web site: *http://www.realaudio.com/*), shown in Figure 7.5.

For acceptable sound quality, these systems require that the visitor to your Web site use at least a 14,400 baud modem, and a high-quality

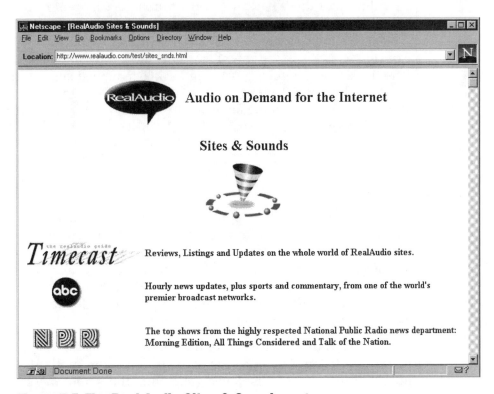

**Figure 7.5 The Real Audio Sites & Sounds page.**

connection. To offer such sound files, the server should have a large capacity and high-speed connection to the Internet.

# Action!

With the increases in modem speed and the processing speed of computers, a new generation of systems is becoming available to add movement, interactivity, and computer processing power to a Web page. This can take the form of movies, animated graphics, 3D navigation systems, and the delivery of small programs to your computer giving your computer new processing functions. These can be accomplished in numerous ways, including the use of Java and ShockWave.

> **Warning:**
>
> While use of these new Web page functions can demonstrate your cutting edge position, and offer genuinely useful functions, they also have the potential of irritating visitors to your Web site. First, of course, is the extra download time needed by some of these features. Second, there is a growing backlash against sites with excessive flashing, movement, and items that cause ongoing hard-drive thrashing. Keep your business's Web site goals and audience in mind when selecting these bells and whistles.

## Movies

Movies are not in wide use now, but their use is increasing. Browsers display external viewers to play movies (some with sound). While almost any digital movie format can be used, those with the filename extensions .mpg, .mov, .avi, and .qt are most widely available on the Web. The installed base of movie viewers is still rather small, so it is good policy to arrange for links to sites offering downloadable viewers on you Web page, if you are offering movies.

A digital movie consists of a file containing a series of still pictures (usually with one or more file size compression methods). The rate these pictures can be displayed (and thus the smoothness of the display) depends on the speed of the visitor's personal computer processing hardware and video display card/system. To improve the chances that the movie will run at a reasonable rate, the movies should be based on relatively small pictures—for example, 320 pixels by 240 pixels, which is 1/4 of a normal VGA size screen, or even 160 x 120 pixels. Even with these reduced picture sizes, a five-second movie can require over 100 kilobytes of data.

Movies are usually assembled into one file from a series of still picture files with a graphics editor designed for that purpose; sound can then be linked to the movie. The still pictures can be made by any of the methods mentioned previously in this chapter—with some incremental change from picture to picture.

Animations are used on the TASC page, *http://www.tasc.com/ENTERTAINMENT/himalayas.html*, shown in Figure 7.6.

**Figure 7.6 The Himalayan Flyover page from TASC.**

## Java/JavaScript

JavaScript (used with Netscape browsers) is not the same as Java, the applet language developed by Sun Microsystems. Both systems have just gotten started. Here's what's brewing.

### Java

Java is a programming language/system developed by Sun Microsystems, Inc. that allows browsers that support Java to read and execute programs stored within an HTML document. These small programs (called "applets") can be used to provide added features and capabilities to the Web browser.

The applets are "platform independent"—they will run on any kind of computer that is using a Java-compatible browser. Web pages with applets therefore let you provide small programs which run on your site visitors' computers, programs that can do almost anything a program written specifically for their computers and browsers could do (there are some exceptions—for example, there are controls on reading and writing to disk to limit chances for hacking and virus problems).

Applet code writing, like most programming, is definitely not a one-evening study, but prewritten applets are increasingly becoming available online for download and use in your own Web pages. Web pages with applets can be stored as normal HTML documents and used with normal Web servers.

Web browsers that are currently Java-compatible include HotJava, and Netscape browsers v. 2.0 and newer (on most platforms).

For further information and updates about Java, contact Sun Microsystem's site: *http://java.sun.com/*, shown in Figure 7.7, and read the newsgroup *comp.lang.java*.

### JavaScript

JavaScript, also under development, is another approach to making Web pages more intensely interactive, both in detection and response to user interaction with the Web page. (Merely moving a mouse over a text link anchor might, for instance, cause a sound file to be played or a graphic displayed.)

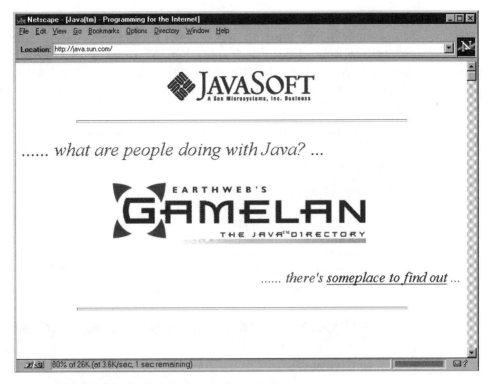

**Figure 7.7 Sun's Java Gamelan page.**

The script language is included within a normal HTML document— often between the HTML tags <SCRIPT> and </SCRIPT>. It can be additionally protected from old browsers that might not know how to interpret the script by using the standard HTML comments tags: <!-- -->.

You can keep track of JavaScript at Netscape's support pages starting at *http://home.netscape.com/comprod/products/navigator/version_2.0/ script/index.html*.

## Animated GIFs

Standard GIF format files (specifically, specification 89a), commonly used for still pictures on the Web, can be used for animations on browsers that support this extra GIF feature (on browsers that don't support animated GIFs, either the first or last image of the sequence is shown as a still image).

The speed of the animation can be adjusted, and the animation sequence can be looped to provide a continuous animation from the single, self-contained GIF file (no further information needs to be received from the Web site). These animations can make use of other GIF features such as background transparency and choice of number of colors (from 2 to 256).

Background information, tutorials, and software (Windows, DOS, Mac, UNIX) for GIF animations are available via these duplicate Web sites maintained by Royal E. Frazier:

*http://members.aol.com/royalef/gifanim.htm*
*http://emoryi.jpl.nasa.gov/royalef/gifanim.htm*
*http://www.ecafe.org/tools/gifanim/gifanim.htm*

As an example, the Lanny Silver Architect page at *http://www.cyberspc.mb.ca/~silver/* has animated GIFs, shown in Figures 7.8 and 7.9. The thumbnails of the buildings each change.

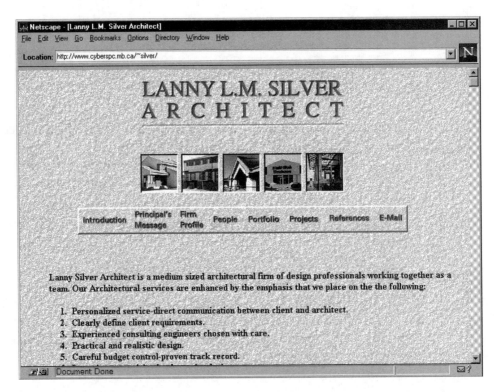

**Figure 7.8 Lanny Silver page in one .gif state.**

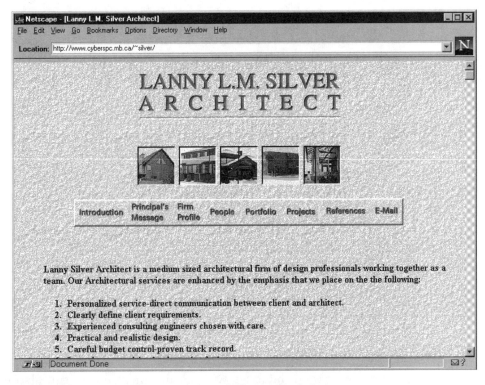

**Figure 7.9 Lanny Silver page in another .gif state.**

## Databases

A database is rather broadly defined on the Web. It can be pretty much any collection of information, whether in single or multiple files. While databases are usually files intended for computer searches, some are lists that are alphabetized or organized by topics in a way that human readers can find items.

Offering databases of general interest, or databases related to your business's area of expertise, is a good way to get return traffic to your Web page. The databases you offer can either be those on other sites, linked to your page, or those prepared and maintained by your business.

In addition, your products, customer support information about them, and other more direct marketing information can be made available via a database.

## Existing Databases

There are thousands of currently existing databases that you can link to a Web page with an anchor just as you would any normal HTML document. This will give access to the database you've found to whoever visits your homepage.

To find databases appropriate to your business, use the search services such as Lycos, AltaVista, and WebCrawler. Check each database site occasionally to be sure the database is still available and up-to-date.

Most Web links are made without any contacts, arrangements, or contracts between the sites involved. However, if your site brings substantial traffic (tens of thousands of "hits") to a nonprofit site, you may offer, or be called on to provide, some support for the site. On the other hand, if the site you are linking to is a commercial site, you may be able to make arrangements to profit from the traffic you send their way. Also consider making arrangements to have the site offer links to your site, either as an enhancement to their site (if you are offering useful content) or for payment.

## Offering Your Own Database

Offering your own database will require more effort, but also will focus more attention on your company. A well done, up-to-date, useful database will also encourage others throughout the Web to add links to your database. Be sure to provide very visible links from each database document to your homepage—some visitors may be arriving at your database via direct links to it from other sites, and you don't want them to miss your homepage's marketing information.

### Browser-Based Databases

Browser-based databases range from simple word searches of text documents to intricate pages with inline images, formatted text, and complex interlinking. Browser-based searches must be kept to a reasonable size, since the browser will download the whole document in order to be able to search it. If your database is over 100 kilobytes, break it into parts in some logical way, and start the database with a small page where visitors choose what portion of the database they are interested in. This will allow you to link them to smaller, more focused portions of the database.

### Word Searches

The easiest form of databases to prepare makes use of the fact that most browsers can search for words within a document (the particular commands vary from browser to browser). With this type of database, any common text file, converted to a basic HTML file, could be used. This method can be used well with lists, especially with lists that will not have very many "hits" for any particular word search (e.g., lists of telephone numbers, where the words being looked for are individuals' names).

In unorganized lists and for text files, these browser-based searches can be a bit frustrating for the visitor to use. This can be overcome by organizing the material in some manner and then, at the top of the document, telling the visitor how it is organized. This will allow the visitor to more accurately select words to search for; in addition, if the material has been grouped, most of the occurrences of the word will be in a single area that is relatively easy to read.

### Links Databases

Another way of offering a database is to use HTML links. As was explained in Chapter 6, links can be made within a document, as well as to other documents. By writing links into the database, providing HTML text formatting, and organizing the database material in some logical manner, you can offer a very high quality database.

For data that changes often, you can provide links to small, non-HTML text files. Then you only need to delete the old text files and put in new ones with the same names to provide fast updates.

In additions to links at the top of the document to various sections and subsections, include repeated links back to the top of the document, and to the tops of any subsections.

This kind of database will require greater initial effort, but the result will be user-friendly and of very high quality.

### Server-Based Databases

For a database that is very large or contains quickly changing data, a server-based database might be the best choice. This kind of database makes use of HTML "forms," which display not only the usual page elements, but also text boxes to allow users to type in input, and check-boxes and buttons for making selections.

For example, if you have a database of retail price histories for a certain group of products, you might create a form with checkboxes for each category of products and a text input area for the visitor to type the range of dates to include in the result.

When the visitor to your database page clicks on the "submit form" area of the screen, the entered information is sent to a particular Web server; there, a stored script tells the server how to make the search using the data the visitor entered, and how to format the results before sending them back to the visitor.

For installation, storage, and maintenance of such a database, you will need to make arrangements with your Internet service provider.

## Input Forms

Input forms can provide very effective collection of information from visitors to Web sites. Your site can make use of database search forms, sales forms, feedback forms, and so on. These forms can include fields for information to be typed in, checkboxes, radio buttons (selection buttons that allow only one choice), and pull-down selection menus. An input form is defined by HTML tags; the form elements are then interpreted and displayed by the browser.

The information sent from the browser after the form is filled out and submitted needs to be interpreted and stored using a script (such as a CGI script) at the Web server's site. Form preparation, therefore, is usually provided by Web site staff or other professionals. Figure 7.10 show the form on the Godiva Chocolate page for ordering a catalog (*http://www.godiva.com/services/catalog-godiva.html*).

## Frames

Another page layout element under current development is that of separate windows to divide a page into several parts or "frames." Each frame has its own scrollbars so the viewer can move around within it without affecting the view in the other frames. The Web page author can also specify that viewers be able to resize each frame. Each frame

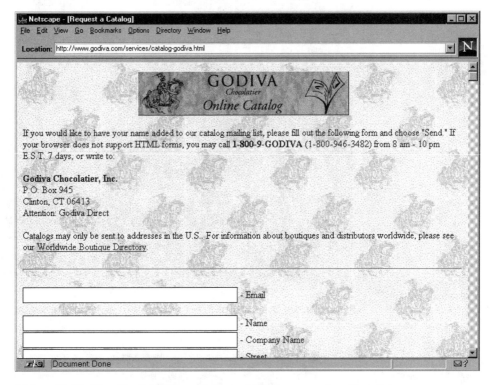

**Figure 7.10 The Godiva Chocolate catalog request online form.**

can have a separate URL and can be made to work interactively with the other frames. Thus, for instance, one frame could include a scrollable table of contents that could call up portions of a large document in another frame, and still a third frame containing copyright and contact information could be held static. Frames are likely to become incredibly interactive devices with the addition of Java and JavaScript.

Figure 7.11 shows the Gif Animation page from Royal Frazier Gallery page (*http://members.aol.com/royalef/galframe.htm*) using frames, and Figure 7.12 shows the non-frame version of that page.

## From Here . . .

Now that the basic elements of authoring and presenting Web pages have been considered, check out Chapter 8 for suggestions on creative ways to assemble these elements into effective business Web pages.

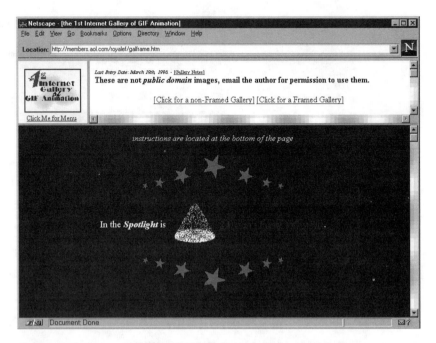

**Figure 7.11 The Animated Gif Gallery page using frames.**

**Figure 7.12 The Animated Gif Gallery page without frames.**

# Homepages That Work:
# Best Practices for Marketing

The Web is an interactive, multimedia medium, and therefore requires structures, visuals, and other adaptations different from those used for mass media when doing marketing and sales.

This chapter will discuss these issues and give suggestions on how to deal with them through good HTML document design.

Marketing and advertising professionals are accustomed to having the ability to maintain tight control over the appearance of paper-based, audio, and video marketing tools. With the Web, however, you have much less control over the exact appearance of your business's advertising and marketing materials presented as Web pages. The quality of a Web page as seen by a potential customer can vary dramatically based on various combinations of these elements:

- How the page was designed, HTML encoded, and written
- Which particular browser the user (potential customer) is using
- How the user's particular browser is configured locally—fonts, styles, colors, and so on

The ideas and guidelines presented here are useful both for writing your own HTML documents and for making Web page plans with a consultant or page author.

## Good Practices

There are a number of commonly accepted practices among HTML document authors that can insure that your page is maintained properly.

### Some Quick Authoring Tips

Here are some good authoring practices:

- Date—Always include the date of the latest version of the page. Remember that the page will have an international audience, so the date formats April 10, 1996 and 10 April '96 are better than the standard U.S. format 4/10/96.

- Creator—Identify the author of the page with a name and e-mail address for feedback.

- Feedback—Offer some method for those who view your pages to provide feedback, suggestions for new links, and reports of problems using your business's Web pages. Displaying your e-mail address on the page is the quickest and easiest way, but you may get more responses using an input form page with checkboxes and text input fields for comments or replies to your questions.

- Cross-linking—If you are linking an individual's *personal* page to yours, it is a good idea to let that individual know that you would like to do this.

- Local vs. linked copies—Make a local copy of remote files that are very likely to be temporary—or to keep an archive of documents as they evolve. Otherwise, it is easier to just put a hotlink out to the information.

- Test—New HTML documents should be tested during development, and then thoroughly tested immediately upon being installed on your Web service provider's computer. Check the appearance and functionality of each link.

### HTML Design Considerations

Keep these methods and considerations in mind when planning a Web page.

### Icons

Very small images or graphics can be used as icons. A set of icons with similar style can give all of your pages a consistent and memorable appearance, and serve to unify the pages into a site. They can be used as the inline click-on anchors for links to other sections or documents. Icons should be kept small so that the page will load into a browser quickly. Each icon image file needs to be downloaded by a browser only once—repeat uses of the same icon in one document won't slow the download.

### Selecting Anchors

Web users very quickly learn that highlighted words and small pictures are used as anchors that can be selected or clicked on to view another document or image. Therefore, awkward sentences that tell visitors to your page that they should *"click here"* are not needed. More information can be included on the page, and smoother text will result, if you choose anchor words within well-written text:

```
The library at the Vatican contains many useful documents from
the 1400's.
```

"Library" is the link, and consequently is highlighted. This is better than saying:

```
Click here to go to the library at the Vatican, which contains
many useful documents from the 1400's.
```

The phrase "click here" breaks the flow of the text and the thought pattern of the reader. Some readers may even mistakenly click on the word "click." Text-based browsers use arrow keys to move around the page and to activate a link—thus the click "here" will be both confusing and impossible—you can't use an arrow key to click *on* anything.

### Titles

Use the <TITLE> </TITLE> pair of HTML tags to surround a title for each Web page. This is useful because some browsers can display this title at all times while a document is in view—visitors to your page will be reminded of where they are even if they have scrolled down many screens into your Web page.

### *Preformatting Consideration*

Care should be taken when using the <PRE> and </PRE> preformatting tags. While preformatting gives you some control over the positioning of characters on a screen, it is not foolproof—if the browser used by the visitor to your page has been configured to display fewer characters per line (e.g., has a larger default character size), or if the visitor has sized the browser window so that it is somewhat narrow, words in the preformatted area may disappear off of the right side of the screen and be unviewable. To reduce the chances of this, keep line lengths short—50 characters or less.

### *Planning the Opening Screen*

Most HTML authors assume the following general font settings:

- Heading 1: Times 20
- Heading 2: Times 18
- Heading 3: Times 14
- Heading 4: Times or Palatino 12

With all of the variations in font size and in the amount of space that each browser takes up on the screen with its own icons, menus, ribbons, and buttons, it is impossible to predict accurately how much of your Web page will show up on the screen. Whether visitors to your page stay and explore or move on to another company's pages often depends on what they see on your first screen.

Try to get in as much information as you can about your pages in the first 25 lines or less. Avoid using too many headlines, or ones that are unnecessarily large (an <H3> headline will still stand out from the rest of the text, and will save a lot of space over an <H1> headline). Also, using inline images that are wide but not high will save space while still offering color and interest. Much of your design planning should be focused on these top lines.

## Writing Styles

Writing documents for use on the Web is very different from writing linear, top-down documents. Documents for use on the Web are meant to be accessed in a generally nonlinear fashion, with so much of the control over the order of the access in the hands of the reader rather than the writer.

The Web, as the homepage at CERN mentions, has no functional top. Any page is an entry page.

Often Web homepages and other documents are written as summaries or "big picture" views of a particular topic. Words or phrases in these summaries are used as anchors for links to Web pages that then summarize subtopics. You are not, however, limited to using links only in the direction of smaller subdivisions of the subtopic—Web documents are usually also written with links back to bigger-picture documents and links to other branches. This differs from linear writing, in which each subject is developed to some extent within one document.

The nonlinear style is excellent for marketing—many points can be made quickly, and the anchors with links to other documents can then be used to more fully explain things. Your summaries at the very top of a document can quickly put all the possibilities and choices before the visitor to your page. At the same time, links back to the homepage or directly to your business's other documents provide repeated reminders of what you are offering.

## Document Size Considerations

How large should your HTML documents be? There is no single answer. Here are some things to consider in making this decision.

Larger documents take longer to load. This can lead to some initial irritation with your business's homepage—not a good way to start. A visitor may even stop the download process of your homepage because of the time it is taking, hit the browser's Back button, and never even see your site.

On the other hand, if you put your information in one long document with many internal links, instead of breaking it up into a number of short linked documents, the potential customer who did have the patience to view your page would be rewarded with lightning-fast links within the document.

If you don't provide internal links, then each document should be kept quite small (say, four pages) and be used primarily as a launching pad for links to your other documents.

In long documents, it is important to offer the chance to break out and go back to the top or bottom. It is also a good idea to use the word "more" and an inline image of a down arrow at regular intervals to encourage the visitor to keep reading down the page.

Many writers include navigation hints at the bottom of each section such as "Up to <section name>" or "Down to <section name>," and include the specific topic of the jump link.

## Images

The use of large inline images is tempting to overdo on the first screen of a page. The impulse is to go for broke with flashy, eye-catching graphics.

The best option is to let viewers make some choices about how they want to view an image-rich top page in the way that Time, Inc. does. Time has options for full-bore bitmapped images, for a page with smaller inline images, and for text only. This way potential customers aren't annoyed with image downloads that can take several minutes.

You can use miniature ("thumbnail") versions of large images inline; viewers can click on these to see the full versions as external images.

## Dealing with Web Browser Variations

All of the Web browsers interpret the HTML formatting information a bit differently even when using the default settings. In addition, individual users can set up their browsers for different backgrounds, colors, fonts, and styles, and some of the browsers have optional toolbars and ribbons that decrease the viewing area for the Web page itself.

This creates special problems for HTML document writers. The best approach to getting acceptable results is to test each HTML document using as many browsers as possible from the three most popular browser platforms—Windows, Macintosh, and X-Windows. Do the testing with the lowest commonly used resolution (e.g., for PCs use the standard 640 x 480 VGA mode, not the 800 x 600 or 1024 x 768 modes). If the page layout looks fine at this low resolution, it will probable work well at any higher resolution mode, but the reverse isn't always true.

It is wise to check your page using different browsers. Figures 8.1, 8.2, and 8.3 show how Cello, Mosaic, and Netscape view exactly the same document with all fonts and styles set to the default settings. Notice how differently the words "Texas-West" and the following lines and bulleted list are treated. In this Cello example, only eight lines of text are displayed, reaching the second bullet in the list, whereas with Netscape, 11 lines are shown, and in NCSA Mosaic, 15 lines are shown, displaying the entire bulleted list, information on specials, and the beginning of some text on RF transistors.

The rendering of colors is quite different as well. In one case, "Texas-West" is in maroon, and in another, it is navy. As you can see, the fonts are different sizes and styles, especially for the line "Retail Throughout. . . . "

Many of those who visit your page will have changed their browser's configurations. Figure 8.4 shows this very same homepage as seen

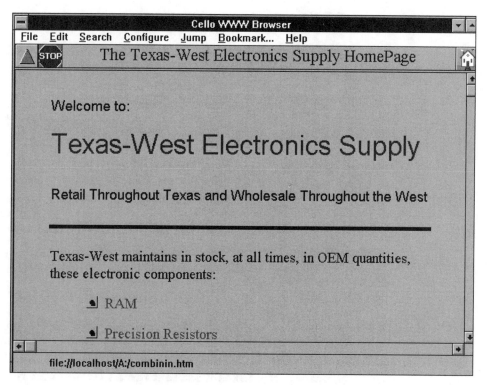

**Figure 8.1 The Texas-West test file as viewed with Cello.**

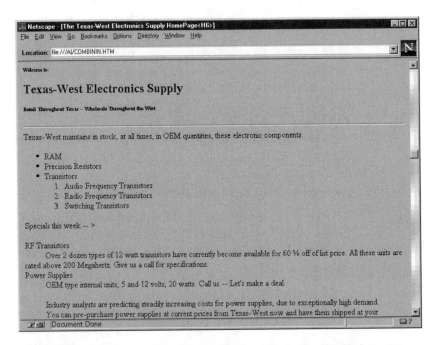

**Figure 8.2 The Texas-West test file as viewed with Netscape.**

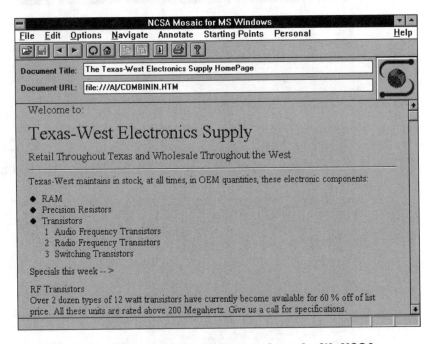

**Figure 8.3 The Texas-West test file as viewed with NCSA Mosaic.**

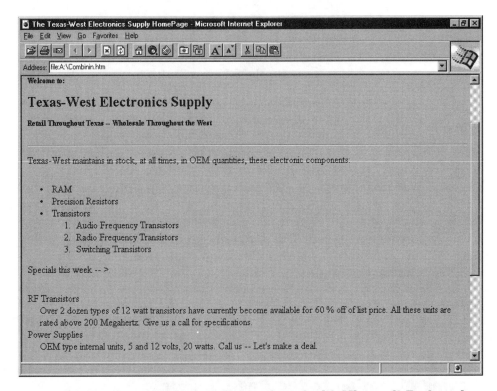

**Figure 8.4 The Texas-West test file as viewed with Microsoft Explorer in a nonstandard configuration.**

using the Microsoft Explorer browser configured to a higher resolution. Notice that the text is quite small, making much more of it visible.

## Text vs. GUI; GUI with Images Turned Off

With all of the discussion about Netscape, Microsoft Explorer, and other GUIs (graphical user interfaces), it is easy to forget that there are other ways someone might access a Web page. Many GUI users still browse the Web using a text-based browser such as Lynx, or use their GUI with image-loading turned off for superior speed and ease of use with dial-up accounts. Some business people use a GUI at work, where they have a full Internet connection, but use a GUI with the images turned off at home, where they have a slower dial-up connection. The evidence is that business users hunting for information often bypass the images in favor of speed.

To demonstrate this problem, Figures 8.5 and 8.6 show the same page as viewed by Lynx and by Netscape. As you can see, the Lynx user is given no clue as to what these markers mean or where they lead. The same would be true for the GUI user with image-loading turned off.

What this means to you as a Web marketer is that you should make your Web pages intelligible to text-only users. Some mixture of icons and text is useful. Figures 8.7 and 8.8 show good Lynx and GUI layout. The menu items show up well in both cases. Notice that the information is easy to use in both, with little sacrifice of colorful icons. Notice too the added feature—that you can choose graphical or text mode right at the top of the page. In this case, both images and text are used for easy navigation. It is also possible to accomplish this by using alternative text anchors—the "ALT" parameter in the HTML document (see Chapter 6). Figure 8.9 shows the same page viewed with Netscape but with the images turned off.

In addition, the various search engines will be able to find you and index your site better if you use text buttons as well as imagemaps—the engines cannot read the words contained on images.

## Paying Attention to the Page Visitor

While planning a Web page, consider how the page will appear to a visitor—how an expert Web user might perceive it, how a novice Web user might perceive it, or how an expert or novice in your industry might perceive it. What actions do you want visitors to take? Do you need to direct customers quickly to separate paths (e.g., if you do both retail and wholesale)? What speed is the connection your customers are likely to be using?

### Jumping In and Navigating

If visitors to your business's page are new to the subject matter or to the page, they will probably move through the page top to bottom, and take the items in order. More advanced users or those who have visited before will more likely go to the links that interest them.

Readers may jump in from anywhere to anywhere, so navigation links are critical. Buttons to jump back to the top or to headings throughout a document are very helpful.

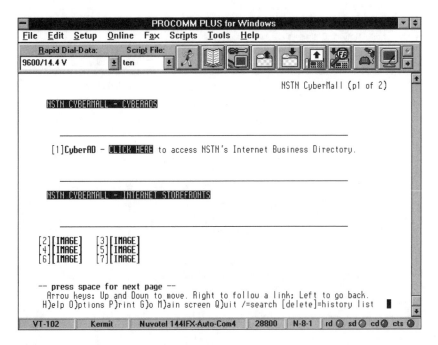

**Figure 8.5 NTSN page viewed by Lynx.**

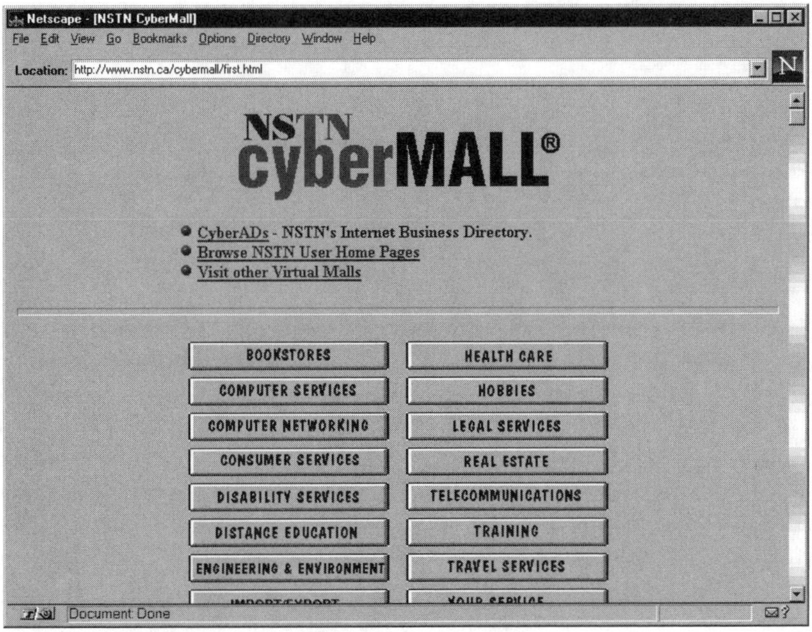

**Figure 8.6 NTSN page viewed by Netscape.**

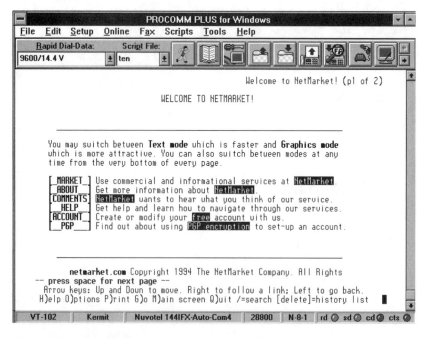

**Figure 8.7 The NetMarket homepage with Lynx.**

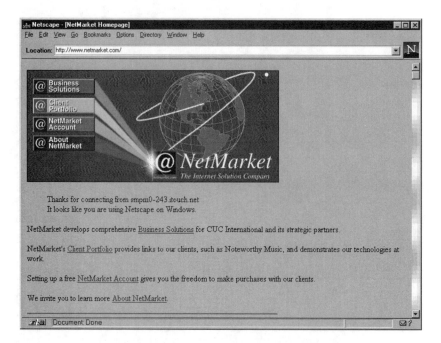

**Figure 8.8 The NetMarket homepage with Netscape.**

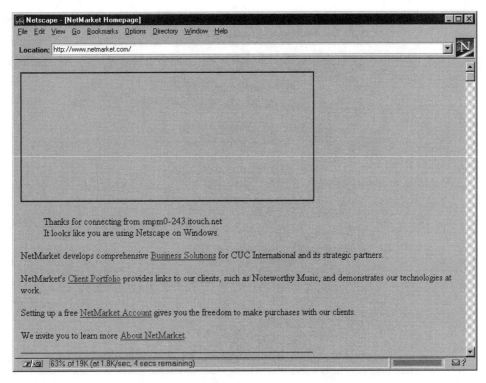

Figure 8.9 The NetMarket homepage with Netscape, with the images off.

## Menu and Tree Structures

The Time Inc. Pathfinder page mentioned previous is a good example of how a page can offer choices to the visitor right at the beginning to make browsing more individualized. Another good example is John December's page on computer-mediated communications *http://www. december.com/cmc/info/).*

John December maintains his page to organize a tremendous amount of information about computer-mediated communication. He has created a useful feature by allowing the user to choose the level of depth of the menus.

On the first level of the access menu (Figure 8.10), only the top level of the main sections are shown—access to information on the Internet, applications, technology, culture, forums, organizations, and bibliography. This is a good way for novices to begin browsing.

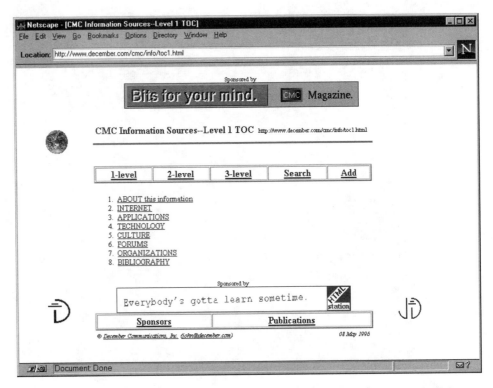

**Figure 8.10 The CMC Information Sources page showing menu level 1.**

The second level (Figure 8.11) expands to include the major sub-headings. For example, under the Internet, the reader would find collections, training, navigating, searching, directories, services, and an introduction.

At the third level (Figure 8.12), The Internet/Introduction level has expanded to show motivation, overviews, facts, and history.

It is often advantageous to provide two or three trees or levels, depending upon your purpose in creating the page. One of these trees can be fairly linear, designed to guide the new visitor to appropriate information. Other trees can feature more technical or specific information higher in the tree for the experienced visitor.

## Okay, What About Java, ShockWave, and RealAudio?

The various computer-user surveys point out that the average Web surfer is hitting the electrons using a low-end 486 machine, with a mo-

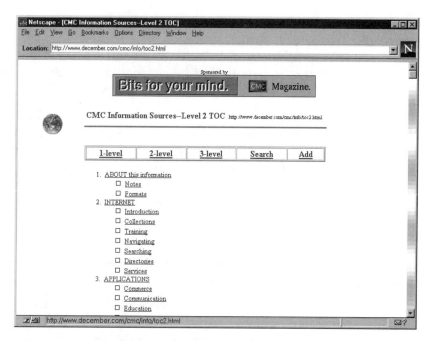

**Figure 8.11 The CMC Information Sources page at menu level 2.**

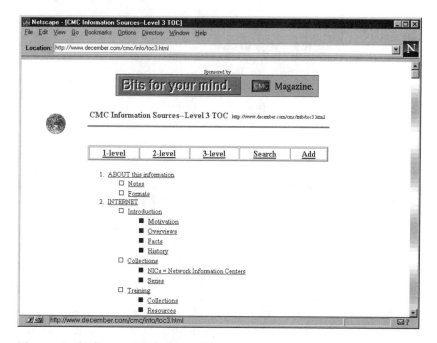

**Figure 8.12 The CMC Information Sources page at menu level 3.**

dem speed average between 9600 and 14,400, using 16-bit applications. What this means is that he or she cannot yet use Java applets or RealAudio plug-ins. Some animation is possible, as is some sound.

The key to successful design is in knowing your customers and designing for them. If your customers are high-end, techno-savvy users, then Java and other sophisticated plug-ins are useful. If your customers are Joe and Jane Average, then approach those with caution. This is another opportunity to offer *options* at the top of the page, one for graphics- and sound-intensive pages, and one for a set of pages that is less intensive.

## Using Forms Successfully

Many Web marketers will want to use the data entry feature of Web pages for customer input, feedback, sales, surveys, and more. Support for data entry forms is not universal, so it is a wise move to provide alternatives on the page for visitors using browsers without forms support.

### Testing Your Forms

Forms can be tested using the site and procedures described in Chapter 6. You can test sample data entry and obtain the results from your data to be sure that what you intend to happen actually happens.

## Using the META HTML Tag for Marketing Success

The META HTML tag is used within the HEAD portion of an HTML document to supplement other information found on your page by providing information you would like used for indexing and cataloging. It is a place to put additional information about products and the page using keywords, descriptions, and other descriptive items. The information supplied in the META element is not normally displayed by browsers but can be read by servers, and is used by search engines and indexing programs. Using the tag can help your page be more visible and more accurately used by the search engines.

If you do not provide indexing information, many search engines will only use the first 250 characters of your pages, although AltaVista and some other search engines will index all words in every document.

This is an example of a set of META tags for the Texas-West page:

```
<HTML><HEAD>
<TITLE>Texas-West Electronics Supply</TITLE>

<LINK REV=made href="mailto:oakridge@world.std.com">

<META NAME="keywords" CONTENT="RAM Resistors Electronics
Transistors RF Texas">

<META NAME="description" CONTENT="Texas-West Electronics Supply
sells retail electronics in Texas and wholesale throughout the
West">

<META NAME="revisit-after" CONTENT="15 days">

</HEAD>
```

# Successful Business Web Sites

Remember that the control of the layout and visuals is jointly vested in the user and creator. You have very little space on the top of your homepage to make your main points.

A successful site has these characteristics:

- *The site is highly visible.* It is registered with search engines such Lycos, Inktomi, AltaVista, HotBot, WebCrawler, Excite, McKinley, and InfoSeek, and with catalog listings such as Galaxy, Yahoo, and the Commercial Sites Index.

- *The content is always fresh.* New pages are added and old pages are updated and given face-lifts.

- *The pages are information-rich.* The site offers good content, content, content, offering more than a visitor can absorb in one visit.

- *The site introduces your business and tells visitors about the site.*

- *The pages have clear navigation aids.* Users can move around and through the site easily. Navigation elements (icons, arrows, etc.) are consistent and intuitive.

- *The pages do not funnel the user out too quickly.* A good site doesn't send visitors out right away with too many prominent links to other sites.
- *The site can be viewed successfully with many browsers.*
- *Every page is treated as a starting point.*
- *The site has true value added.* It offers services, content, products, or other resources. It is not just a place to market and sell. Users can get real information, products, and services for free.
- *The site maintainers are responsive.* Visitors receive no dreaded "404, URL not found" messages.
- *The site has organizational and/or institutional support.* It is not run by the guys "out back." It has budget and personnel support—it is not dependent, like Blanche Dubois, on hand-outs.
- *The site is capable of gathering information.* Information about users is routinely gathered through contests, newsletters, surveys, and so on, so that the maintainers know who has been visiting the site, and their preferences and reactions.
- *The site is a marketing channel integrated with other channels.*
- *The site is supported through other Internet tools such as e-mail and FTP.*
- *The site has good design:*
  - there are text and small image alternatives for large images;
  - interactivity with people is available;
  - the site has a good balance between what's sensible and what's "hot"—graphics, design, and colors are in synch with the corporate image;
  - the site has relatively consistent imagery and content from page to page, providing a sense of visiting one *site*, not just a collection of pages;
  - the page is technologically compatible with customers.
- *The URL is easy to remember.* It is not a "funny-looking" URL with lots of mixed cases and tildes.

There are some informal and formal ways to measure Web site success. You should get a real Return on Investment (ROI) and/or sales analysis, but also consider these factors:

- How many times has the site been accessed? How many hits did it receive and from how many different hosts?
- Are other sites asking for formal cross-links? What kinds of sites, what volume of traffic are they getting, and of what quality are they?
- Are you getting awards such as the "top 5%" sites?
- How many mailing list sign-ups have you gotten from the site?
- How many transactions were carried out, over what time interval?
- How many guest book signings, contest entries, or feedback forms were transmitted?
- How much attention are you getting from traditional and nontraditional media?

## From Here . . .

Part IV of this book, starting with Chapter 9, will take you to "the fire-hose" of resources for Internet marketing.

# Online Resources for Internet Marketing

# *Power-Searching the Web*

While surfing from site to site, following interesting paths, and collecting "bookmarks" can lead you to useful information and sites, it is obviously a haphazard way to explore what is probably in excess of 40 million Web pages currently on the Internet. Fortunately, several types of Web search systems are currently developing and expanding at high speed:

- Web catalogs
- Web search engines
- Synergistic search sites

Familiarity with these catalogs and engines can serve two functions in Internet marketing—first and most obviously, the search tools can assist you in finding the information you need about companies, products, competitors, and data from the huge variety of databases that are online. Second, such familiarity will provide you with information for listing or registering your Web site to make it visible on the Internet so that customers can locate your business.

Each of these search systems will be described, and some of the bests sites in each category will be reviewed. Note that as the Web and these sites evolve, the categories of search sites are becoming less well defined. Most sites are moving toward becoming synergistic sites featuring many search tools.

# Web Catalogs

Web catalogs are Web sites that offer lists of other sites on the Internet. The lists are organized by topic categories and subcategories not unlike those used in library card catalogs. To use a Web catalog, visit the catalog site as you would any other Web site, and then scroll down the top-level list of categories. When you locate an interesting category, click on it. The catalog will then take you either to a list of subcategories from which to select, or to a list of sites. When you find a Web site of interest, click on its name and you will be linked to it in the usual way.

Many catalogs provide brief descriptions of each site they list. Some catalogs provide additional features such as lists of new sites, frequently visited sites, and highly recommended sites. Many of the larger sites also offer a search feature that will hunt for sites listed within the Web catalog, based on words you type into a search form. The combination of these features makes Web catalogs very powerful aids in doing business research, and very powerful aids to customers trying to find your business's products and services. Many Web users start each online session with a Web catalog, and come back to the catalog frequently to start new surfing routes.

> **Note:**
>
> Some catalogs allow searches by "keyword." On the Internet this is commonly understood to mean that using the on-screen text box, you type in *any* word or words that you can think of that are related to the topic you are interested in. When you then click on a "Submit" or "Search" button on the screen, the catalog will return a list of topic subsections or Web sites related to the word or words.

Here are some of the best catalogs on the Web.

## Yahoo

*http://www.yahoo.com/*

In the hyperspeed history of the Internet, Yahoo, started in April, 1994, is the old-timer of major Internet catalogs (Figure 9.1). No listing of excellent catalogs could be without it. It is well organized, and very

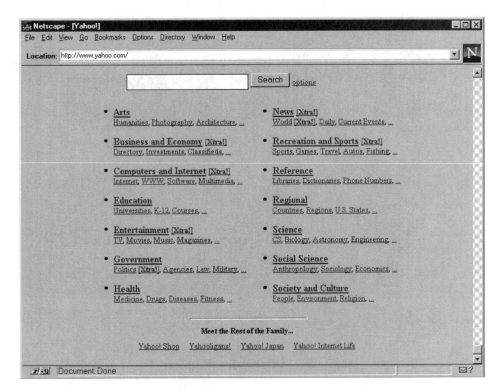

**Figure 9.1 Yahoo's top-level categories.**

well maintained and updated. The catalog can be searched by keyword, including use of "and," "or," and substrings (see the search tips
in the Search Engines section later is this chapter). Yahoo also provides
search abilities for e-mail addresses and Usenet newsgroup postings.
In addition it has an assortment of features such as listings of the
newest Web sites and links to search engines. Have a look under the
categories of business and economy, government, Internet, and computers particularly.

> **Note:**
>
> Consider creating a personalized starting page for Yahoo by going
> to *http://my.yahoo.com*. Every time you visit, you will find a cus-
> tomized page of news and information.

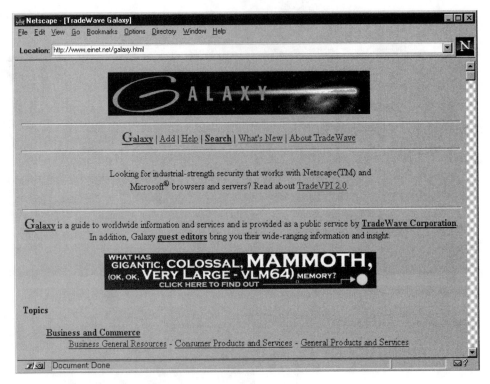

**Figure 9.2  Galaxy's categorized topics list page.**

## Galaxy

*http://www.einet.net/galaxy.html*

Tradewave Corporation's Galaxy is an example of one of the things a business can provide on the Web to help attract visitors to its site. The Galaxy catalog can be browsed from topic to topic (Figure 9.2), or the effective search form can be used to find sites listed within the catalog. Of particular interest are business and commerce, engineering and technology, government, law, and reference.

## Xplore

*http://www.xplore.com/xplore500/medium/menu.html*

Xplore (Figure 9.3) seems to be holding the line on information overload. This catalogs keeps its size stable at around 500 carefully se-

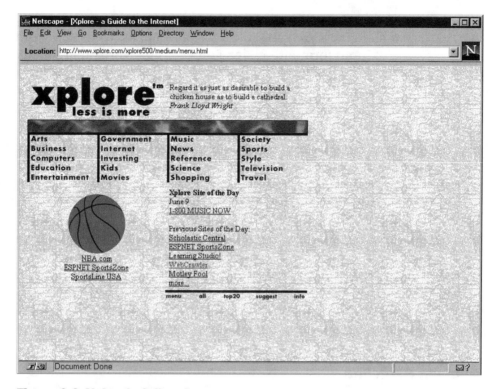

**Figure 9.3 Xplore's full welcome screen.**

lected sites—their motto "less is more." The categories of business, investing, and shopping are particularly useful.

# Search Engines

Another approach to finding Web pages is to utilize one or more of the increasing number of Web search engines. The different groups offering search engines on the Web vary in the software and techniques they use (and in the resultant search quality, too), but here are the basic concepts.

To begin, an individual, company, or other group with high-speed access to the Internet uses some software to automatically and systematically visit as many Web pages on the Internet as it can. The full text of those pages is saved and then analyzed by special software that develops an index of words along with lists of page URLs (addresses) where those words can be found.

To start a search of Web pages about a particular subject, you visit a search engine's Web site in the usual manner. Here you will find some type of input form into which you can type words that you expect to be found on Web pages dealing with your current topic of interest. The site then checks its previously developed index and responds to you with a list of sites that contain those words. You can then visit any of these Web sites by just clicking on the site's name.

As you can imagine, a large list (sometimes thousands) of Web site names might present quite a challenge to explore. Search engine sites therefore provide a number of features to make it easier to decide which sites to visit and how to refine the search.

Some sites automatically generate descriptions of a Web page by listing its section headings. Other sites provide the first few lines from the top of each Web page. Neither method is perfect, but both are a definite improvement over providing just the site's name. Some search engines use the META tag for keywords and descriptions, where these have been provided by the page authors (see Chapter 8 for more on the META tag).

## Boolean Searches

Some sites provide more exact searches by allowing you to use several "Boolean" control words in the searches. The techniques you must use vary from site to site (so you will need to read the site's help and tips pages to make the best use of its search capabilities), but here are examples of some of the more common search techniques:

- OR

  *Example*: `phone OR telephone OR cellular`

  OR works well for broadening a search when the things you are after can be described in more than one way.

- AND

  *Example*: `tape AND recording`

  Use AND when you aren't sure what order the words will be in but you want them both to be present on the Web page. The results of this particular search would be more likely to get Web pages selling or discussing recording tape than pages discussing sticky kinds of tape.

- NOT

  *Example*: `bears NOT Chicago`

  This search would more likely yield a list featuring big furry mammals, rather than pages about a certain Chicago sports team.

- NEAR

  *Example*: `Harrison NEAR John`

  NEAR can be used for many kinds of searches, but it is particularly useful for names. This search, for example, would retrieve Web pages with any of these forms of the name:

  > Harrison, John
  >
  > John Harrison
  >
  > John G. Harrison

- Quotation marks

  *Example*: `"George Washington"`

  Some sites interpret two words typed one after another as two separate keywords joined by AND or OR. In that case you might receive a huge list of sites including anything from a George Carlin fan page to a page telling about Washington apples (George OR Washington), or pages mentioning anyone named George who had anything to do with Washington—the state, the city, and so on (George AND Washington). At some sites the quotation marks can save you from this.

- Substrings and wildcards

  *Examples*: `comput`

  computers

  `comput*`  (when you are looking for computing, computer, computers, computed, computation, etc.)

Sites vary considerably in how they handle substrings and wildcards. Some sites accept the word you type in as a substring and look for all words that contain it that are in the site dictionary. Other sites will search for the full form of the word you type in, as well as for the substring they derive from it (if you type in `computers`, for instance, a site might search for all words containing "comput" as well as for "computers"). Still other sites will only search for all words starting with the substring "comput" if you use the asterisk wildcard character by typing `comput*`. Search sites now are increasingly letting you choose what method to use by way of a checkbox.

Here are some of the best search engines on the Web.

## AltaVista

*http://altavista.digital.com/*

AltaVista claims to "give you access to the largest Web index: 30 million pages." Searches can be done with either the "Simple" or "Advanced" search forms. The Simple search form gives you less control over the breadth of your search, using just a few search modifiers like the plus and minus signs and quotation marks; but it often does an excellent search. The Advanced queries (Figure 9.4) use a different, larger set of modifiers, including AND, OR, NEAR, NOT, and parentheses, and provide you with control over the order in which the sites found are listed.

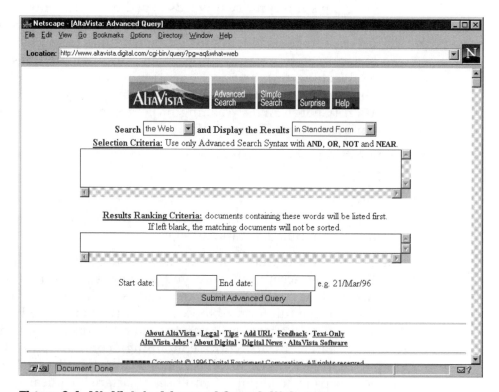

**Figure 9.4 AltaVista's Advanced Search Web page.**

AltaVista can also be used to search the test postings on 14,000 Usenet newsgroups.

Read the Help files to greatly increase the precision of your search. (In searches that can yield more than 10,000 responses, accurate searching is more than just a minor matter.)

## Hotbot

*http://www.hotbot.com/*

Sponsored by HotWired and Inktomi (University of California at Berkeley), Hotbot, like many other search engines, is aiming at indexing 100 percent of the Web as well as providing an index to Usenet news postings. Its user interface is likely to become very popular because most of the search criteria can be selected using an on-screen form, thus minimizing the learning curve (Figure 9.5). Searches can be narrowed by date, geographic location, media type, and how the keywords the

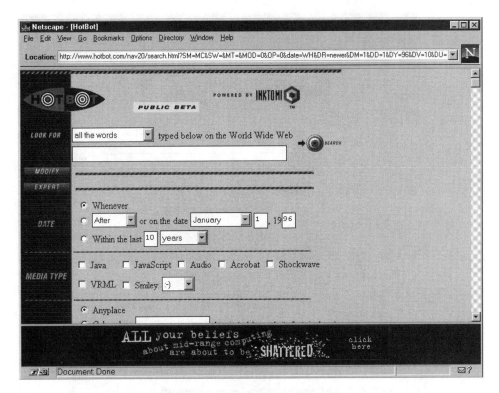

**Figure 9.5 Top of Hotbot's Expert search form.**

user enters are to be handled (e.g., *all* of the words listed should be on each page, *any* of the words listed should be on a page, the words should be taken as a phrase, etc.).

## WebCrawler

*http://www.webcrawler.com/*

While the WebCrawler is know to most on the Web as a search engine, the WebCrawler site, sponsored by AOL, also illustrates the evolution of many Web search engine sites toward multi-featured Web search systems (Figure 9.6). In addition to a computer-generated index of Web sites, it includes Web site reviews, and a system to find Web sites similar to those reviewed. The search engine allows an easy search and an advanced search, along with options on how the resulting lists and descriptions of sites will be displayed. The WebCrawler page also offers access to GNN's Best of the Net by category.

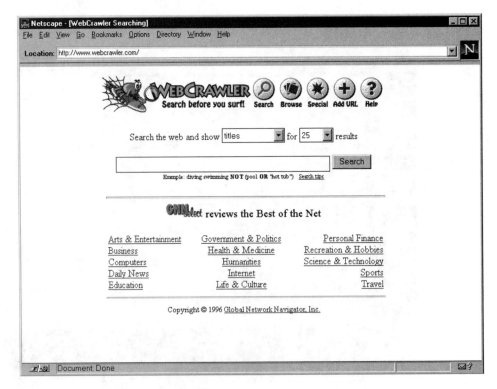

**Figure 9.6 WebCrawler's welcome screen.**

## Synergistic Search Systems

The distinction between catalogs and search engines is rapidly blurring. Some sites are combining the catalog and search engine systems at one site. Others provide access to many catalogs and/or search engines from one site—sometimes searching multiple sites automatically. These synergistic or "meta" sites are evolving through active experimentation with Web search systems. Here are some of the most powerful and most interesting.

### search.com

*http://www.search.com/*

c | net's search.com provides access to over 250 search engines, catalogs, and databases (Figure 9.7). Many of these can be searched from forms right on search.com's pages. You can search the list of sites by

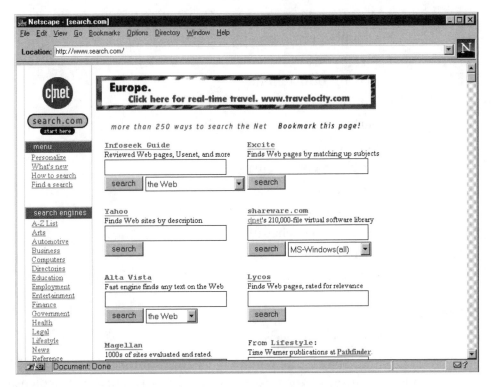

**Figure 9.7 search.com's opening search page and menu.**

browsing the full list, by using a keyword search, or by first clicking on one of the top-level categories of searches. You can also customize a page of search tools and return to the customized page in future sessions.

The tools available can be used to search for almost any type of information that is currently available on the Internet. In the area of business, here are just a few examples:

- Edward Lowe Digital Library of approximately 5,000 documents about starting a business
- Thomas Register of American Manufacturers
- Hoover's online corporate directory, with more than 10,000 company profiles
- Better Business Bureau
- FedEx and UPS package tracking sites
- Advertising Law Internet site
- American Demographics/Marketing Tools
- Chamber of Commerce Directory
- Communications Law
- c|net Product Finder
- Fannie Mae
- *Fortune* and *Money* magazines
- business directories
- employment services
- OSHA
- SBA Shareware Library
- U.S. Airline Schedules
- currency converter sites
- yellow page sites

## Savvy Search

*http://savvy.cs.colostate.edu:2000/*

Savvy Search adds another useful tool for searching the Web: a single search input form for you to fill out (Figure 9.8), which automati-

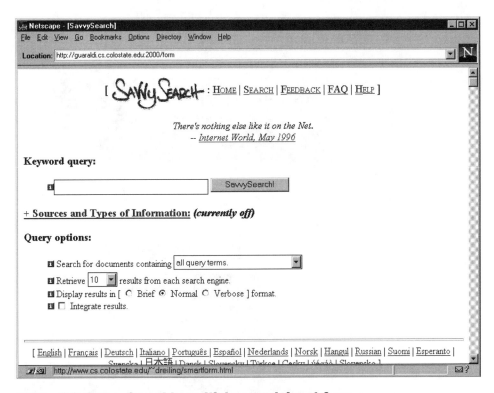

**Figure 9.8 Savvy Search's multiple search input form.**

cally submits your search request to all appropriate search engines on its list. The results are returned to you in one list (which you can control in several ways, such as by determining how detailed you want the site descriptions to be). In addition to a general help file, Savvy Search has help buttons for each section of the search input form.

Savvy is also remarkable in that it supports 20 language interfaces, including French, Japanese, Swedish, Italian, German, Portuguese, Spanish, and Finnish.

## A2Z

*http://a2z.lycos.com/*

A2Z provides a categorized catalog of Web sites as a "complement to the Lycos catalog of the Internet, which provides more than 30 million links." Each A2Z catalog link has a brief human-generated descrip-

**Figure 9.9 A2Z's top-level directory categories.**

tion. More in-depth Web site reviews and ratings are available via links to Point Communication. The A2Z directory can be searched by keyword or browsed from category to category to find major sites covering a topic. Lycos provides a powerful search engine for hard-to-find information and idiosyncratic sites.

## Excite

*http://www.excite.com/*

Excite (Figure 9.10) provides several search tools. NetSearch is Excite's search engine for Web pages, Usenet, and classifieds. In addition to keyword searching, sites can be searched by "concept"—that is, the search engine responds with lists of pages containing not only the search words, but also words with related meanings. This site will

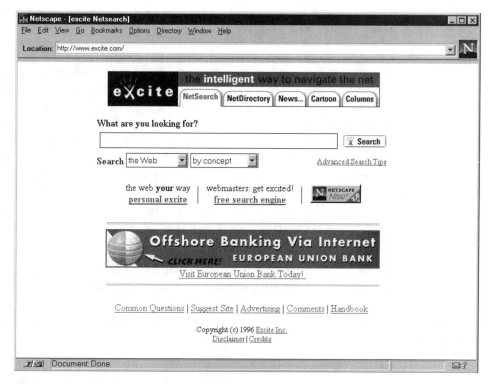

**Figure 9.10  The top of Excite's search entry form.**

search the Web, Usenet, and classifieds, and their NetDirectory provides a catalog of over 60,000 Web pages with reviews. Business-related cataloged sites are available under subtopics such as:

- Electronic Commerce
- Patents and Intellectual Property
- Taxes
- Products
- Investments
- Directories
- Business News

Excite also allows you to create your own top page with news, information, and search options.

## Register, Register, Register

As has been mentioned several other places in this book, you should register (list) your business's Web site at as many places as possible so that others on the Web can find you. Search engines use their automatic data gathering software (searchbots) to gather Web site information from the Web, and catalogs use these and other techniques to gather their information. They do a great job, but the Web is so large, and growing so fast, that no catalog or database of sites is complete. A search engine may find your business without your help, but then again, it may not. To be sure you are listed, and to speed up the process, check in at each search and catalog site and look for the page where you can register your Web site and perhaps provide a description of it. (Almost all registrations are free.)

In addition, you should check your site logs to see that all of the places you are listed are referring traffic to your site.

## From Here . . .

These search tools will help you locate almost any information, but the next two chapters will provide you with some specific marketing data, sites, and resources.

# CHAPTER 10

# *Important World Wide Web Resources and Sites Supporting Internet Marketing*

There are a large number of resources on the Internet that are of high value to businesses interested in using the World Wide Web for marketing. Because of the explosive growth of the Web, there are useful sites and resources springing up and changing constantly; the resources given here were chosen for their stability and for the breadth of their materials.

This chapter will cover a wide range of useful tools for marketing on the Internet, including mall/business directory services, Web resources, guides, and utilities of general interest, marketing and business services and sites, and other business-related resources.

Industry analysts estimate that the number of Web sites, Web service providers, and cybermalls will continue to grow very rapidly—recently the number has been doubling every three months. The sites discussed have been chosen to demonstrate the range and kinds of activities available and are excellent starting points. It is important to remember that sites come and go, URLs change, and new pages and sites are coming to the Web each day. Therefore the search tools discussed in Chapter 9 will be very important in staying up to date, by helping you to locate sites that move and to find new ones.

## Helpful Web Resources

The World Wide Web has some rich resources for online business and marketing. Some of them are large sites with sections of useful information, while others are more narrowly targeted. These resources are some of the most useful and most durable on the Net.

### W3

*http://www.w3.org/pub/WWW/*

The World Wide Web Consortium is the mother of the World Wide Web. The World Wide Web initiative began at the CERN European Laboratory for Particle Physics as a way of networking information for physicists, but has turned into a body of software, protocols, and conventions joining participants around the world.

This site offers access to:

- WWW software—including clients, servers, gateways, and tools
- Discussion groups—newsgroups, mailing lists, WWW interactive talk, and conferences relating to the Web
- Technical information—including details on WWW protocols, formats, and program codes
- Bibliographies—papers regarding WWW, references, and manuals

This site arguably provides the most extensive access to materials on WWW, HyperText Transfer Protocol (HTTP), and HyperText Markup Language (HTML) in the world. This is the place to look for information on HTML, HTTP, WWW, WWW software, and more. It is designed for the casual as well as the serious user of the WWW and HTML. All of this can sound pretty technical and daunting, but this site has a great deal of very practical information. It has sections on graphics and 3D, fonts, style, SGML, technology, the social implications of technology, disabilities, privacy, demographics, security, architecture, the WWW Library, and of course, electronic commerce.

Of particular interest to the business user is W3's relatively new initiative to create protocols to make the network easier to use in support of commerce. These new initiatives include increasing the automation of routine procedures, maintaining an open architecture, improving network efficiency, and creating new mechanisms for privacy, data in-

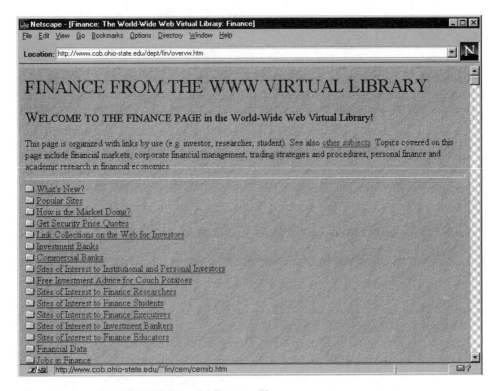

**Figure 10.1 The WWW Virtual Library: Finance.**

tegrity, and the authentication of transactions for commercial or confidential use. In addition, W3 is working on enhanced document capabilities to include distributed virtual reality using Virtual Reality Transfer Protocol (VRTP).

The main page of the WWW Virtual Library is organized by subject; the Finance Virtual Library is shown in Figure 10.1. The URL for the Virtual Library is *http://www.w3.org/vl*.

The Virtual Library subject menu shown below covers a lot of ground, from engineering and the sciences to commercial services, education, and more, and each subject links to further menus, lists, documents, and images. This site is worth return visits, since W3 adds links and information regularly.

- Aboriginal Studies
- Aeronautics and Aeronautical Engineering

- Aeronomy, Solar-Terrestrial Physics and Chemistry
- African Studies
- Agriculture
- AIDS
- Animal Health
- Anthropology
- Applied Linguistics
- Archaeology
- Architecture
- Art
- Asian Studies
- Astronomy and Astrophysics
- Autos
- Aviation
- Beer & Brewing
- Bio Sciences
- Biotechnology
- Broadcasters
- Cartography
- Ceramics
- Chemistry
- Coal
- Cognitive Science
- Collecting
- Commercial Services
- Communications
- Community Networks
- Complex Systems
- Computing
- Conferences
- Cross-Connection Control/Backflow Prevention
- Cryptography, PGP, and Your Privacy

- Crystallography
- Culture
- Dance
- Demography & Population Studies
- Design
- Developmental Biology
- Drosophilia (fruit fly)
- Earth Science
- Education
- Electronic Journals
- Energy
- Environment
- Epidemiology
- Finance
- Fish
- Forestry
- Furniture & Interior Design
- Games
- Gardening
- Geography
- Geophysics
- German Subject Catalogue
- Gold
- Hazards and Risk
- History
- Home pages
- Human Computer Interaction
- Humanities
- India
- Information Quality
- Information Sciences
- International Affairs

- International Development Co-operation
- International Security
- Ireland
- Italian General Subject Tree
- Journalism
- Landscape Architecture
- Languages
- Latin American Studies
- Law
- Libraries
- Lighthouses, Lightships & Lifesaving Stations
- Linguistics
- Literature
- Logistics
- Mathematics
- Medicine
- Medieval Studies
- Men's Issues
- Meteorology
- Middle East Studies
- Migration and Ethnic Relations
- Museums
- Music
- Mycology (Fungi)
- Neurobiology
- Non-Profit Organizations
- Nursing
- Oceanography
- Pacific Studies
- Paranormal Phenomena—Archive X
- Pharmacy (Medicine)
- Philosophy

- Physics
- Physiology and Biophysics
- Political Science
- Politics and Economics
- Publishers
- Recipes
- Recreation
- Religion
- Remote Sensing
- Retailing
- Roadkill
- Russian and East European Studies
- Secular Issues
- Social Sciences
- Sociology
- Spirituality
- Sport
- Standards and Standardization Bodies
- Statistics
- Stress
- Sumeria
- Sustainable Development
- Technology Transfer
- Telecommunications
- Theatre and Drama
- Tibetan Studies
- Transportation
- Treasure
- Unidentified Flying Objects (UFOs)
- United Nations and other international organizations
- U.S. Federal Government Agencies
- U.S. Government Information Sources

- Vision Science
- Whale Watching Web
- Wine
- World-Wide Web Development
- Writers' Resources On The Web
- Yeasts
- Zoos
- Other virtual libraries

## Washington and Lee University Netlink

*http://netlink.wlu.edu:1020/*

Washington and Lee University sponsors Netlink, a very broad compendium of resources on the Web. An extensive subject-organized menuing system provides top-level links to resources. Of particular interest are areas such as commerce, business, accounting, careers, and statistics. The main subject categories are:

- Non-classified
- Agriculture
- Animal Culture, Veterinary Science
- Anthropology, Archeology
- Architecture
- Bibliographic Indexes
- Biology, Genetics
- Botany
- Careers, Jobs, Employment
- Chemistry
- Commerce, Business, Accounting
- Computers
- Directories of People / Institutions
- Earthquakes
- Economics
- Education
- Education—Primary / Secondary (K-12) Schooling

- Engineering (Civil, Electrical)
- Environment, Health/Safety
- Film, Television, Radio
- Fine Arts
- Forestry
- Games, Sports, Recreation
- General Reference
- Geography
- Geology, Paleontology
- Grants, Funding
- History
- International Law
- The Internet
- Journalism
- Language & Literature
- Law
- Law—Primary Materials (legislative, executive, judicial)
- Library and Information Science
- Library Catalogs
- Library Catalogs (Major U.S. and Canada Libraries)
- Mathematics
- Medicine
- Military Science
- Music
- Naval Science, Navigation
- Oceanography
- Pharmacology
- Philosophy
- Physics
- Plants, Gardening
- Politics
- Psychology, Mental Health
- Religion

- Retail Trade
- Science
- Social Science
- Social Science Statistics, Census
- Space Science, Astronomy
- Weather, Meteorology
- Z39.50 Information Retrieval Clients
- Zoology

In addition, a user can sort by type of resource (database, Gopher, Telnet, etc.). This site is one of the most useful when looking for subject-oriented information. The Washington & Lee Netlink homepage features a breakdown by subject, and by Net service (Telnet, Gopher, FTP) is seen in Figure 10.2.

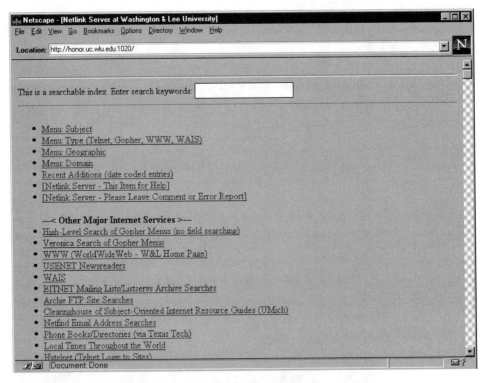

**Figure 10.2 Washington & Lee University Netlink homepage.**

## Yahoo! — A Guide to WWW

*http://www.yahoo.com/*

Begun as a kind of personal bookmarks file by some Stanford University graduate students, Yahoo has become one of the premier catalog sites on the Internet. It is a hierarchical hotlist for the WWW and it covers a huge range of topics, all linked to WWW sites:

- Arts
  Humanities, Photography, Architecture, . . .
- Business and Economy
  Directory, Investments, Classifieds, . . .
- Computers and Internet
  Internet, WWW, Software, Multimedia, . . .
- Education
  Universities, K-12, Courses
- Entertainment
  TV, Movies, Music, Magazines, . . .
- Government
  Politics, Agencies, Law, Military, . . .
- Health
  Medicine, Drugs, Diseases, Fitness, . . .
- News
  World, Daily, Current Events, . . .
- Recreation and Sports
  Sports, Games, Travel, Autos, Fishing, . . .
- Reference
  Libraries, Dictionaries, Phone Numbers, . . .
- Regional
  Countries, Regions, U.S. States, . . .
- Science
  CS, Biology, Astronomy, Engineering, . . .
- Social Science
  Anthropology, Sociology, Economics, . . .
- Society and Culture
  People, Environment, Religion, . . .

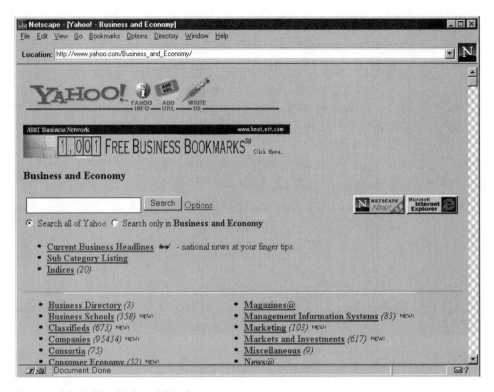

**Figure 10.3 The Yahoo! Business page.**

It has a menu system for navigating the hierarchies and searching. You can add to the hotlist with your own WWW entries. The homepage has links to pages for What's New, What's Popular, What's Cool, Statistics on Web growth, and a chance to have a look at a Random Link—click on it and it picks a link from Yahoo's database—you never know what you'll find. The business hierarchy (Figure 10.3) is very complete, and I find that I can often find company information using Yahoo.

## The Electronic Commerce WWW Resources Guide

*http://e-comm.iworld.com.*

Created and maintained by Thomas Ho, The Electronic Commerce WWW Resources Guide is extensive, and contains links to sites, information, and services (Figure 10.4). This resource is unique in that it focuses exclusively on electronic commerce in all of its current in-

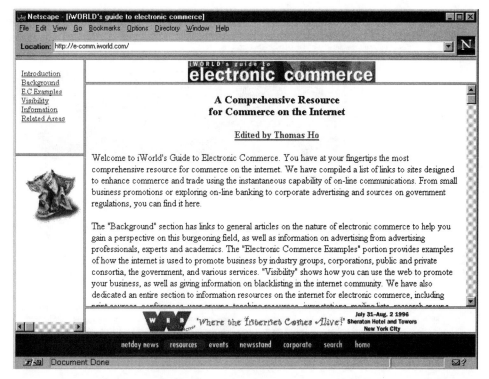

**Figure 10.4 E-Comm/iWorld Electronic Commerce WWW Resources page.**

carnations. It is organized into thematic headings covering the background and development of electronic commerce.

The Background section, for example, has information about the foundations of electronic commerce in general, which offers the context and perspectives on the field. This section also covers advertising. The section on Electronic Commerce (E.C) Examples uses specific cases to show how various companies carry out electronic commerce—it covers industry groups, corporations, consortia, the government, and services. The Visibility section covers promotion, blacklisting, spamming, and more. The Information portion includes print, online, conferences, teaching resources, jumpstations, discussion lists, and research. The Related Areas category covers policy, regulations, standards, and more.

This is one of those Web sites worth regular visits to track new developments in commerce on the Internet.

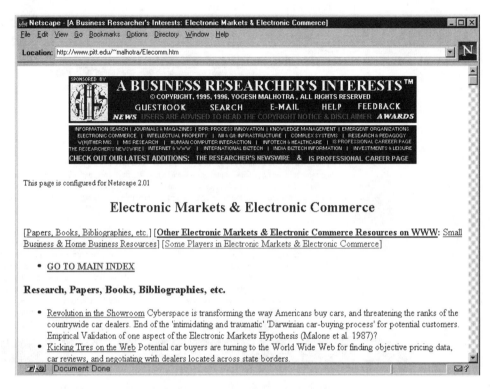

**Figure 10.5 A Business Researcher's Interests page.**

## A Business Researcher's Interests: Electronic Markets & Electronic Commerce

*http://www.pitt.edu/~malhotra/Elecomm.htm*

This page, created by Yogesh Malhotra (see Figure 10.5), organizes a great deal of the information available online about business, electronic commerce, and marketing. Primarily a jumpstation, it covers a lot of ground:

- Starting Points for Information Search & Retrieval—search tools and information repositories
- Business, Social Sciences & Technology—accounting, finance, communications, computing, marketing
- The Business Researcher's News.Wire—news, newspapers, reference libraries

- Management Information Systems Research & Reference—papers, conferences, journals, resources, working papers, companies and research
- Business Process Reengineering/Innovation—handbooks, reviews, workflow, books, periodicals, bibliographies
- Tools for Process Reengineering
- Organizational Knowledge Management
- Organizations as Complex Systems
- Emergent Organizational Forms & Virtual Organizations
- Research & Articles on New Organization Forms—outsourcing, Intranets, virtual communities
- Electronic Markets & Electronic Commerce—SOHO resources
- Intellectual Property & Legal Issues
- National Information Infrastructure (NII)
- Information Technology & Healthcare
- Human Computer Interaction
- Research, Pedagogy and Information Technology
- Information Systems & Management Journals & Magazines
- International Business & Technology Information
- Business & Information Technology in India
- Tool Box: Designing Web Applications
- The Information Professional's Career Page

## CommerceNet

*http://www.commerce.net*

Increasingly, companies, organizations, educational institutions, and consortia are hard at work investigating and supporting commerce on the Net. CommerceNet is an ambitious nonprofit consortium of organizations and companies, largely located in California, with matching federal funding. The Core Development Team includes such organizations as Stanford University, BARR-Net, the State of California, and others. This WWW electronic commerce project supplies high-technology product information, secure ordering, and data exchange systems; it also provides services such as secure multimedia messaging, network access control, and payment facilities.

Information and service providers can use CommerceNet toolkits to contract with third parties, make use of network services, and use CommerceNet authentication and remittance protocols. Its Electronic Commerce Jumpstation is particularly useful (*http://www.commerce.net/jump*).

CommerceNet is creating applications targeted at electronic commerce and connectivity to the Web. The working groups include:

- CALS—Electronic commerce applications focusing on virtual enterprise formation and integrated product development
- Collaboration Tools
- Connectivity—Internet connections, service integration, network administration, etc.
- Electronic Catalogs & Directories—Online access and ordering
- Directory, messaging, searching/indexing services; information directories
- Electronic Data Interchange—EDI messaging on the Internet and Value-Added Networks
- Marketing
- Network Services—Security, etc.
- Payment Services—Payment systems
- Public Policy

CommerceNet supports the Internet Consultant's Directory and CommerceNet Directories of resources and sites. Its members are engaged in extensive work on issues surrounding privacy and authentication, secure HTTP protocols, and secure payment systems promoting the use of encryption. (See the information page shown in Figure 10.6.)

CommerceNet seeks sponsors and cooperating businesses. It provides an online customer interaction form designed to assist visitors in getting the information they need to become involved. The form solicits information on interest (as a provider, customer, journalist, consultant, etc.), membership category, connectivity, information on your company, its incorporation status, contact person, and a range of business data including annual sales, number of employees, line of business, and type of organization. You will receive an individualized response to your query.

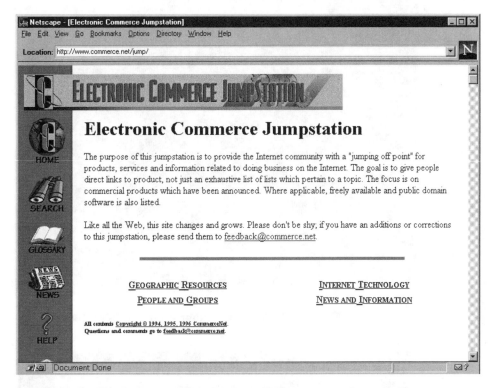

**Figure 10.6 The CommerceNet Electronic Commerce Jumpstation.**

## SBA: Small Business Administration Homepage

*http://www.sba.gov/*

The Small Business Administration has a very content-rich site with online documents and links (Figure 10.7). The site has very practical information for doing business online or off. One particularly useful link is to "the one-stop electronic link to government for business"—the U.S. Business Advisor, *http://www.business.gov/*.

## University of Houston College of Business Administration WWW Yellow Pages

*http://www.cba.uh.edu/ylowpges/ylowpges.html*

This listing of several thousand companies with Web pages is presented alphabetically by business category (Figure 10.8). The list was developed at the university by researching publicly available informa-

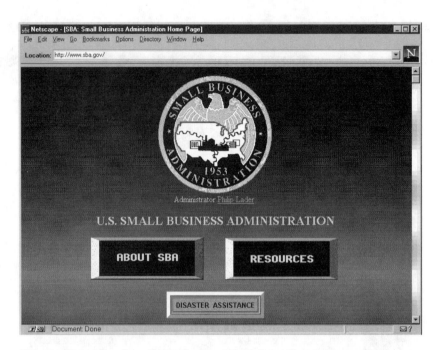

**Figure 10.7  The Small Business Administration homepage.**

**Figure 10.8  The UH WWW Business Yellow Pages homepage.**

tion. A listing of the categories under "B" gives a good sampling of the range of businesses using the World Wide Web:

- Banking Services
- Bartering Services
- Bedding
- Bed & Breakfast Inns
- Biotechnology
- Books and Book Publishers
- Books and Publishers: Adult
- Books and Publishers: Avant-Garde
- Books and Publishers: Business-Related
- Books and Publishers: Canada
- Books and Publishers: Fiction and Literature
- Books and Publishers: General
- Books and Publishers: Health Related
- Books and Publishers: History
- Books and Publishers: Home and Garden
- Books and Publishers: Latin America
- Books and Publishers: Marriage and Family
- Books and Publishers: Old, Rare, and Out-of-Print
- Books and Publishers: Religious
- Books and Publishers: Search Services
- Books and Publishers: Science Fiction & Fantasy
- Books and Publishers: Specialty Books
- Books and Publishers: Sports, Recreation and Travel
- Books and Publishers: Technology
- Books on Tape
- Book Reviews
- Braille
- Building Inspection

- Bulletin Board Referrals
- Business Services
- Business Opportunities
- Business: Entrepreneurship/New Business
- Business: Financing & Financial Service
- Business: General Business Services
- Business: Property Management
- Business: Specialty Items & Services
- Business: Accounting
- Business: Africa
- Business: Asia
- Business: Australia
- Business: Brazil
- Business: Canada
- Business: Central America
- Business: Europe
- Business: International
- Business: Israel

The providers of these yellow pages request that you fill out their online Web Users Survey in order to help them in their Web demographics research.

## TradeWave

*http://www.tradewave.com*

TradeWave is a multifaceted company that provides software such as MacWeb, WinWeb, TradeVPI, Trade Server, and a variety of commercial Web services. It supports electronic commerce through its software and services, and through TradeWave Galaxy.

TradeWave Galaxy (*http://galaxy.tradewave.com/*), shown in Figure 10.9, provides a guide to the Web through a page that organizes information into broad subject areas. This listing has particular strength in business, engineering, and technology. The directory includes access to both public and commercial information, by topic:

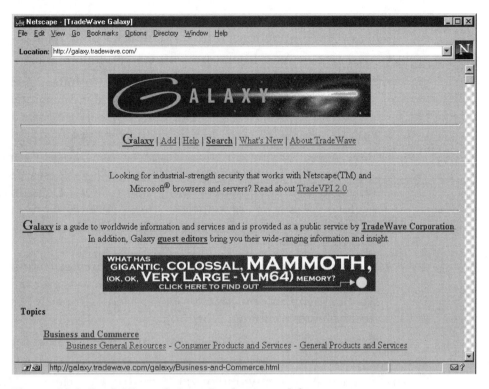

**Figure 10.9 TradeWave Galaxy Business and Commerce page.**

- Business and Commerce: Business General Resources; Consumer Products and Services; General Products and Services

- Community: Births Deaths and Weddings; Charity and Community Service; Consumer Issues; Crime and Law Enforcement; Culture; Education; Environment; Family; Gender Issues; Health; Home; Immigration; Law; Liberties; Net Citizens; Networking and Communication; News; Parascience; Politics; Religion; Safety; US States; Urban Life; Veteran Affairs; Workplace; World Communities

- Engineering and Technology; Agile Manufacturing Information Infrastructure; Agriculture; Biomedical Engineering; Chemical Engineering; Civil and Construction Engineering; Computer Technology; Electrical Engineering; Human Factors and Human Ecology; Manufacturing and Processing; Materials Science; Mechanical Engineering; Nondestructive Testing; Technical Reports; Technology Transfer; Transportation

- Government: Government Agencies; Government Publications; Laws and Regulations; Military; Politics; Public Affairs

- Humanities: Arts; Literature; Philosophy; Religion

- Law: Administrative; Commercial; Constitutional; Criminal; Environmental; Intellectual Property; Legal Profession; Military; Personal Finance; Research; Societal; Tax

- Leisure and Recreation: Amateur Radio; Automotive; Aviation; Beverages; Birding; Boating; Collectibles; Dance; Fashion; Film and Video; Food; Games; Gardening; Hiking; Horses; Humor; Interactive Web Fun; Just For Kids; Magic; Metal Detecting; Motorcycles; Music; Personalities; Pets; Photography; Pictures; Pyrotechnics; Radio; Reading; Recipes; Restaurants; Speleology; Sports; Television; Theater; Travel

- Medicine: Chiropractic; Community Medicine; Dentistry; Exercise; History of Medicine; Holistic Medicine; Human Biology; Medical Applications and Practice; Medical Specialties; Medical Technologies; Nursing; Nutrition

- Reference: Census; Dictionaries; Directories; Grants; Internet and Networking; Libraries

- Science: Astronomy; Biology; Chemistry; Geosciences; Mathematics; Physics

- Social Sciences: Anthropology; Business Administration; Communication; Education; Geography; History; Library and Information Science; Political Science; Psychology; Sociology

## The Global Network Navigator: The Whole Internet Catalog

*http://www.gnn.com/GNNhome.html*

The Global Network Navigator, created by O'Reilly & Associates and now part of America Online, offers access to their Whole Internet Catalog, which indexes and organizes Internet resources. Figure 10.10 shows the GNN Whole Internet Catalog homepage.

GNN also offers access to publications and news services such as the American City Business Journals, Briefing: Concise Market Analysis, Business Update @ internetMCI, CNN Financial Network, The Financial Times, Computer News Daily, Interactive Age, Money Daily,

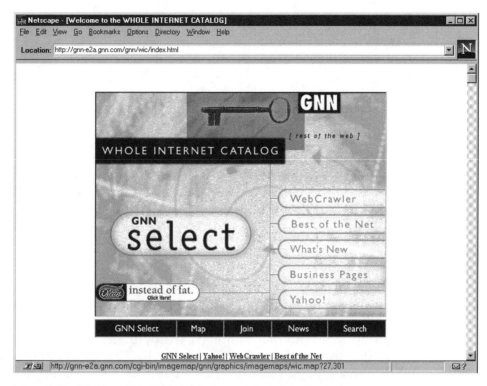

**Figure 10.10  The GNN Whole Internet Catalog homepage.**

Multichannel News, NewsPage, Nikkei Net, PR Newswire, Reuters Money Network, SimbaNet, and Wall Street Journal Interactive.

The GNN Catalog includes the following categories:

- Arts & Entertainment
- Business
- Computers
- Daily News
- Education
- Government & Politics
- Health & Medicine
- Humanities
- Internet

- Life & Culture
- Personal Finance
- Recreation & Hobbies
- Science & Technology
- Sports
- Travel

"Business" covers subject areas such as agriculture, careers, government information, information systems, Internet commerce, labor, magazines, management, marketing, nonprofits, real estate, small business, and yellow pages listings.

## Net.Value: Interesting Business Sites on the Web

*http://www.owi.com/netvalue*

This resource grew out of something called, plainly enough, "Interesting Business Sites on the Internet." It is now a full-fledged online magazine about Internet commerce maintained by Bob O'Keefe at Rensselaer Polytechnic Institute (Figure 10.11). The "Interesting Sites" area offers carefully chosen resources including sites, publications, news, and more about commercial use of the Web.

A sample "Picks of the Month" includes:

- Services
  Amazon.com Books—online book store
  Big Book—searchable yellow pages with maps
  Eldan—A car hire company in Israel
  The Federal Marketplace—subscription-based help with obtaining U.S. government contracts
  Map Quest—interactive, personalized maps

- Financial
  Met Life
  Nationwide
  Poulton Associates
  Reuter's Money Network

- Electronic Markets

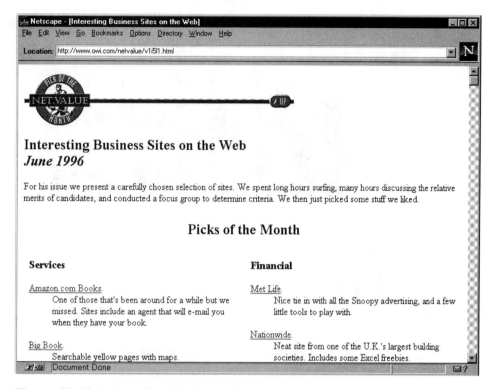

**Figure 10.11  Interesting Business Sites on the Web homepage.**

> Banx Quote—apply for loans or credit cards
> LithoQuoter—printing brokerage

- Large Companies
  Hyundai
  LEGO

## The Tenagra Corporation

*http://www.tenagra.com/*

The Tenagra Corporation started out as a member of the NASA Technology Commercialization Center, but rapidly moved out on its own. It provides a broad range of services focusing on assisting organizations and businesses in creating what it calls a "net.presence." Tenagra places a heavy emphasis on assisting organizations in finding,

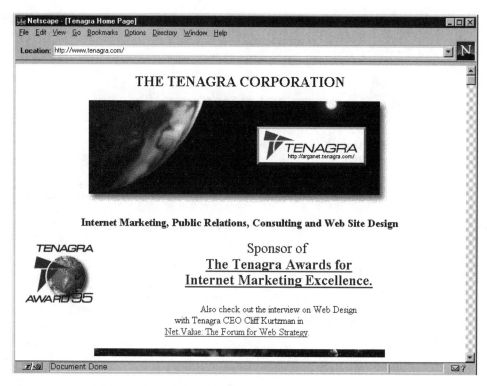

**Figure 10.12 The Tenagra homepage.**

using, and providing information. Not surprisingly, Tenagra has created the World Wide Web Aerospace Business Development Center. Because of its location, it supports many Houston businesses, and provides links to Rice University, local restaurant reviews, a theater guide, windsurfing information, and community information. Figure 10.12 shows its homepage. One very interesting link is to a document called "net.acceptable," which is a collection of information on acceptable use of the Internet and "netiquette" for doing business on the Internet.

Tenagra is a Web presence provider. An example of one of the pages it has orchestrated the creation of is the WWW Tennis Server (get it?), which includes the Racquet Workshop—the first tennis pro shop on the Web (Figure 10.13). This site was created by doing a competitive market assessment, defining the page content, processing the images, and setting up the electronic Web site.

**Figure 10.13 The Tennis Server homepage.**

## Open Market Commercial Sites Index

*http://www.directory.net*

This directory was begun at the MIT Laboratory for Computer Science as an informal listing—one of those examples of the gift economy of the Internet—and quickly became one of the premier listings of commercial services on the Web. Open Market now maintains the list as a free public service to the Web community. Open Market also facilitates commerce on the Internet through assisting in the development of virtual storefronts and other services involving store creation, account management, buyer authentication, and secure payment processing.

The Index can be searched by keyword or browsed alphabetically. Open Market plans to provide categorizations of the listings in the future. The homepage, showing the search feature, can be seen in Figure 10.14.

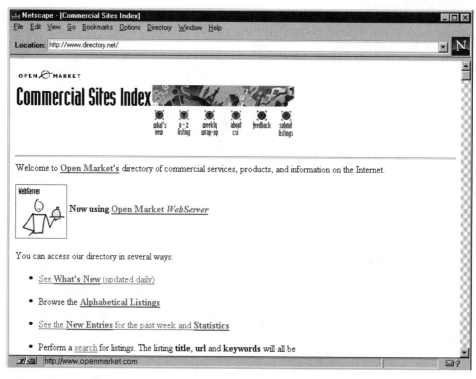

**Figure 10.14 The WWW homepage of Open Market's Commercial Sites Index.**

You can list your site in the Commercial Sites Index using the online form at *http://www.directory.net/dir/submit.cgi.*

## The Apollo Directory

*http://apollo.co.uk*

The Apollo Directory, based in the United Kingdom, offers WWW ads for services and goods arranged in geographical indices covering the United States, Canada, the United Kingdom, Europe, and the rest of the world. It has online advertising services, offering pictures, sound, and video—everything from text documents to multimedia commercials—and currently, for small ads, it is very inexpensive. The site has keyword searching; Figure 10.15 shows the homepage with its world map, from which you can choose the part of the world you wish to search.

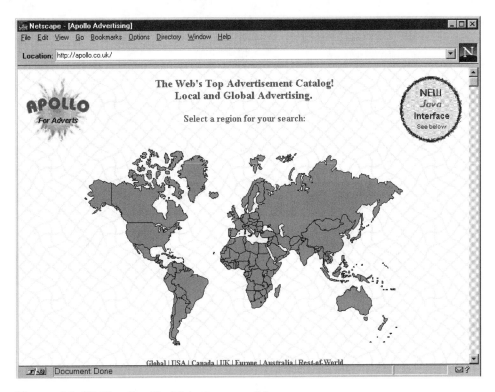

**Figure 10.15 The Apollo Directory world map.**

## BizNet—Blacksburg Electronic Village

*http://www.bnt.com and http://www.bev.net*

The Blacksburg Electronic Village is a wired community, with all sorts of electronic way-stations including a mall, banks, and grocery stores, created in association with BizNet Technologies.

BizNet offers two kinds of services. Local businesses can post a free "business card" listing on BizNet's Gopher. Global businesses can get started for as little as $20 a month for the Basic Ad package, which includes a listing and Gopher access, and a homepage with graphics and text. BizNet also offers custom services for Web customers. Biznet's homepage is shown in Figure 10.16.

One of the most popular areas for local residents are the community discussion groups which range from *bburg.general* for general talk, to *bburg.environment* about environmental issues, and *bburg.bev.volunteers* for disucssion of BEV volunteer activities.

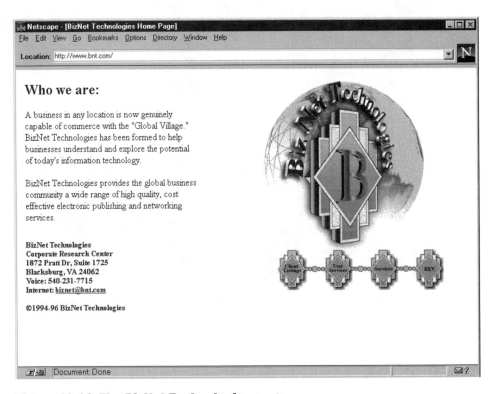

**Figure 10.16  The BizNet Technologies page.**

## GoldSite Europe

*http://www.gold.net/*

One of the largest commercial Web servers in Europe, GoldSite (Figure 10.17) has more than 12 million accesses per month. It offers information on 26,000 Internet-connected companies, and a broad range of services including HTML design, advertising, and Web server rental. In addition, it offers directory services and news.

## The British Broadcasting Corporation (BBC)

*http://www.bbcnc.org.uk/babbage/*

The venerable BBC offers the BBC Babbage page, including a compendium of search information and tools. It offers links to all of the various Web searching engines, including a Veronica server (Figure 10.18).

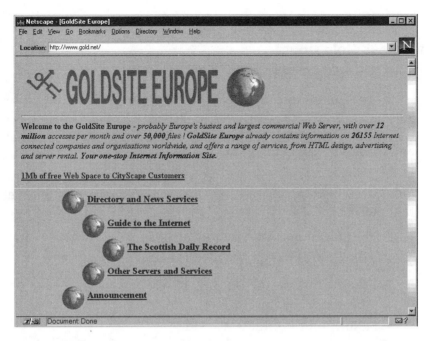

**Figure 10.17  GoldSite Europe homepage.**

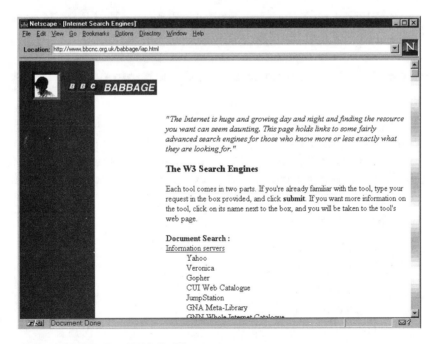

**Figure 10.18  The BBC Babbage page.**

## Small Business Help Center

*http://www.kciLink.com/sbhc/*

Khera Communications is in the business of providing Internet consulting, training, and World Wide Web server space leasing. Khera's site (Figure 10.19) provides a good example of how a business can present and explain itself on the Web.

The site offers, free of charge, articles by nationally syndicated business columnist Raj Khera concerning small businesses, marketing, and the Internet.

In the area of marketing, these are some of the articles offered:

- Getting Free Publicity for Your Small Business
- What to Include in Your Capability Brochure
- Where to Look for Leads
- Selling Your Products Abroad
- How (and Why) to Write Your Own Newsletter
- How to Publish Your First Article
- Marketing Your Services: 1993 Reader's Poll Results
- How to Sell Your Steak by Selling Its Sizzle

## Business on the Web, Management and Technology

*http://www.euro.net/innovation/*

Information Innovation provides an assortment of resources to help businesses improve management and aid them in conducting business on the Internet (Figure 10.20). The over 150 resources are grouped several ways, but all can be viewed from the "Power Launch Pad" at *http://www.euro.net/innovation/Power.List.html.*

The site includes:

- The DeskTop Web
- The DeskTop Manager
- The Electronic Banker
- Our Web Sites
- The Web Word
- The Web Newsbase

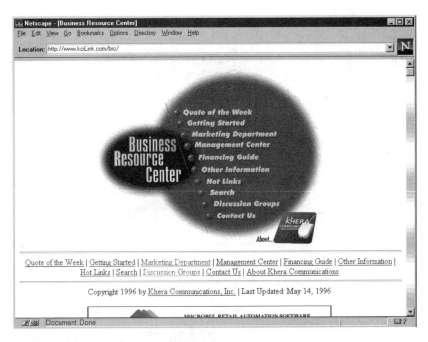

**Figure 10.19 The Small Business Help Center homepage.**

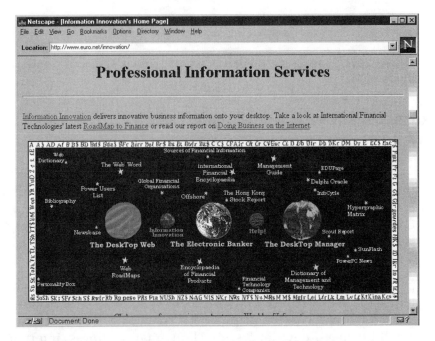

**Figure 10.20 The Business on the Web, Management and Technology homepage.**

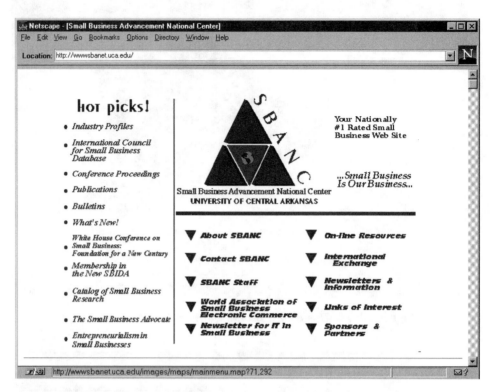

**Figure 10.21 The Small Business Advancement National Center homepage.**

## Small Business Advancement National Center

*http://wwwsbanet.uca.edu/*

The primary goals of this center are "to provide information, training, and counseling to help small businesses succeed. This includes gathering information on small business, entrepreneurship, international small business, and collegiate programs as well as providing research on these subjects."

The site (Figure 10.21) has areas for industry profiles, conference proceedings, the International Council for Small Business database, bulletins, the White House Conference on Small Business, a catalog of business research, The Small Business Advocate, entrepreneurialism in small business, newsletters for IT in small business, international exchange, and online resources.

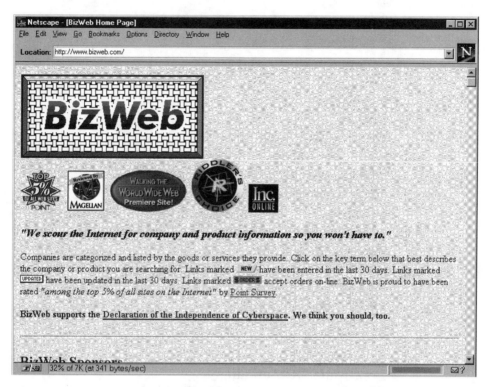

**Figure 10.22  The BizWeb homepage.**

## Malls, Product and Sales Sites

Malls and other sales sites offer "how-to" lessons and examples of the current state of affairs in online selling.

### BizWeb

*http://www.bizweb.com/*

BizWeb maintains a very large free listing of commercial products, now numbering over 7,000. Each month it has a "what's new" section with featured companies and products. A company joins the listing by simply filling out the online form. You can see the BizWeb homepage in Figure 10.22.

BizWeb's listings are organized by categories:

- Automotive
- Aviation
- Clothes
- Computer
  CD-ROM
  Hardware
  Hardware: Graphics
  Hardware: Misc.
  Hardware: PC
  Hardware: Risc
  Retailer
  Retailer: Accessories
  Retailer: CD-ROM
  Software
  Software: Accounting
  Software: Database
  Software: Graphics
  Software: Misc
  Software: PC
  Software: Programming
  Software: Programming: Embedded
  Software: UNIX
  Software: Windows-NT

- Consulting
  Network
  Network: Internet
  Software
  Technical

- Educational
- Electronics
  Consumer
  Devices
  Distributor

- Finance
  Bank
  Insurance

> Investment
> Mortgage
> Personal

- Florist
- Food
  > Alcohol
  > Coffee
  > Guide
  > Health

- Fortune 500
- Games
- Gifts
- Hobby
- Housewares
- Imaging
- Info
- Internet service provider
- Jewelry
- Manufacturing
  > Equipment
  > Supplies

- Marketplace
- Medical
- Music
- Network
  > Hardware
  > Hardware: Misc
  > Hardware: PC
  > Provider
  > Software
  > Software: Misc
  > Software: PC
  > Software: UNIX
  > Software: WWW

- Other
  Art

- Photography
- Publishing
  Bookseller
  Electronic
  Publisher
  Publisher: Book
  Publisher: Magazine
  Publisher: Newspaper

- Real estate
- Service
  Business
  Business: Import/export
  Business: Management
  Business: Opportunity
  Business: Shipping
  Employment
  Graphics
  Info
  Law
  Marketing
  Printing
  Telecom
  Training
  Translation
  Web

- Sports
- Travel
  Agent
  Carrier
  Guide
  Places

- Video

Clicking on a category will usually lead to more listings and further hierarchies.

**Figure 10.23 The Internet Shopping Network page.**

## The Internet Shopping Network

*http://www.isn.com*

This is a wholly owned subsidiary of the Home Shopping Network (TV retailers), making it unusual on the Net. ISN has over 35,000 products available for purchase. Its homepage has a useful feature up-front allowing you to choose full graphics or text only. It offers searching by alphabetical listing, by product category, or for individual companies. Figure 10.23 shows the ISN homepage. Product groups include:

- Accessories
- Desktop
- Computers
- Drives
- Memory & Processors

- Modems
- Monitors & Video
- Multimedia
- Networking
- Notebook Computers
- Printers
- Scanners
- Software

ISN offers secure data entry for shopping using an ID number. Businesses may explore merchant status by sending e-mail to *newvendor@ internet.net*.

## Branch Information Services

*http://branch.com:1080/*

Branch operates what it calls a commercial Internet information service provider—using Gopher, WWW, e-mail, and FTP to deliver information. Among its services is the Branch Mall—as they say, "exit 1, just off the information superhighway." The Branch Mall is one of the largest and longest-established virtual shopping malls on the Internet, and offers the following types of services:

- Corporate Web Site Design and Development
- On-line Storefronts and Catalogs in the Branch Malls
- High-end Web Hosting Services
- Direct Entrance (tm) virtual hosts (http://yoursite.com/, a Branch invention)
- Internet Image (tm) Service
- Firewall Secured, SSL Encrypted Servers (using Netscape's Commerce Server)
- Database Retrieval Systems
- Internet Marketing Plans
- Complete Firewall Solutions

Branch's homepage is shown in Figure 10.24—you can click on the "voice" link to hear a welcome message.

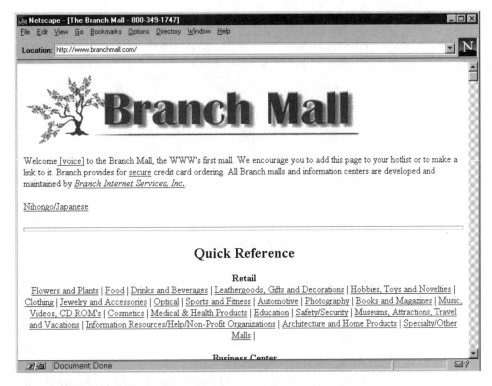

**Figure 10.24 The Branch Mall page.**

The Branch Mall features vendors such as flower shops, choco-latiers, a logging and timber company, and storefronts that sell T-shirts, flags, exercise devices, tuxedos, books, and educational videos. These shops are listed with a hotlink to their page. Vendor categories include:

- Flowers and Plants
- Food
- Drinks and Beverages
- Leathergoods
- Gifts and Decorations
- Hobbies
- Toys and Novelties
- Clothing

- Jewelry and Accessories
- Optical
- Sports and Fitness
- Automotive
- Photography
- Books and Magazines
- Music
- Videos
- CD ROMs
- Cosmetics
- Medical and Health Products
- Education
- Safety/Security
- Museums
- Attractions
- Travel and Vacations
- Information Resources/Help/Non-Profit Organizations
- Architecture and Home Products
- Specialty/Other and Malls

For example, would you like fresh live lobster flown overnight to your doorstep? If so, Lobsternet (*http://branch.com/lobster/lobster.htm*) is for you (Figure 10.25). They have Lobster Claw t-shirts and take Visa and Mastercard.

## Keeping Up to Date and Additional Resources

How can you keep up to date on all of this? There are some tools that may prove useful.

One of the best ways to keep up with one part of the Net—Usenet news—is to use the Reference.COM (*http://www.reference.com*) service. It provides on-the-fly newsgroup and list searching, but more importantly, a personalized news delivery service through e-mail. You can

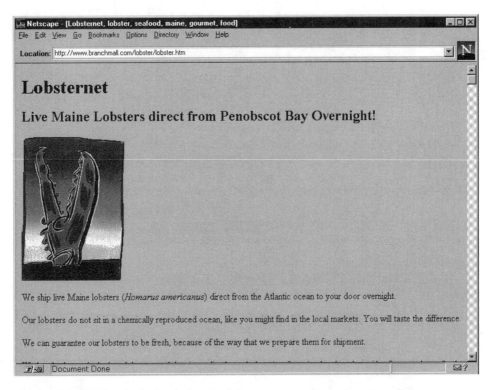

**Figure 10.25 The Lobsternet page.**

submit a profile of the subjects you wish to search for, and it will e-mail you abstracts of the items that meet your criteria. It provides options for either a weighted or Boolean system, and a method for giving feedback to the system. At the homepage (Figure 10.26), enter your subscription online.

Also, be an active Internaut, and visit some of the hot spots on the Web. Join a couple of marketing-oriented lists like IMARCOM, or a list concerned with the commercialization of the Internet such as *com-priv*. You can find good information on this at *http://www.bayne.com/wolf-Bayne/htmarcom/mktglist.html*. Read *net-happenings* regularly to find new pages, lists, newsletters, and ideas.

There are some other resources useful to businesses wanting to market on the Internet, for gaining information, doing research, or locating other sites and references.

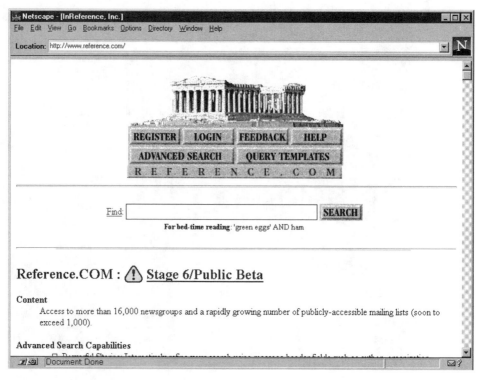

**Figure 10.26 Reference.COM homepage.**

- **Discussion Group and Newsgroup Searching**—Nova University makes a very complete searchable index of discussion groups available through its Inter-Links at *http://www.nova.edu/Inter-Links/cgi-bin/lists*, and its index of Usenet groups at *http://www.nova.edu/Inter-Links/cgi-bin/news.pl*. Another great place for searching Usenet for ideas and contacts is DejaNews (*http://www.dejanews.com*).

- **Information Sources**—The Internet and Computer Mediated Communication, maintained by John December, is an extensive guide of all manner of Internet information, including a section on WWW, at *http://www.december.com/cmc/info/*.

- **Inter-Links**—The Inter-Links Internet Access page contains one of the largest collections on the Web. To visit, go to *http://www.nova.edu/Inter-Links/*. The homepage featuring dolphins is seen in Figure 10.27.

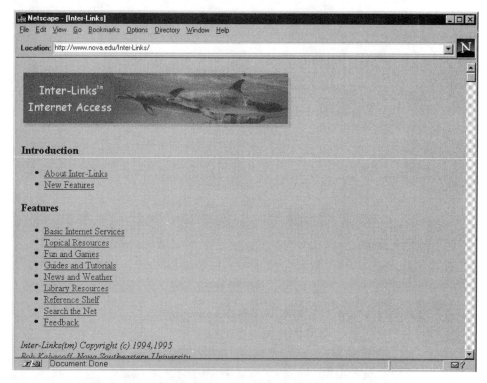

**Figure 10.27  The Inter-Links Internet Access homepage.**

- **Internet Conferences Page**—Automatrix makes a WWW page listing of Internet-related conferences available at *http://conferences. calendar.com*.

- **BOBAWORLD**—An off-beat site on the Web, Bob Allison's Bobaworld (Figure 10.28) connects you to thousands of sites. The links can be accessed through a page that sorts them into categories. This site has one of the best sets of links to WWW resources on the Web. The Tech Stuff link page points you to the various Web FAQs, HTML writing resources, sources of images, and more. The URL is *http://miso.wwa.com/~boba/*.

- **In Business Forum**—This AOL forum provides information for doing business on the Internet, offering resources, documents, message boards, live events, transcripts, and more. The site is arranged topically around marketing, commerce, selling, customer service, interactive communication, Web site development, and research ( find it at keyword "inbiz"), as seen in Figure 10.29.

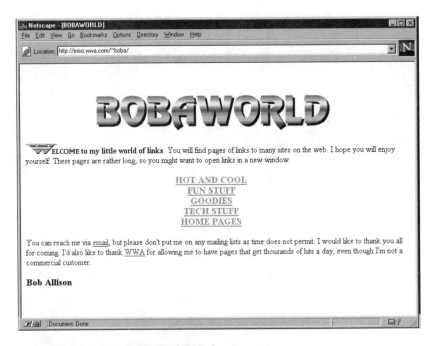

**Figure 10.28  The BOBAWORLD homepage.**

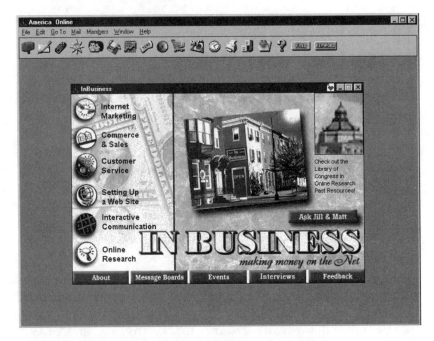

**Figure 10.29  The Internet Business front screen.**

# From Here . . .

Use the resource sites mentioned in this chapter, along with the browsers mentioned earlier, to get out on the Web—experiment, look around, and get a sense of the "look and feel" of the Internet. Have a look at what competitors are doing. The following chapter will help you connect with online advertising agencies and business-to-business support.

# CHAPTER 11

# Business to Business: Cyber-Advertising Agencies, Venture Capital, Web Services, and Information

The number of businesses providing services to online entrepreneurs on the Net is growing every day. This chapter offers a look at a sample of advertising firms, venture capital firms, and other business services available to assist you in your online marketing efforts. You can use these examples to help you make decisions about your needs.

## Advertising Agencies

As business and marketing on the Internet and Web have become more mainstream, many advertising agencies have come online as well. Some of these are virtual ad agencies, existing only in cyberspace, while others are new channels for old line ad agencies. These listed below might prove useful to both existing Net businesses, and to start-up ventures.

### adfx—Virtual Advertising

*http://www.adfx.com*

Virtual (Figure 11.1) specializes in "nonintrusive" ways to explore opportunities. They offer consulting, design, and publication of infor-

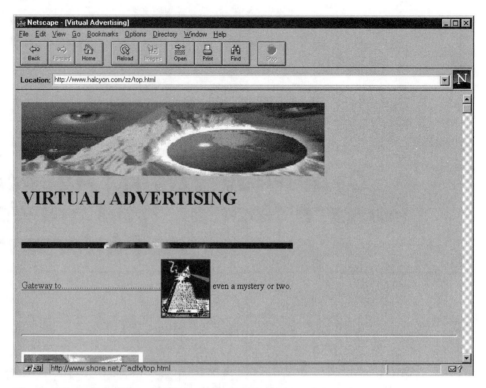

**Figure 11.1 The Virtual Advertising homepage.**

mation. As a part of their services, they offer Ultimate Solutions, for helping their clients sell online advertising.

They publish the Net@Work, which helps clients keep up to date with electronic marketing. For more information, send e-mail to *arnold3a @halcyon.com*.

## Dainamic Consulting

*http://www.netpart.com/dai/*

Dainamic Consulting (Figure 11.2) specializes in marketing strategy and management services for high-technology companies. Services include:

- Strategic Partnering and Joint Marketing Programs
- Business Plans for Corporate Intrapreneurship or Entrepreneurs

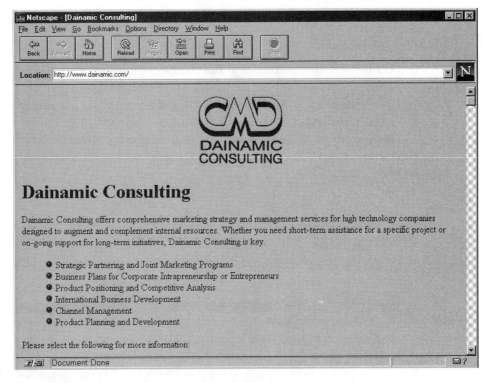

**Figure 11.2 The Dainamic Consulting homepage.**

- Product Positioning and Competitive Analysis
- International Business Development
- Channel Management
- Product Planning and Development

Contact Dainamic Consulting at:

*cyn@Dainamic.com*

Dainamic Consulting

3529 25th Street

San Francisco, CA 94110

Phone: (415) 285-4855

Fax: (415) 285-4874

## Dataquest Interactive

*http://www.dataquest.com/*

Dataquest Interactive is a market research and consulting company focusing on high-technology and financial institutions. The company provides market analysis, data and statistics, and market coverage on the semiconductor, computer systems and peripherals, communications, document management, software, and services sectors of the information technology industry. Dataquest is an international company of the Gartner Group.

Their Web page (Figure 11.3) offers information on:

- What's New
- DQi Today
- DQ Insight

**Figure 11.3 The Dataquest homepage.**

- Data Views
- DQ News
- DQ Events

Contact them at *info@dataquest.com*.

## Directrix Advertising

*http://www.directrix.com/directrix/*

Directrix Advertising specializes in Web advertising, maintaining directories of Web sites that offer advertising and sponsorship opportunities (Figure 11.4). Their SiteMatch service is designed to assist businesses with the challenging task of matching businesses with appropriate sites to advertise on.

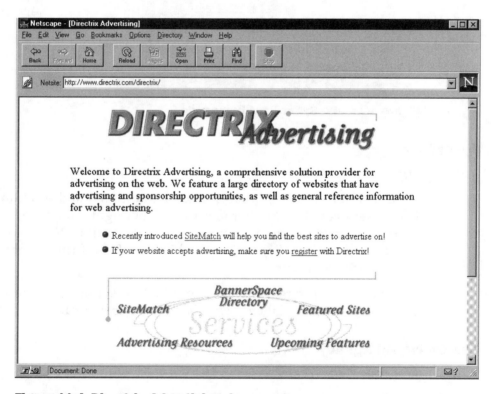

**Figure 11.4  Directrix Advertising  homepage.**

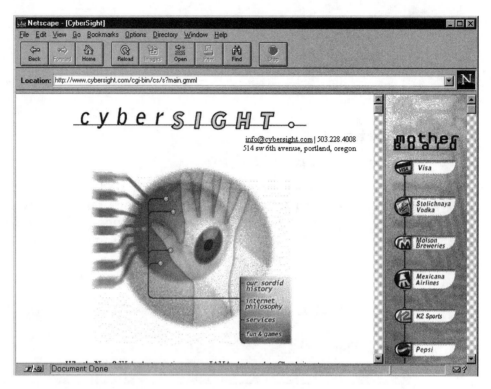

**Figure 11.5 The CyberSight homepage.**

## CyberSight

*http://cybersight.com/*

CyberSight offers a broad range of traditional and electronic marketing services. The Motherboard on CyberSight's homepage (Figure 11.5) features information about their clients, such as Visa, Stolichnaya Vodka, and Molson Breweries, the history of the firm, its philosophy and services, and "fun."

CyberSight offers design and production services, including database and Java. E-mail them at *info@cybersight.com* or call (503) 228-4008.

## The Online Ad Agency

*http://www.advert.com/*

The Online Ad Agency (Figure 11.6) focuses on getting content to your customers via both traditional and new media, with a strong em-

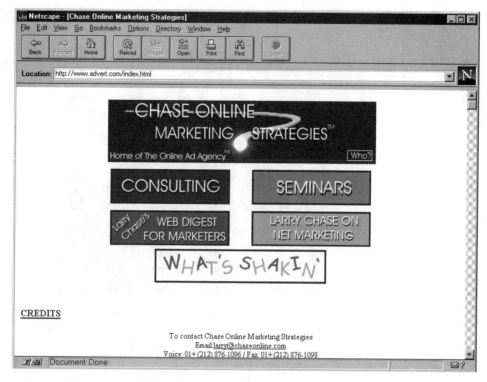

**Figure 11.6  The Online Ad Agency Welcome page.**

phasis on brand name recognition. Their homepage provides access to menus emphasizing content, delivery, audience target, the opening of new channels, clients, and Online's portfolio.

Contact them at (212) 876-1096, or e-mail Larry Chase at *larry@ chaseonline.com*.

## Poppe Tyson Advertising

*http://www.poppe.com/*

Poppe Tyson Advertising (Figure 11.7), founded in 1924 as a business-to-business advertising agency, is a subsidiary of Bozell, Jacobs, Kenyon & Eckhardt, the world's fourth largest marketing communications company. Poppe Tyson has an online PR division, and database marketing capabilities.

**Figure 11.7 The Poppe Tyson Advertising homepage.**

The company emphasizes the mix of marketing strategies that include integrated online activities such as:

- New Advertising
- Electronic Bounce-Back and Follow-up
- Virtual Stores

Contact them at:

Poppe Tyson New York

40 West 23rd Street

New York, NY 10010-5201

Phone: (212) 727-5600

Fax: (212) 727-5662

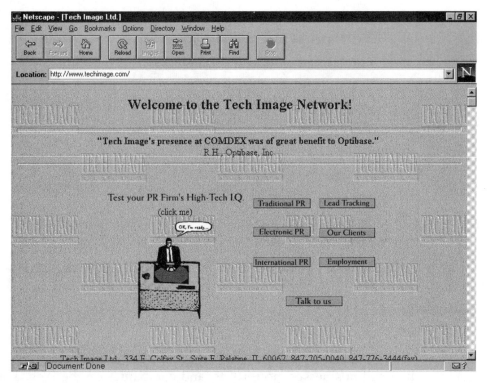

**Figure 11.8 The Tech Image homepage.**

## Tech Image

*http://www.techimage.com/*

Tech Image (Figure 11.8) specializes in public relations for the computer hardware/software, telecommunications, digital video, and interactive/multimedia industries.

The company utilizes both traditional and electronic media. Its Electronic Public Relations service is designed to include:

- HTML authoring
- E-mail, FTP, and WWW server management
- Disk-based demos
- Fax-on-demand server management
- CompuServe and AOL forum management

- Online market research
- Usenet newsgroup monitoring
- Internet shopping and conferences
- Electronic newsletters

Contact them at:

*pr@techimage.com*
Tech Image Ltd.
334 East Colfax Street
Palatine IL 60067-5343
Phone: (708) 705-0040
Fax: (708) 776-3444
CIS: 70233,42

## Webvertising

*http://www.webvertising.com/*

Webvertising (Figure 11.9) is a firm that specializes in bringing all kinds of businesses, nonprofits, and companies on the Web. The idea is to support advertising that is "consistent with the culture and etiquette of the Internet."

Webvertising assists businesses in creating a presence on the Internet, particularly with a Web-based vehicle.

Current customers and projects include a variety of travel attractions such as Reynolds Plantation and Moody Gardens, travel services such as Sailboard Vacations and Star Travel, sports and recreation projects with a heavy emphasis on windsurfing and sailboarding, outdoor recreation, and a variety of software, television, and music sites. Contact Webvertising at:

*info@webvertising.com*
Webvertising
2727 NASA Road 1, Suite 615
Seabrook, Texas 77586
Phone: (713) 326-4886

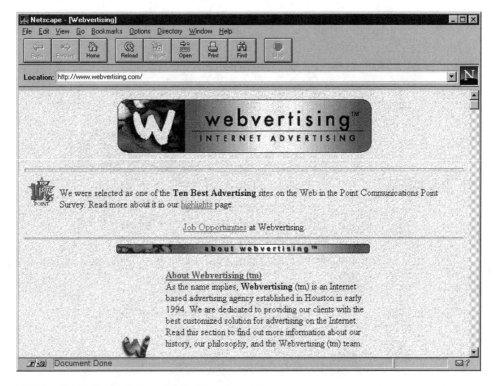

**Figure 11.9 The Webvertising homepage.**

## Werbal: Advertising Agency

*http://www.werbal.ch/*

This is a Swiss company, located in Bern, that is very involved in new media such as the World Wide Web. It offers design, image building, sales and promotion, and public relations services.

The homepage (Figure 11.10) offers the visitor the chance to find out more about Werbal's services, clients, conferences, marketing information, prices, and people. There are two parallel sets of pages, one in English and one in German.

Contact:

*info@werbal.ch*

Werbal: Advertising Agency

Thomas Bollinger

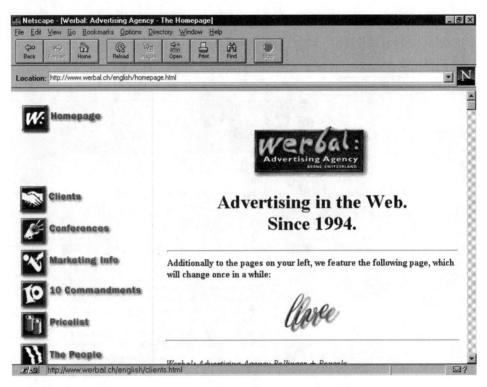

**Figure 11.10  The Werbal: Advertising Agency homepage.**

Berner Technopark

Morgenstrasse 129

CH-3018 Bern, Switzerland

Phone: ++41 (0)31-998-44 99

Fax: ++41 (0)31-998-44 98

## Winkler McManus Advertising

*http://www.winklermcmanus.com/*

Winkler McManus is a traditional advertising agency branching out to the Internet. The homepage (Figure 11.11), which displays a large graphic of the Lobby, features the Virtual Agency, and offers links to the Portfolio, Staff Office, Philosophy, Late Breaking News, and the Boardroom.

**Figure 11.11 The Winkler McManus Lobby homepage.**

The Portfolio page (Figure 11.12) lists some of Winkler McManus's clients, including:

- Sony
- Nikon Precision Inc.
- Adaptec
- Ascend

Contact the company at:

Winkler McManus Advertising
150 Spear Street, 16th Floor
San Francisco, CA 94150
Phone: (415) 957-0242

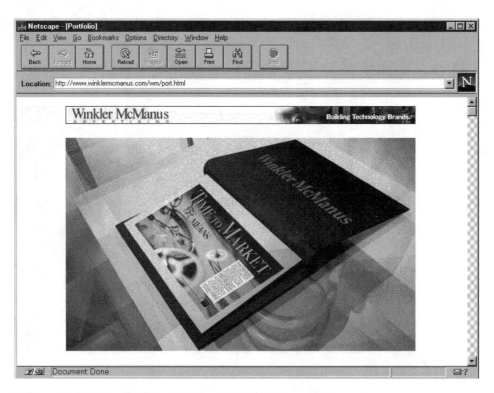

**Figure 11.12  The Winkler McManus Portfolio page.**

## Sources of More Net Advertising Information

The University of Houston's College of Business Administration maintains a large listing of all kinds of WWW information called the WWW Yellow Pages at *http://www.cba.uh.edu/ylowpges/ya.html#Adve* (Figure 11.13). The Advertising and Marketing entry currently contains a tremendous number of hotlinks, including some of the agencies just discussed.

The listing is, like the Web itself, dynamic, so this resource is worth regular visits.

The Advertising Law Internet Site (*http://www.webcom.com/~lewrose/ home.html*) offers access to a large body of advertising and marketing information. Its What's New page (Figure 11.14) draws visitors to the recent additions to the site.

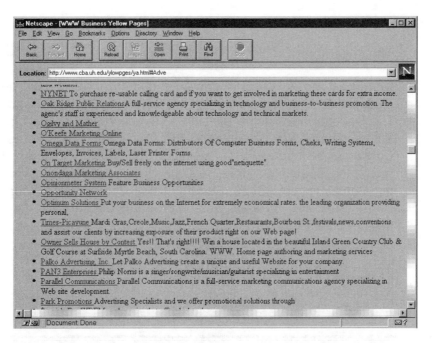

**Figure 11.13 The College of Business Administration WWW Yellow Pages Advertising page.**

**Figure 11.14 The What's New page at the Advertising Law Internet Site.**

The page covers:

United States Advertising Law—Fundamental Advertising Principles, Articles About Advertising Law, Review of Decisions Issued By The National Advertising Division, FTC Advertising Guidelines and Enforcement Policy Statements, FTC Trade Regulation Rules, FTC Consumer Brochures, FTC Business Compliance Manuals, Testimony and Speeches; Links To Other Internet Advertising/Marketing/Consumer Law Sites, Federal Trade Commission, Council of Better Business Bureaus, Inc., European Commission Advertising/Consumer Law.

Yahoo maintains a list of advertising resources at URL *http://www.yahoo.com/Computers_and_Internet/Internet/Business_and_Economics/Advertising_on_Web_and_Internet/*.

# Venture Capital

There are a number of venture capital firms with an Internet presence, as seen in Figure 11.15. These include Graylock Management, Accel Partners, Sierra Ventures, and Merrill, Pickard, Anderson.

## Accel Partners—Venture Capital for the Internet

*http://www.accel.com/*

The earliest firm of this kind to have a Web site, Accel Partners is a private venture capital firm that invests in entrepreneurial companies in technology-driven markets. It has a large capital base (over $500 million). Its homepage (Figure 11.16) offers information on Accel's investment strategy, background on the partners, networks of companies, resources for entrepreneurs, CEO day pictorial: a look inside venture capital at work, and jobs at Accel portfolio companies.

In addition, Accel's page provides access to information under these headings:

- Looking for Venture Capital
- Advice for First Time Entrepreneurs—our most popular page
- How to Win a Venture Capitalist—the five characteristics we look for in entrepreneurs

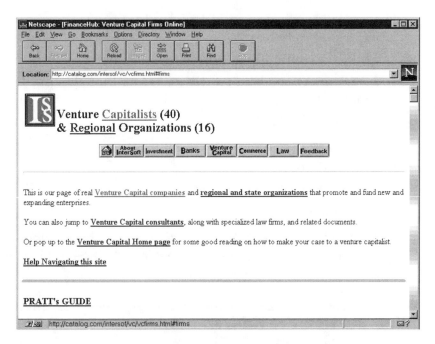

**Figure 11.15  Venture Capital Firms on the Net page.**

**Figure 11.16  The Accel Partners homepage.**

- Challenges in Building World Class Technology Companies
- Communications Week Articles—some thoughts on networking opportunities
- Financing Internet Entrepreneurs
- Other Resources for Entrepreneurs
- General Resources
- Organizations & Universities
- Publications

Contact Accel via e-mail to *rcoeby@accel.com*, by telephone at (609) 683-4500 or (415) 989-5656, or by fax to (609) 683-0384 or (415) 989-5554.

# Finding Web Service Providers

For many businesses trying to get on the Net, the task of finding a Web service provider is still a daunting one. This selection is meant to provide a few examples of the types for providers "out there," not an exhaustive listing; the following section lists some sources on the Web for further information. Check out *http://thelist.com* for a searchable database of providers.

## Bedrock Information Solutions

*http://www.bedrock.com/*

Bedrock (Figure 11.17) provides WWW services of all kinds, including Web page creation and serving, CGI script processing, HTML authoring, FTP, e-mail, Gopher, DNS registration, and application development. In addition, extensive computer-based training is provided in all areas of interconnectivity and client-server technology, including Novell, Banyan, LAN Manager, Windows NT, Internet, UNIX TCP/IP, ATM, SONET, and LAN/WAN troubleshooting. Bedrock also provides a help desk, telephone support, and system integration services.

Contact Bedrock at its URL, and at *webmaster@end2.bedrock.com*.

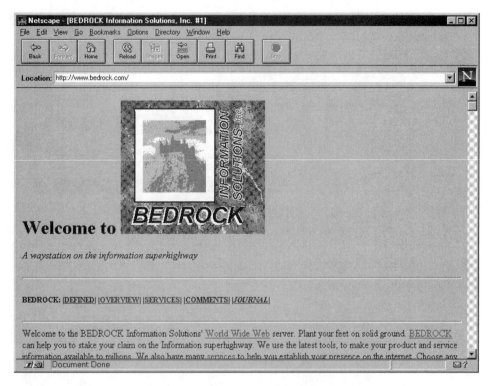

**Figure 11.17  Bedrock Information Solutions homepage.**

## InfoMatch Communications, Inc.

*http://www.infomatch.com/*

InfoMatch, located in British Columbia, is a full-service ISP/Web service provider. It provides Web pages, CGI scripting support, WAIS, HTML authoring, FTP, auto-response e-mail, Gopher, and registration services.

The homepage (Figure 11.18) offers the following options:

- Accounts
- Business
- Software
- Users

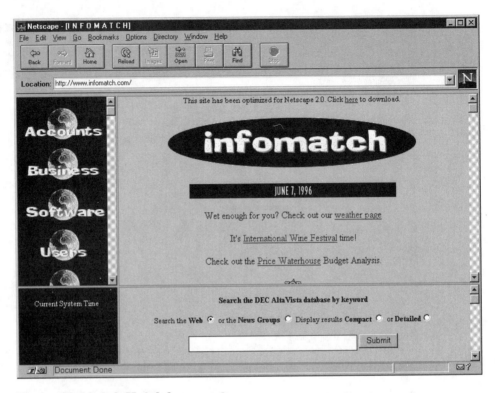

**Figure 11.18  InfoMatch homepage.**

- Buy & Sell
- InfoMatch Network Stats

For more information, contact *accounts@infomatch.com*, or (604) 421-3230.

## ITRIBE

*http://www.ip.net/*

ITRIBE, the Internet Presence & Publishing Corporation (Figure 11.19) is a provider of Web services and electronic publishing services.

They provide network connections, marketing, and advertising. Their Web services include CGI script support, HTML authoring, FTP, e-mail auto-response, registrations services, the Internet Shopkeeper, and Internet Business Reply ™. Contact them via e-mail at *info@tcp.ip. net* or by phone at (804) 446-9060.

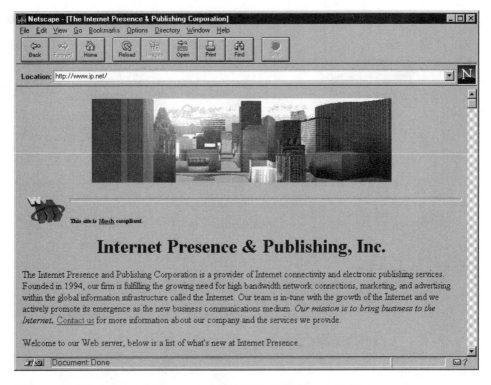

**Figure 11.19 Internet Presence & Publishing homepage.**

## Mainsail Marketing

*http://mainsail.com*

Mainsail (Figure 11.20) provides electronic directory services for direct marketing. Through Mainsail's Web Site Development Group, you can put together a single page or a whole unit. Mainsail's clients include:

- GCI-GROUP: "Strategic, Innovative and Effective Public Relations"
- Arthur D. Little: "one of the world's premier consulting firms"
- Invention Dimension—Massachusetts Institute of Technology
- Direct Marketing World
- International Male
- Childswork/Childsplay

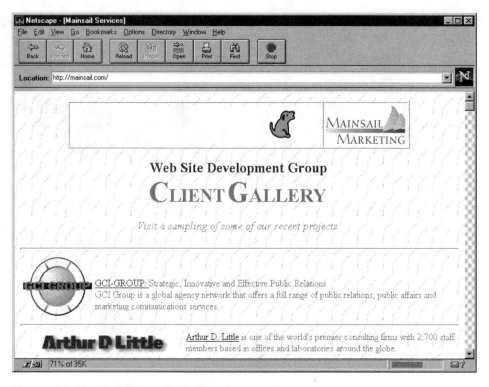

**Figure 11.20  The Mainsail Mall welcome page.**

- The Vivarin® There's No Place Like Home Pages Contest
- APCO Associates Inc.: "an international public affairs firm"

Contact Mainsail at *mmi@mainsail.com*, or (510) 486-0876.

## Teleport

*http://www.teleport.com*

Teleport (Figure 11.21),"Home of 4371 Web Sites and Growing," is a regional company offering Net services including FTP, Gopher, and DNS registration. All accounts come with full Internet access. Planned expansion includes CGI scripting, WAIS, HTML authoring, and Web application development.

Currently, the local dial-up area includes Oregon and southwest Washington state, with more expansion in the works.

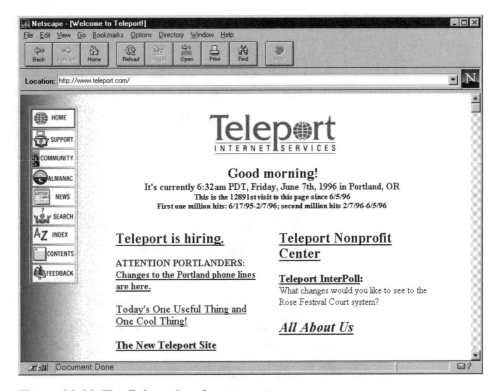

**Figure 11.21 The Teleport welcome page.**

Contact Teleport via e-mail at *www@teleport.com* or phone at (503) 223-0076.

## XOR Network Engineering/The Internet Plaza

*http://plaza.xor.com/*

XOR Network Engineering (Figure 11.22), at *http://www.xor.com*, offers numerous Web services, including basic Web page support, CGI scripting, WAIS, HTML authoring, FTP, Gopher, and registration services. The site's Internet Plaza is a forms-capable cybermall.

They began as a Gopher-based service (*gopher://plaza.xor.com*), which is still functioning.

Contact them at *plaza@plaza.xor.com* or (303) 440-6093.

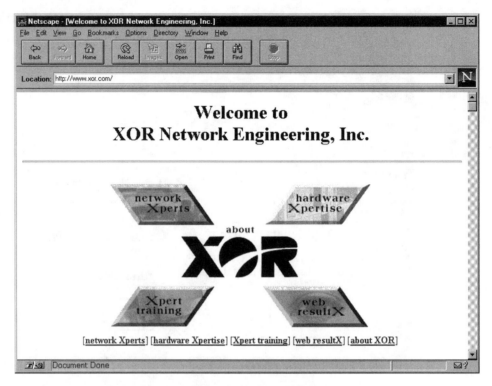

**Figure 11.22  XOR Network Engineering homepage.**

## Locating Web Services

There are a few sites that will quickly offer access to listings of Web service providers, hosting services, and other related services.

### Open Market

*http://www.directory.net/dir/servers4.html*

*http://www.directory.net/dir/servers3.html*

*http://www.directory.net/dir/servers2.html*

*http://www.directory.net/dir/servers1.html*

Open Market (Figure 11.23) maintains a very complete listing of "Companies Providing Web Space," broken down by the number of sites that they host: companies providing Web space and hosting more than seventy-five listings, those hosting from fifteen to seventy-five list-

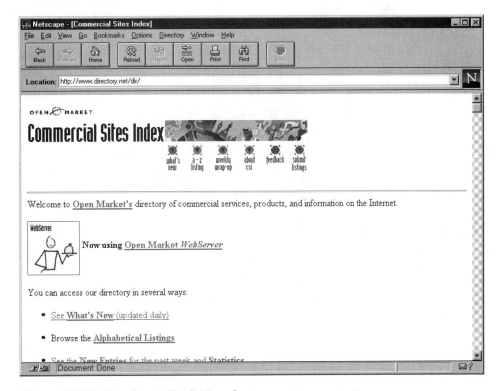

**Figure 11.23 The Open Market web space servers page.**

ings, those with six to fifteen listings, and finally, those providing Web space and hosting from three to five listings.

### Yahoo

*http://www.yahoo.com/Business_and_Economy/Companies/Internet_Services/ Web_Presence_Providers/*

It is no surprise that Yahoo provides an extensive, searchable listing of Internet and Web services providers. They have categories for:

- Announcement Services
- Free Web Pages
- Industry Specific
- International
- National
- Web Page Designers

### Leasing a Server Page

*http://union.ncsa.uiuc.edu/HyperNews/get/www/leasing.html*

Alex Chapman maintains an index of information for leasing a server. This site provides access to other listing services as well:

- List of low-cost Web space services
- Leasing a Server list of Presence Providers
- Yahoo index of Internet Presence Providers
- Web Developer's Virtual Library: Providers
- Shell accounts & home pages

### TradeWave Galaxy

*http://galaxy.einet.net/galaxy/Business-and-Commerce/General-Products-and-Services/Internet-Services.html*

TradeWave (Figure 11.24) provides catalog listings of Internet, Web, and related providers. Services and companies are listed under these headings:

- Articles
- Announcements
- Software
- Product and Service Descriptions
- Organizations
- Commercial Organizations

### Budget Web

*http://budgetweb.com/budgetweb/*

Budget Web (Figure 11.25) is a listing of low-cost services designed to help individuals, home offices, and small businesses establish a Web presence. These include both virtual hosts and domain hosting, as well as firms that provide design and scanning services at reasonable rates.

## From Here . . .

Its time to move on to the last chapter and have a peek at some group conferencing tools for enhancing Web marketing and for managing an online business and marketing venture.

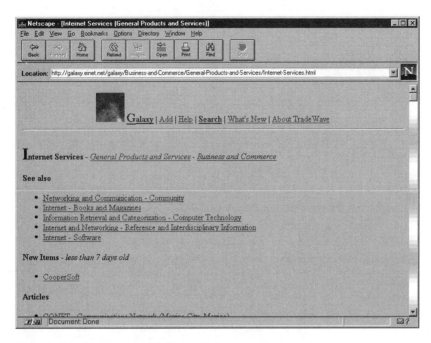

**Figure 11.24  The TradeWave Galaxy page.**

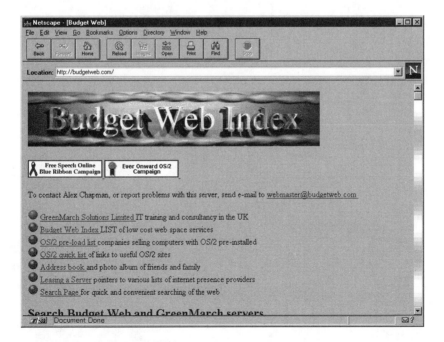

**Figure 11.25  Budget Web.**

# CHAPTER 12

# *Expanding Your Internet Marketing Tool Kit*

This chapter is designed to help you think about extending your Internet marketing efforts into real-time chat, web chat, real-time audio, online conferencing, whiteboarding, and more—the current applications "out there" that might prove useful to the Internet marketer. There are applications to help you with:

- Real-time audio
- Real-time conferencing
- Internet videoconferencing
- Interactive chat on your Web site
- Virtual Worlds interactive environments

These tools can assist you in providing information, gathering information, bringing traffic to the site, getting users involved, getting them to act and interact, building customer loyalty through community, and more.

All of these can be used to enhance Web marketing and to create additional channels for marketing, brand recognition, customer and vendor communication, and various business functions.

## Real-time Audio and Conferencing

There are an increasing number of Internet real-time audio and real-time conferencing systems available. Some of these, like IPhone, are Internet telephone applications with attendant telephone-like functions including Caller ID, voicemail, and so on; they may also include document transfer and text-based chat. Some of these are one-on-one, while others allow conference calls.

The conferencing systems often add whiteboarding—the ability to mark up and edit text and images—and often allow for movement to a Web page and tours among groups of people.

## IPhone

*http://www.vocaltec.com*

Internet Phone from VocalTec (Figure 12.1) offers the ability to make phone calls (local and long distance) over the Internet. It supports a variety of features, for just the cost of your Internet connections:

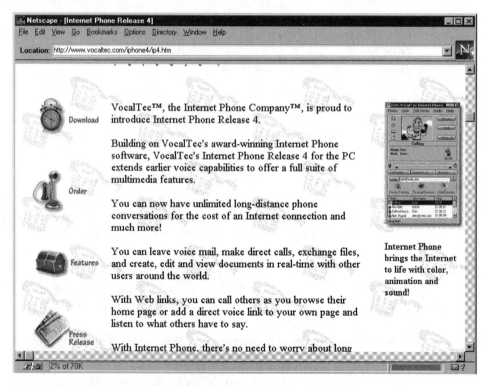

**Figure 12.1 The Internet Phone page.**

- Voicemail—including call waiting, Caller ID, screening, muting, and blocking
- Whiteboarding—document sharing and marking up
- File transfer—for file exchange
- Chat—text-based
- Full-duplex
- Online directory of users
- Automatic voice activation
- Web links—you can call others while browsing

How the regulating agencies and telcos view applications like this remains to be seen.

## NetMeeting from Microsoft

*http://www.microsoft.com/netmeeting/learn/overview.html*

NetMeeting is included with the 3.0 version of Microsoft Internet Explorer. This is a powerful collaboration tool which combines an Internet telephone function with the ability to share applications. It contains an object-oriented whiteboard, a file transfer facility, a shared clipboard, and a real-time chat area.

NetMeeting allows for groups of people to work online together. There is a Moderator who initiates the session, and controls the activities such as editing so that everyone does not try to do everything at once. There are tools to set some users as watch-only, while others can watch, talk, and edit at will (see Figure 12.2).

NetMeeting can interoperate with many other conferencing products from PictureTel, OnLive Technologies, White Pine Software, and Databeam.

Currently this is ported for Windows 95 and Windows NT, and versions for Win 3.x and Macintosh are in development.

## CoolTalk from Netscape

*http://www.netscape.com/comprod/products/navigator/version_3.0/communication/cooltalk/ index.html*

CoolTalk is included in the 3.0 version of the Netscape Navigator. CoolTalk is an Internet telephone that can provide for audioconferenc-

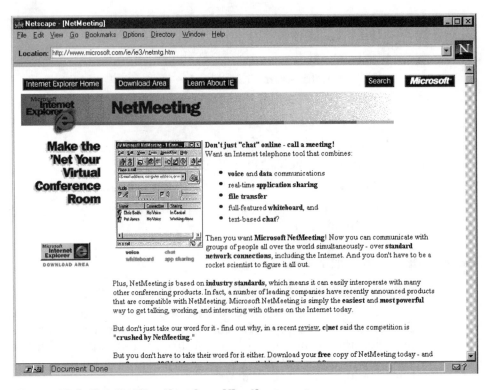

**Figure 12.2 The NetMeeting Specifications page.**

ing, a full-featured whiteboard, and text-based communications using its chat tool (Figure 12.3).

This is an online real-time collaboration tool, currently providing for one-to-one (as opposed to group) collaboration. It has:

- Audioconferencing—live interactive full-duplex talk, which includes Caller ID, call screening, dialer, and mute
- CoolTalk Phonebook—Web-based phone book for locating other users
- Answering machine—voicemail-like features
- Whiteboard—while talking, you can view and mark up the same images
- Chat tool—a text-based interactive messaging system

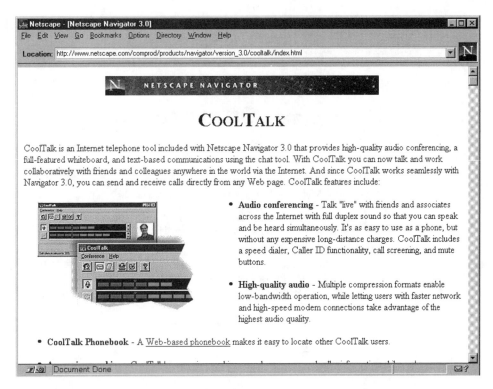

**Figure 12.3  CoolTalk Information page.**

CoolTalk is currently available with Navigator 3.0 for Windows 95, Windows NT, Windows 3.1, SunOS, Solaris, HP-UX, Digital Unix, and IRIX. Versions for Macintosh and for additional UNIX platforms are in development.

## Internet Conference

*http://www.vocaltec.com/conf.htm*

Internet Conference (Figure 12.4) is conferencing software for up to 255 users at once. Users can communicate even using 9600 baud modems and cellular connections. The software lets users view and comment on (mark up) shared images, and view Web sites together. It integrates Internet Phone with real-time chat, file transfer, whiteboarding, document markup, cutting and pasting, and public and private discussion. It is available for 32-bit and 16-bit Windows platforms.

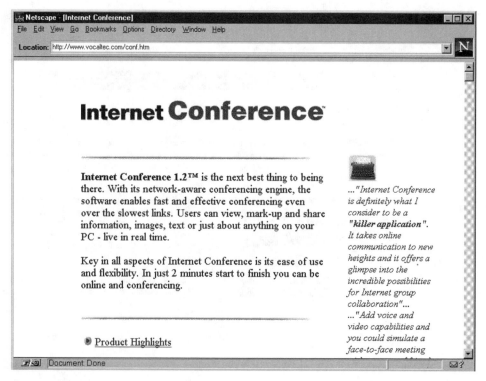

**Figure 12.4 The Internet Conference page.**

# Videoconferencing

Videoconferencing builds on the features of some of the conferencing software just described by adding video to the mix.

## CU-SeeMe

*http://cu-seeme.cornell.edu/*

CU-SeeMe (Figure 12.5) is a free videoconferencing program from Cornell University. It allows users to videoconference anywhere, and by using a reflector, numerous groups at different locations can participate in a CU-SeeMe conference. It was developed in 1992 at a time when the only real-time videoconferencing software for the Internet required very expensive hardware.

Craig Luecke's CU-SeeMe page (*http://www.crosslink.net/~craig/directory/page1.htm*) is a great collection of CU-SeeMe information and links.

**Figure 12.5 The Cornell University CU-SeeMe Welcome page.**

Enhanced CU-SeeMe from WhitePine (Figure 12.6) is a commercial version of CU-SeeMe (*http://www.wpine.com/*).

CU-SeeMe is a software-based desktop real-time videoconferencing system used on the Internet. The commercial version has color video, audio, a chat window, and whiteboard. In addition, you can participate in "Live over the Internet" conferences, broadcasts, or chats. CU-SeeMe can be used directly from Web pages with a Web browser, using a 28.8 modem. If you are using it for audio-only, it can run on a 14.4 connection. The Cornell (non-commercial) version lacks voice and color video. It is used for training, conferencing, and communications with customers, vendors, and others.

CU-SeeMe is compatible with video and audio standards found on both Windows and Macintosh systems. CU-SeeMe works with up to eight video participants, with unlimited access for audio and talk windows. In addition it offers security measures such as passwords and Caller ID.

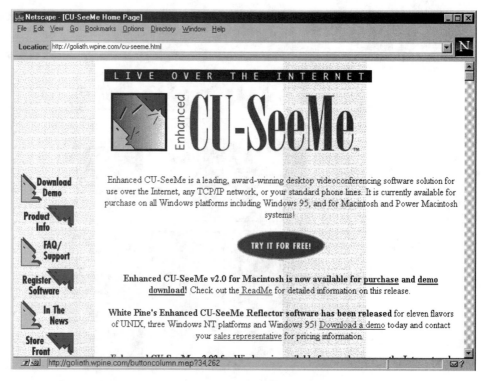

**Figure 12.6 The Enhanced CU-SeeMe page.**

## Other Video Applications

There are some other video applications with features that are signifi-cantly less rich than those of CU-SeeMe; these include Intercom and Video Phone.

### Telescape's Intercom

*http://www.telescape.com*

Intercom from Telescape is a free utility to talk to others, and to share pictures, files, and information in a store-and-forward fashion rather than with full interactivity. You can use it to show digital images and talk one-to-one.

This is a still-picture–enhanced e-mail–based program. With an en-hanced product called Viewport, it lets you display a visual signature, scanned-in photograph, or any other graphic file.

### Connectix Video Phone

*http://www.connectix.com*

To accompany its small video camera called Quick Cams, Connectix offers Video Phone, which adds audio to its existing video transmissions. It allows simultaneous video, talk, and the sharing of a markup board.

## Broadcasting

The Internet is capable of providing real-time audio at speeds of 14.4 kbaud or faster, including live streaming at 28.8 using such applications as RealAudio. In addition, there are some industrial-strength applications such as Mbone Multicasting that can provide high-quality audio and video broadcasting.

### RealAudio

*http://www.realaudio.com*

RealAudio from Progressive Networks (Figure 12.7) brings real-time, on-demand audio to Internet users through a combination of a free player and a commercial server. With a connection of 14.4 or faster, you can use the Player like a cassette or CD player, pausing, rewinding, fast-forwarding, stopping, and starting. Once the connection is established, it can stream the audio steadily.

The Player is available for Windows, Macintosh, and UNIX platforms. Most browsers allow for RealAudio as a supported plug-in. The Player can play existing clips as well as live cybercasts. The RealAudio Server allows your Web site to deliver this real-time on-demand sound to the user. In addition, Progressive Networks produces Timecast, a guide to the daily news broadcasts available through RealAudio on the Net in a customized form.

### MBONE

*http://www.best.com/~prince/techinfo*

MBONE (Figure 12.8) is the Multicast Backbone of the Internet; it is an overlay network running on top of the Internet, providing real-time multimedia presentations in broadcast mode. Broadcast events include NASA Select, Internet Talk Radio, U.S. House and Senate debates, and more. MBONE was used by the Rolling Stones for their live-to-the-Internet broadcast.

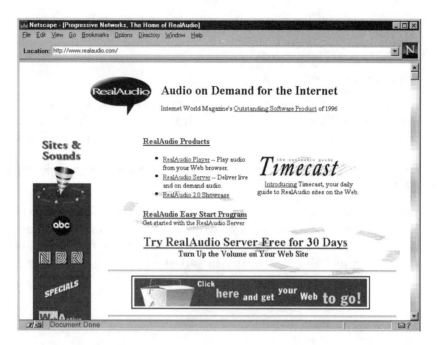

**Figure 12.7 The RealAudio page.**

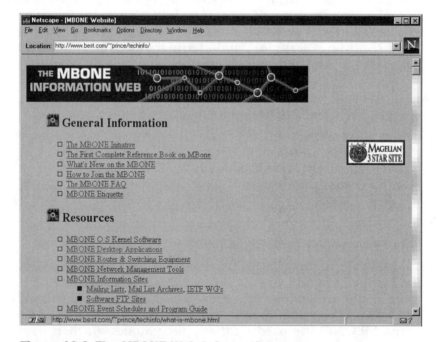

**Figure 12.8 The MBONE Web Information page.**

MBONE began as audio only but now offers video, whiteboarding, and more through a variety of programs. Still primarily for large servers and robust connections, it is migrating to desktops.

The MBONE FAQ by Steve Casner is available at *http://www.best. com/~prince/techinfo/mbone.faq.html.*

# Virtual Worlds

In the text-based portion of the Internet are MOOs, MUDs, and MUCKs, which are all text-oriented "virtual world" sites where the user enters spaces, creates characters, manipulates objects, and interacts with others in a pseudo-physical environment created by the users. MUDs are Multi-User Dialog/Dimensions; MOOs (MUD Object-Oriented ) offer a richer virtual environment. The web-based virtual environments tend to be cumbersome in their manifestations, but more visually interesting.

Currently there are a few 2D and 3D graphical versions of these, called virtual worlds, which offer some interesting opportunities to the marketer. They can be used to create a very rich environment for real-time interaction. They all provide for meeting and launching in Web space. Some of them have capabilities for a moderator or leader to set up the places and moderate the action. These are ideal environments for businesses to display their wares, and create marketing and business situations emulating "real life."

## AlphaWorld

*http://www.worlds.net/alphaworld/*

AlphaWorld is a virtual world, emphasizing what it calls "social computing." It uses the language of a virtual country where you immigrate, become a citizen, and help shape the environment.

As in some of the MUCKs (which predate the Web), you acquire and develop property, assume an online persona, and interact with others in the environment. When you enter a new zone or world, the software downloads the art that you need for that environment.

The metaphors play out in highly graphical, almost science-fictional settings as seen in Figure 12.9, and the various worlds are quite different from each other.

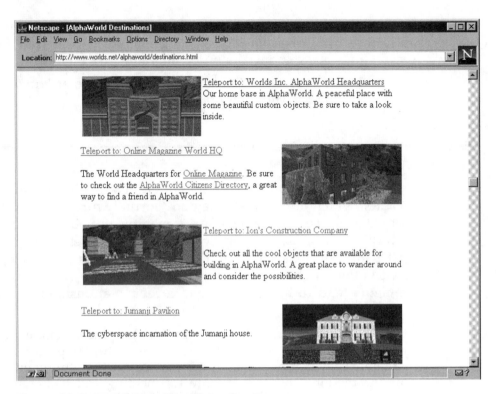

**Figure 12.9  Some AlphaWorld destinations.**

## The Palace

*http://www.thepalace.com*

The Palace is a virtual online environment that works with Web browsers to provide for real-time chat and interaction. In this environment, users choose the appearance and characteristics for their avatars (virtual online representations, faces, or cartoons, as seen in Figure 12.10).

Users can create these by importing photos or other images, or by rummaging through a set of props that comes with the software. Online in a Web environment, The Palace can use hyperlinks, and has been called a cross between IRC chat and a hypermedia environment.

Once you enter the environment, you can see and talk with others, roam through various existing rooms, or create your own private talk

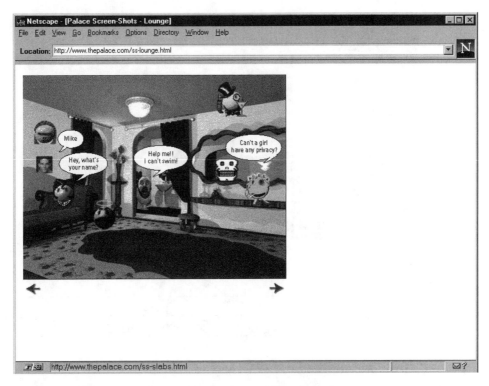

**Figure 12.10 The Lounge with Avatars at The Palace.**

areas. You can make sounds, change avatars, and jump to other Palace sites. The Palace supports as many as 20 users.

To use the Palace, you must download the browser plug-in. There is a shareware version for the server that is more limited in capability, but can be upgraded.

The Palace server and client both are available for Windows, Mac, and UNIX platforms, and at your server site, you create the scenes using a scripting language called IptScrae.

The InterActive Agency (Figure 12.11, *http://www.iagency.com/*) is one company that makes use of The Palace. InterActive is a firm that provides an "understanding of new media technologies and experience in traditional marketing and promotion."

The InterActive Agency offers traditional public relations services, online marketing and promotion for Web sites, and a Palace venue designed to be an interactive marketing vehicle.

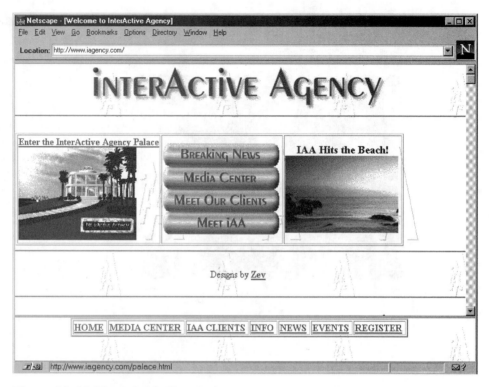

**Figure 12.11 The InterActive Agency page.**

## Virtual Places

*http://www.vplaces.com/index.htm*

Created by Ubique and now owned by AOL, this tool is a chat room over the Web (Figure 12.12).

When launched, Virtual Places attaches itself to your browser, and makes pages into chat rooms; users of VP can then meet at a page and have a chat. You can control the size and characteristics of the chat room. In addition, you can create private conversations with anyone who is VP enabled at the site. Another option is Tours—you can move from site to site with the same group, or invite new members as well. Virtual Places lets you locate other users by their nickname.

Like other virtual environments, Virtual Places lets you create an on-screen avatar to represent yourself in the environment. This can be customized, or you can choose one from the VP library. There is even a

**Figure 12.12  Virtual Places examples page.**

mood and gesture tool. The right mouse button lets you show "emotions" by displaying smiles, waves, throbbing hearts, and more. You can change your "identity" on the fly, which can include your e-mail address, too.

## Live3D

*http://www.netscape.com/comprod/products/navigator/live3d/index.html*

Live3D from Netscape is a viewer for VRML (Virtual Reality Modeling Language). This includes text, images, animation, sound, music, and even video. This VRML viewer provides for distributed 3D spaces that are rendered with background processing. You can manipulate objects, walk, fly, and point. Live3D provides for selectable camera views and optional gravity. Multimedia-Live3D offers integration with Live-Media for streaming audio and video in 3D space.

Potential applications include multiuser chats, GIS (geographical information systems), authoring, interactive advertising, and online presentations.

Currently, Live3D is available with Netscape Navigator 3.0 for Windows 3.1, Windows 95, Windows NT, and Power Macintosh. Versions for 68K Macintosh and UNIX are under development.

## PowWow

*http://www.tribal.com/powwow/*

PowWow (Figure 12.13) is an Internet program for Windows that, in its native "Personal Conference" mode, lets up to seven people cruise the Web together, chat, send and receive files, and view images. You can chat via text (typing) or voice.

A new part of PowWow called Conferencing permits up to fifty people to chat together at one time. A conference can be run by a moderator

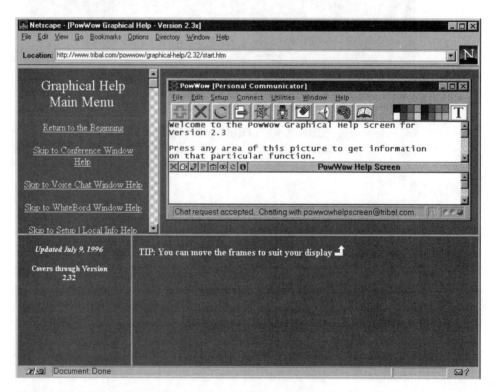

**Figure 12.13 The PowWow Graphical Help page.**

or left un-moderated. The Moderator controls the interaction as well as the display of pages.

You can page someone using your Web browser to have them join a PowWow session by entering their PowWow Address into the URL (location) field of the browser. In PowWow lingo, the Leader is the person who initiates a group Cruise session and has control of cruising the Web.

## Web Chat

There are a number of products allowing sites to put live chats on their Web pages. Usually this is accomplished by opening up public rooms for chatting on the site, since this is a faster method of access than some of the group chat/tour packages like PowWow.

### Global Stage Chat—Prospero Systems Research

*http://www.prospero.com/*

Global Stage Chat provides server-based software solutions that enable Web sites to offer chat rooms in a variety of sizes and with varying levels of sophistication (Figure 12.14).

The Cafe is for personal and very small sites, and includes both moderated and un-moderated channels, transcripting, and up to 50 users at once. Somewhat larger is The Theater, which is aimed at small commercial sites and can handle up to 100 simultaneous users.

Larger yet is The Stadium. Designed for much more robust sites, it is enhanced for 1,000 users, and provides for private chat sessions and can offer advertising. A Stadium for even larger groups is planned. Branded versions are available, so that you can have a customized "Your Company Stadium."

### The Chat Server

*http://chat.magmacom.com/info/*

The Chat Server is a real-time, continuous stream, multimedia-capable, Web-based communication server.

The Chat Server lets you set up public and private chat rooms of all kinds, for seminars and meetings (Figure 12.15). It provides for logging, password-protected rooms, and the setting up of "walls" (similar to bulletin or message boards). It supports a Java interface as well.

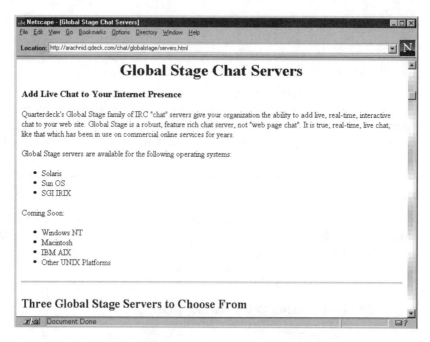

**Figure 12.14 Global Stage server specifications page.**

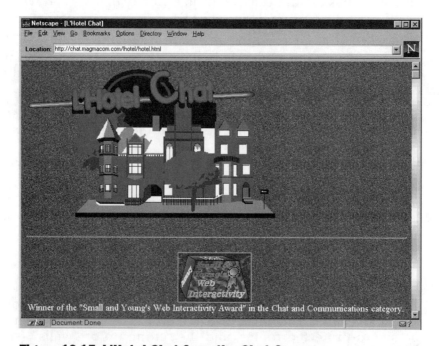

**Figure 12.15 L'Hotel Chat from the Chat Server.**

## Finding More Information

There are lots of good places to find more information on these kinds of Internet tools. Among them are:

- Internet telephone: Internet Telephony Resources Page (*http://rpcp.mit.edu/~itel/resource.html*)
- Internet multimedia and telephone: Real-Time Multimedia Web (*http://www.inria.fr/rodeo/personnel/hoschka/bof-list.html*)
- Internet multimedia resources: Index to Multimedia Information Sources (*http://viswiz.gmd.de/MultimediaInfo/*)
- Information on Web chat: Links ~R~Us—Chattin' on the Web (*http://rampages.onramp.net/~gegomez/den3.htm*)

## From Here . . .

At this point, you should be bristling with ideas for how to market on the Internet. Now is the time to create or revise those Web pages. Check the Epilog that follows for a look at where this might all be headed.

# Epilogue: The Future—
# Think Months, Not Years

What can be expected for the future? Long-term forecasts will require a working crystal ball or a long chat with the Psychic Friends Hotline, but near-term trends can be determined without tea leaves. Here are some of the trends and issues for Internet marketing.

## Data Transmission—Emphasis on "The Last Mile"

The technological and financial aspects of high-speed worldwide data transfer systems are well established, but the techniques for interaction between the end user and the telecommunications system are still up in the air. Modem speeds have increased and may increase somewhat more, but substantial improvements in getting data over the "copper" to and from the individual may await widespread, affordable ISDN access, and/or some dramatic improvements in data compression technologies. ATM (Asynchronous Transfer Mode) will also play a part.

Interactive cable systems, cable modems, radio, wireless, and satellite systems may also be predominant, or will at least play a role. For the near term, however, businesses need to keep in mind that a large portion of their potential customers may have access only to the slower systems.

**307**

## More Multimedia

Audio and video Web site enhancements are rapidly being incorporated for product demonstrations and to attract visitors to sites for sales and marketing of many products, but the low-cost online delivery of audio and video products themselves is also likely to increase dramatically as those outside the usual audio and video distribution channels become aware of the possibilities.

Net video, real-time video and audio, whiteboards, and Internet videoconferences are in use already, and are coming packaged with browsers—CoolTalk with Netscape, and NetMeeting with MSIE, for example. As the multimedia capabilities of the Internet improve, you can expect more access to, and use of, full-motion real-time video and audio online broadcasting and interactive audio- and videoconferencing, along with better integration of these and other multimedia elements in connection with Web sites. These kinds of multimedia and interactive systems can be expected to be integrated into business Web sites for much more extensive interactivity between businesses and the public. Java will play a role, ActiveX will, and companies such as RealAudio and Macromedia are moving along as well.

Web chatting and interaction on sites offered by such products as PowWow are likely to have a greater impact in the short term. In addition, Java applets appear to be greatly adding to functionality, but will be less useful until the installed base of consumers have better access and more powerful hardware.

## Virtual Reality

Virtual reality is likely to become one mode of online interaction sometime in the future, but software, standards, and online bandwidth problems will probably keep the more robust incarnations on the slow track.

Some less full-featured systems like AlphaWorld are beginning to offer some VR functionality. These are definitely worth watching; but VR probably will not be a factor for most businesses until more users have the capabilities of faster connections and more sophisticated computers.

## New and Improved Transfer Protocols

The Internet's phenomenal growth is often attributed in part to the development of an open standard protocol (TCP/IP), and the Web's even more phenomenal growth is also based in part on the open HTTP/HTML protocols. These have allowed additions and improvements to be added to these systems without having to remake them. As the next generation of protocols develop, there is a continuing strong push to keep developing standardized, open protocols that are also backward compatible—keeping individuals currently on the Web actively engaged without the requiring them to upgrade systems and software.

## More Sophisticated Search Engines

Web search systems have improved dramatically in the last year, but there is much that can be done to improve search accuracy and user-friendliness—and with large numbers of search sites competing for advertising dollars, improvements should be dramatic and ongoing. In addition, the search tools will most likely allow for personalized agents or "searchbots" (search robots) that can hunt specifically for the information you want, even in your absence. These will make incredibly powerful and up-to-date searches available to individuals and businesses.

## Increased Security

Security issues of many kinds are being addressed now regarding the Internet and the Web. The Web is starting to include more secure transactions, better authentication of messages and virtual signatures, enhanced-privacy e-mail (S/MIME), and more sophisticated encryption.

Many companies are working on more sophisticated virtual banking and virtual credit cards to create more secure transactions, the most promising of which seems to be in the area of standards development for online credit card use. As the number of options and methods increase, so too will marketing and sales opportunities change. These standardized and user-friendly systems will increase confidence in on-

line transactions, but as with checks, credit cards, and telephone ordering, there will be some time lag while consumers develop trust in the
new systems.

## Some Final Thoughts

Each new development and improvement on the Internet should lead
each business to a re-evaluation of the potential for online marketing.
Many of these changes will provide never-before-available opportunities for marketing and sales. This is an excellent time to put your business on the Web—the key elements needed to do business online are
already in place. Get on the Web now, learn the ropes, iron out the wrin-
kles, stay plugged in to the high-speed evolution of the Internet, and
open your business's virtual doors to the estimated 100 million people
predicted to be online worldwide by 1998.

Bon voyage!

# *Getting Internet Access for Marketing on the World Wide Web*

For the business user, especially one interested in using the World Wide Web for marketing, there are a number decisions to be made regarding Internet access, connections, and services. This appendix will explore the types of services most likely to be useful, considerations for making choices among the options, and information on Internet service providers. First, though, let's look briefly at the software needed to view Web pages.

## Browsers

Using the World Wide Web requires the use of a *browser* program to view files, look at or download images and movies, or listen to or download sound files. There are two main kinds of browsers.

### Graphical User Interfaces (GUI) Browsers

These are the mouse/icon-oriented programs that often run under GUI operating systems such as Windows, Mac, or X-Windows (Figure A.1 shows the c l net homepage as an example). Most of these programs automatically display the formatted text with various fonts, pictures, sounds, and movies, with a simple click of the mouse—they provide Internet multimedia.

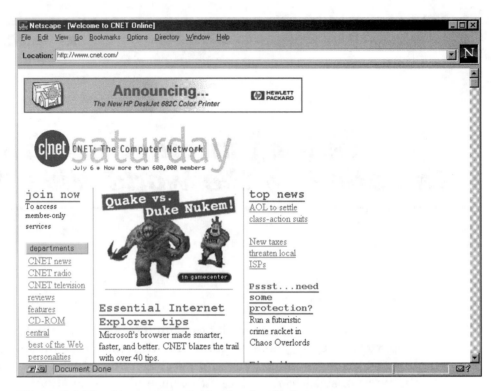

**Figure A.1 The homepage of c|net using Netscape.**

Some of these browsers provide not only access to the World Wide Web but also GUI-oriented direct access to Gopher, FTP, Telnet, Usenet news, and other Internet resources. Many of these programs, such as the popular Netscape, Microsoft Internet Explorer, HotJava, and Mosaic (in various forms), require a TCP/IP connection to the Internet. This type of connection can be obtained from an Internet access provider who offers either SLIP or PPP dial-up service, ISDN, or permanent connection to the Internet, and even through some of the commercial online services.

## Text-Based Browsers

Back in the Internet olden days—about three years ago—text-based browsers were the only game in town, and they are still used by many educational institutions. They work well and require less sophisticated computers/terminals than GUI browsers. Text-based browsers read the same HTML text files that the GUI programs do, but they display them without formatting, varied fonts, and so on. They do not display inline pictures from the document being read, but they will allow for some of the picture and sound files to be downloaded and viewed or played on your local computer at a later time, if your computer has the proper software and hardware.

Text-based browsers allow you to use the Web even with simple computer equipment, monochrome monitors, and systems without a mouse. Without the time required to display pictures, fonts, and so on, text-based browsers are often faster than GUIs. Lynx is probably the best of the text-based browsers (see Figure A.2).

## Access to the Internet

There are numerous ways to be connected to the Internet: direct or via telephone lines. Businesses may want to consider a number of alternatives before making a decision to connect or change their connections.

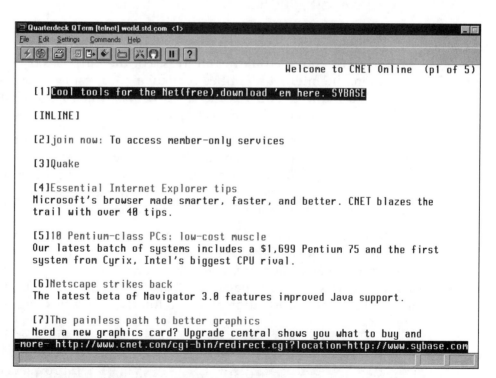

**Figure A.2 The c l net page seen using Telnet and Lynx.**

There are four common types of Internet access: node, ISDN, PPP, and (much less frequently) dial-up shell accounts; in addition, access is provided by the commercial services such as America Online, CompuServe, and the Microsoft Network.

Medium-size and large businesses, or any business that makes extensive use of the Internet, should consider a full-time connection as a node. This can be done through a full-time dial-up SLIP/PPP connection or ISDN, or directly using one of several kinds of dedicated leased lines.

SLIP/PPP and ISDN accounts can be maintained either full-time with dedicated lines or as dial-up accounts. This type of Internet access can be less expensive than the creation and maintenance of a node with a corporate identity, while still maintaining full Internet interaction and a good selection of GUI browser software. Depending on intensity of use, a SLIP/PPP account would be appropriate for businesses of all sizes, although increasingly ISDN should be considered.

Dial-up shell accounts are very low cost but have become scarce as inexpensive SLIP/PPP have supplanted them.

## Becoming a Node

Each node is a unique Internet address. For the purposes of routing information, the Internet identifies particular sites or places on the Internet with a numeric address like *192.74.137.5*. Each node also has an alphabetic domain name such as *binford.com*.

When you have a full, permanent connection to the Internet, you will have your own domain name, like *oak-ridge.com* or *cybernetics.org*. It is also possible to obtain a domain name for your organization to use with other access providers, with ISDN, or on part-time SLIP or PPP accounts as well. They look the same to the Internet.

Registering a domain name for your company can be done by your ISP or by your own system administrator. The forms (templates) for domain name registration are available via FTP from *ftp://rs.internic.net* and via InterNIC's homepage at *http://www.internic.net/*. The InterNIC homepage offers information about all InterNic activities (Figure A.3).

### Is It a Node or Is It Memorex?

A node is a computer that forms a permanent part of the Internet and has registered a name with InterNIC. Most commercial ventures want to have their own domain, such as *oak-ridge.com, wiley. com,* or *ibm.com.* Increasingly, however, there are pseudo-nodes available through Internet service providers (ISPs). These ventures will rent you space on their machines and create addresses that look like nodes.

The value of a well-chosen domain name has been affirmed by some recent legal challenges over the ownership of domain names. In one situation there was controversy over whether MTV had any claims to the domain name *mtv.com,* which was obtained by a former employee on his own while still at the firm. Some people have also been registering names on speculation that they would be of value some day. You may have to use some extra creativity if the obvious name for your company is already in use. For example, if you are that certain large beverage company, you should know that someone already has *coke.com*—how about *fizz.com* or *notpepsi. com*?

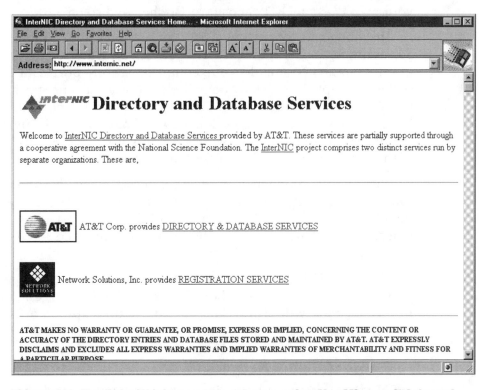

**Figure A.3 The InterNIC homepage (shown using the Microsoft Internet Explorer browser).**

## SLIP and PPP

These are a type of Internet connection usually made through Plain Old Telephone Service (POTS) using fast modems. They allow the use of the Internet's TCP/IP protocol using normal phones, and can be either full-time or on demand. This category of service is still one of the fastest growing due to the new GUI browsers that require it.

SLIP stands for Serial Line Internet Protocol, and PPP stands for Point-to-Point Protocol. SLIP is an older, less-used style of connection, while PPP is the more popular.

These kinds of connections are usually made at 14,400 or 28,800 baud. Because they are slower and have less capacity than a *direct* connection or an ISDN connection, large companies find them limiting.

PPP provides support for GUI WWW browsers, making it a moderately priced but highly versatile alternative to dedicated Internet connections. A full-time PPP style of connection would allow you to run your own Web site, FTP repository, Gopher, and so on.

Installing and configuring a PPP connection can be a bit challenging. For example, on a Windows-based system, you will need to install a program designed to enable your communications port as a dedicated socket. Trumpet Winsock by Peter Tattam is one such program. Information on your IP number, various parameters of the connection, and so on have to be configured. In addition, you will have to install any of a number of the existing WWW browsers, such as Netscape, MS Explorer, one of the variations of Mosaic (NCSA Mosaic, Spry, etc.), or Cello.

PPP dial-up, on-demand service connections usually run from $20 to $40 a month, often with unlimited time access, or sometimes with additional per hour charges for use at $1 to $2, plus any telephone long-distance service charges. Some services provide toll-free 1-800 telephone connections as part of their services.

Full-time 24-hour PPP connections cost from $80 to $150 per month, plus any long-distance or other telephone service charges. A full-time PPP connection will also require a dedicated computer, or access to a mainframe running 24 hours a day.

## Integrated Services Digital Network (ISDN)

ISDN is a digital telephone line between your site and the telephone company's central switching station. It has been available since the mid-1960s, but is now becoming more popular. It is widely available in metropolitan areas, but much less so in smaller towns or rural settings. In Europe it has been easily available for many years.

ISDN is still sometimes jokingly referred to as "I still don't know" because in some small and medium-sized phone companies it is difficult find out who knows about this kind of service. In my own small town, it took six phone calls to a variety of individuals just to locate someone who knew what in the heck ISDN was.

ISDN is fast and offers a very flexible connection to the Internet, combining the ability to transfer data with telephone communication.

## Shell or Dial-up Access

These connections, popular for many years, offer the use of a mainframe or large computer for programming and access to the Internet, and use regular voice phone lines and modems. You can obtain an account on an ISP's machine, but in this case your computer does not directly become a part of the Internet. Such an account can have good Internet access, but you would have to arrange with the service provider to offer a Web site, Gopher site, FTP archive, or other publicly accessible resources; such services are often, but not always, extra-cost items.

While there are a number of Internet co-ops, free-nets, and other kinds of connections, generally they are not appropriate for business marketing.

## Getting Connections

Connections to the Internet are obtained through Internet Service Providers (ISPs). These providers will offer a range of services, some more than others. Full-service ISPs will help you locate and install all equipment needed to become a node with a T3 connection, while others supply services for dial-up connections only. ISPs get their services from the mid-level and national access providers.

The most popular connections for small and medium-sized businesses are SLIP/PPP and ISDN. Part-time PPP connections have what are called dynamic or temporary IP addresses—while signed on, you have a temporary Internet address for FTP and other uses. ISDN can provide either part-time or full-time connections.

Although they are becoming increasingly popular, full-time direct Internet connections using T1 lines are still usually found in larger corporations because the setup, maintenance, and associated personnel costs are often too high for small companies.

In choosing a connection to the Internet, one of the most important considerations (beyond cost) is the bandwidth that you need—how much "stuff" do you want to try to push or pull through the pipe? Each type of connection has a different speed of data flow.

Normal telephone service, or Plain Old Telephone Service (POTS), is an analog communications system designed for transmitting human voice frequencies. Modems currently are able to convert digital (on/off) computer signals into sound and back again into digital signals at the other end of the phone line at a rate of 14,400 bits per second. Increasingly, modems with 28,800 bits per second speed are the standard for new modems.

While the evaluation of what is slow and fast is personal, most experienced users find that GUI browsers should not be used with modems below 14,400 baud—things will work correctly at any speed, but the delays for large files and graphics will get in the way of productive use of the Internet. Table A.1 offers some comparisons of the speeds of various Internet connections. Figure A.4 gives a graphical comparison of some of these connections.

---

### Corporate and Academic Connections

It is not uncommon in large businesses for the research or technical departments to already have an Internet connection, so you should check this out first. To find out, you should check with the person in your company who is in charge of your computing systems or local area network. If you are not already connected, you will need to choose from among the flavors of data transfer and type of Internet connection.

---

## Integrated Services Digital Network (ISDN)

ISDN can support slow-scan video for video conferencing as well as computer data. ISDN has three full duplex channels, an A and two B channels that each carry a nominal 64 kbps. (Computer lines are like

**Table A.1  Internet Connection Speeds**

| Type of connection | Speed of connection |
| --- | --- |
| POTS with shell account | 0.3 to 28.8 kbps |
| POTS with PPP | 9.6 to 28.8 kbps |
| Switched/dedicated | 56 kbps |
| ISDN | 64 kbps to 128 kbps |
| T1 | 1.54 mbps |
| Cable TV | 4–10 mbps |
| T3 | 45 mbps |

lumber—a 2-by-4 is less than 2 inches by 4 inches, and a 64 kbps line actually carries 56 kbps after the control signals overhead is removed.) For data, the two 64 kbps lines can be combined to give a throughput of 128 kbps. ISDN can be full-time or switched on demand.

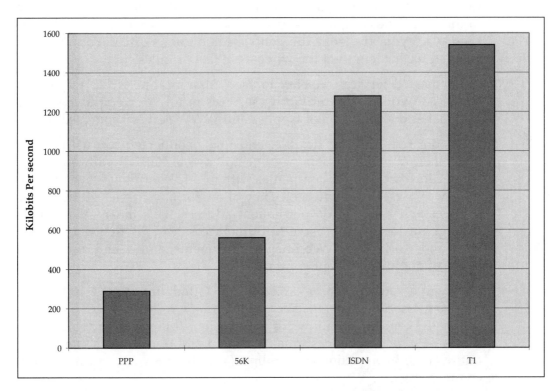

**Figure A.4  A comparison of the speed of some types of Internet connections.**

Increasingly, telephone companies are providing dial-up digital ISDN services. This means that the user does not pay for full ISDN services but, rather, uses the connection through access servers called ISDN devices, bridges, or routers (similar to modems) on a part-time, on-demand basis. These situations are typically cheaper than standard full-time dedicated ISDN services, and can be used over normal voice phone lines. This kind of configuration will also allow for small business LANs or homes to connect at higher speeds to the Internet. An ISDN interface will range in cost from $1500 upward. Monthly services are in the range of $40 to $180, plus fees for actual connect time. This kind of service is ubiquitous in some areas but it is not available everywhere.

A number of ISPs do not yet have much experience with ISDN, so this may require investigation on your part.

## Dedicated Leased Lines

Dedicated 56K, T1, and T3 are direct, or point-to-point, connections—this means that there is a wire or fiber optic cable connecting your site to the telephone company. Setup costs are very high, especially the farther away you are from the central telephone switch. You are then charged for the length of the wire—be it feet or miles.

Dedicated services are easy to use with a local network, so you can connect to your LAN, providing services to all your employees. This also makes the provision of Gopher and WWW services much easier.

Dedicated lines are flexible, and those connected can use Mosaic and other WWW browsers needing to have a TCP/IP address. These connections are best for companies with multiple employees wanting to be power users of the Internet. They allow for a full-time Internet node to be established, with a permanent address. This means that others throughout the Internet have full-time access to FTP archives, Gopher sites, and World Wide Web images, documents, audio, and data stored in the public areas of your computer system.

To give you an idea of capacity, a 56K line will allow a jerky 8–15 frames-per-second partial-screen video image to be sent; a T1 connection at 1.54 mbps can allow for full-motion, full-screen video and audio—just barely. Broadcast-quality digital audio and video can be put out over a T3 connection at 45 mbps. (Yes, there is a T2, but it is not in common use.)

Usually a T1 installation will cost from $2000 to $6000 to start, and then $1000–$4000 per month plus mileage charges of $20–$50 per mile from the central switch. A 56K line may run from $400 a month to $900 plus local phone company charges. In addition, the purchase cost of the router may run $5000 or more. You will need to set up a computer (often a workstation) dedicated to maintaining the link. As the old saying goes, "your mileage may vary" (YMMV).

A permanent connection (through dedicated lines or full-time SLIP) almost always requires that you provide support personnel for the system and for assisting and training employees, adding to these costs.

## Locating Internet Service Providers

The business of providing Internet services is growing like wildfire. As you can see, there are many things to consider in selecting an access provider for your business; but it is also important that you gain access to the Web as soon as possible, for practice and learning as you read this book.

In many areas, you can find provider services in the telephone yellow pages and via ads in local newspapers. Computer user groups and stores selling computer equipment often have information as well. Some local and regional telephone companies have provider services.

InterNic maintains a listing of providers, at *http://www.internic.net/ cgi-bin/tochtml/provider/0intro.provider*. Usually this listing is among the most current and complete.

For InterNic, AT&T Corp. provides Database Services, and Network Solutions, Inc. provides Registration Services—assigning network addresses and top-level domain names (usually needed only by those setting up their own node).

To reach them:

> http: *www.internic.net/*
> Gopher: *gopher.internic.net*
> FTP: *rs.internic.net*
> e-mail: *info@internic.net*
> Phone: (800) 444-4345; (619) 455-4600

Open Market maintains a listing of Web space and hosting services by size: those with more than 75 clients, 15 to 75 clients, six to 15 clients, and three to five clients:

*http://www.directory.net/dir/servers4.html*

*http://www.directory.net/dir/servers3.html*

*http://www.directory.net/dir/servers2.html*

*http://www.directory.net/dir/servers1.html*

Yahoo has listings at *http://www.yahoo.com/Business_and_Economy/ Companies/Internet_Services/Internet_Access_Providers/*

TheList is a large Web site offering a searchable database of providers at *http://thelist.com*. It is a very quick way of searching by area code, state, and so on.

To find ISDN services, have a look at Dan Kegel's list of ISDN providers: *http://mirror.cs.miami.edu/isdn/*.

POCIA maintains a directory of providers in the United States, Canada, and in other countries, and hotlinks to numerous other listings: *http://www.celestin.com/pocia/index.html*.

Usenet newsgroups offering information about various types of connections include:

*alt.internet.services*

*alt.internet.access.wanted*

*alt.online-service*

*news.answers*

Here are some national and international Internet service providers:

### Institute for Global Communications

18 DeBoom Street
San Francisco, CA 94107
Phone: (415) 442-0220
Fax: (415) 546-1794
email: *support@igc.apc.org*
*http://www.igc.apc.org/igc/igcinfo.html*

## JVNCnet

Global Enterprise Services
3 Independence Way
Princeton, NJ 08540
Phone: (800) 358-4437
Fax: (609) 897-7310
e-mail: *market@jvnc.net*
*http://www.jvnc.net*


## Mindspring

1430 West Peachtree St. NW, Suite 400
Atlanta, GA 30309
Phone: (404) 815-0082; (800) 719-4332
e-mail: *sales@mindspring.com; info@mindspring.com*
*http://www.mindspring.com*


## PSINet (owned by Mindspring)

510 Huntmar Park Drive
Reston, VA 22070
Phone: (800) 827-7482
Fax: (800) 329-7741
e-mail: *info@psi.com*
*http://www.psi.com*


## Netcom On-Line Communication Services

3031 Tisch Way
San Jose, CA 95128
Phone: (408) 983-5950; (800) 353-6600
Fax: (408) 241-9145
e-mail: *info@netcom.com*
*http://www.netcom.com*

### UUNET Technologies

3060 Williams Drive
Fairfax, VA 22031-4648
Phone: (703) 206-5600
Fax: (703) 206-5601
e-mail: *info@uu.net*
*http://www.uu.net*

### Iosphere

Sonetis Corporation
280-55 Metcalfe Street
Ottawa, Ontario, Canada K2P 6L5
Phone: (613) 236-8601
Fax: (613) 236-8764
e-mail: *getwired@sonetis.com*
*http://www.sonetis.com*

### Demon Internet

322 Regents Park Road
Finchley
London N3 2QQ, England
Phone: (44) 181-371-1000
Fax: (44) 181-371-1150
e-mail: *internet@demon.net*
*http://www.demon.net*

## Choosing Services: Browsing vs. Marketing Presence

Business users wanting to use the Internet for WWW marketing have
two different needs for Internet services. They need to have the ability
to browse sites and gain information; and they may want to actually
create a WWW site with marketing materials.

The key to your choice of service provider is, of course, your answer to this question: What are the services that you will want to have access to in order to make use of the Internet as a marketing strategy? The following will offer some guidance regarding services needed for becoming a power Internet user, and options for using a site to provide marketing services to others.

## Access as an Individual User

Access to the following Internet tools should guarantee you complete Internet access. Check to be sure that the Internet provider you are considering has these:

- E-mail
- Telnet
- FTP
- Gopher
- WWW/Lynx
- Usenet newsgroups
- Internet Relay Chat (IRC)

These tools will insure that the individual business user can fully browse the Web, keep up with all Net-related business activities, and communicate with others. Access to these tools will also permit the WWW marketer to integrate WWW activities into a larger Internet business presence as discussed in Chapter 4.

### Commercial Online Services

The commercial services such as Prodigy, CompuServe, MSN, and America Online offer the Web, Gopher, Telnet, and more. The range of services differs with each, but, for example, AOL provides two megabytes of free Web space with each screen name (mailbox). With five mailboxes per account, that totals 10 megabytes of space. In addition, AOL provides PrimeHost, a commercial Web site hosting service.

## Connections for Marketing—Making Decisions

Purchasing services requires that you have an idea of what you are looking for, and have constructed some kind of matrix for comparison shopping, as well as some basis for constructing a bid for services if you decide on that course of action.

- *What are your plans for WWW marketing strategies?*

  Do you want to create your own node and WWW site? What business activities and marketing strategies are you after? See Chapters 2 and 4 for more information on these matters. Depending upon the level of your WWW marketing plans, you may need to consider the creation of a company node.

- *What equipment and software do you have or are you prepared to purchase?*

  An IBM-compatible 486, Pentium, many workstations, or a variety of Macintosh computers such as the Quadra will support a PPP, ISDN, or higher connection. But if you are going to go whole hog with a dedicated line, you will need heavier computing "iron" on your desk.

  The Microsoft Windows 95 and OS/2 (Warp or otherwise) come TCP/IP-ready, making connections even easier. If all you are doing is simple dial-up, pretty much any machine or operating system will do.

- *What kind of personnel do you have, or are you prepared to hire?*

  If you are planning to use a PPP connection or better, you will need some computer-savvy employees (or be a techno-wonk yourself). Setting up and configuring a SLIP connection is not for sissies—it takes considerable knowledge and patience.

  If you are going to be providing WWW services from your local machine through dedicated PPP, ISDN, or leased lines, you will need to have a system administrator who is able to make and maintain the connections, and some staff time to work on the creation and design of WWW/HTML documents.

- *Are there limitations on what services are available?*

  The types of phone services available and their costs are going to influence your access choices as well. Can you get ISDN, a 56K or

T1 line? In some locales, these are readily available (for a price), but in others, services are still two to three years away, and you will be limited to dial-up.

Are you long distance from everywhere? If you are outside a metropolitan area, you may find that your only access is through a system such as AT&T, MCI, or Sprint. If the Internet provider is a long distance call away, you most likely will not want to use a full-time PPP connection.

- *Do you want to create and maintain your own Web site or do you want to contract for Web and/or HTML services?*

In deciding upon the services you will need, one key decision is whether or not you want to set up, support, and maintain your own World Wide Web site in-house. You can create your own Web site, or you can job it out to one of the growing number of Web services sites.

You can prepare your own HTML documents and images in-house and then place them at a site, or you can contract for the whole job. Part II of this book can help you understand HTML and get information on Web services.

## And in the Future . . .

The whole arena of Internet service providers is very dynamic right now. The number of providers and methods of providing services are expanding constantly. Soon, you may find the following kinds of services:

- Cable TV—Several cable TV companies are looking at the delivery of Internet connectivity to enable interactive video, shopping, and more. Look for companies to offer Internet services bundled with video and other services.

- Microwave—Some companies are looking into the use of microwave equipment and repeaters for the delivery of Internet services. Some of the telcos that already own the towers and systems are interested in starting services or leasing equipment to others.

- Other wireless technologies—*RadioMail* is already delivering e-mail using wireless technology. Several companies are attempting to gain access to portions of the radio spectrum in order to provide Internet and other services to consumers.

- Satellite—Look for the use of smaller digital satellite dishes similar to those already delivering cable-like TV to include Internet connectivity.

# *Using Browsers to Get Online*

This appendix is a quick guide to hopping online, and to using the GUI Web browsers, and some other client software. Appendix C is a short guide to the text-based browser, Lynx.

## The Keys to the Internet

Your basic Internet on-ramp tool kit begins with:

- a computer
- a phone line
- a modem

While you can use a DOS computer without Windows to get on the Internet, the approach is pretty plain, and is entirely text-based. Your best bet is a machine running under Windows or a Macintosh, with at least a 14.4 modem.

Next, you need to locate a local Internet service provider. Information about this can be found in Appendix A, but hunt for these in local newspapers, the telephone book, at computer users clubs, at local computer equipment dealers, and at *http://www.thelist.com*.

Most providers will supply you with software, and some, like Mindspring (*http://www.mindspring.com*), with an easy-to-install package. The commercial services like AOL and CompuServe will also supply you with complete solutions. To continue with your basic tool kit, on Windows, you will need:

- an ISP account
- a Winsock (built into Win 95)
- e-mail software
- a Web browser

Other tools might include an FTP client, an IRC chat client, and a Telnet client.

There are lots of different ways to go about installing browsers and the equipment needed to get them running, but the information that follows will give you a quick idea of what has to be done.

## Web Browsers

Web browsers are programs that act as an interface between you and the Internet. They can be run on your personal computer that you connect over the phone lines via modems to an Internet access provider, or to a corporate or organization's large computer that your desktop terminal or computer is wired to.

These are what are called "client" programs—programs that take commands from you and then get information and services by sending requests to "server" programs. One server can provide information to many thousands of client programs.

Though browsers were initially designed primarily to interact with the World Wide Web, most browsers now also interact directly with Gopher servers, FTP sites, and other Internet tools and systems, thus providing a uniform, easy-to-use interface with many services and protocols of the Internet, even for individuals without experience with these services and protocols.

Browsers can be divided into two basic groups: text-mode and GUI (graphical user interface). Text-mode browsers (words only, no pictures) are often faster and usable with more types of hardware and software systems, but have just about disappeared from the landscape for the business user. GUI browsers are often easier to learn and faster to control.

The GUI browsers perform their functions largely through mouse point-and-click operations in keeping with the native interface, be it Windows, Macintosh, or X-Windows.

When most GUI browsers are started, they automatically retrieve and display a homepage. This default homepage is often the homepage of the site where the browser was developed. You can change this default page to any other page for which you have a URL; that page will then be displayed when you start a session with the browser. (Many GUI browsers display the URL of the page currently being viewed.)

Generally, the anchor links in a page are shown by a GUI browser as color highlights and/or underlining, and often the cursor will change shape as it moves across links and selectable fields—sometimes it will change from an arrow to a hand, or from a plus to an arrow.

Most of the GUI browsers have mouse scroll bars along the bottom and side of the window, allowing movement around the loaded page.

The GUI browsers usually offer a variety of configuration options, including colors and choice of which screen elements, such as toolbars and ribbons, are shown on screen. They also allow you to choose some style elements such as fonts and colors, and to choose options for printer configuration. In addition they have options for add-ins or plug-ins like Java, Real-Audio, ShockWave, and Acrobat.

GUI browsers keep a record of pages that you have viewed. Those pages can be revisited by opening this "history" list and clicking on the appropriate page name. If your visit to that page was recent, the page may still be in your computer's memory, and thus it will be displayed rapidly. If it is no longer in the memory, a new copy of the page will be downloaded and displayed. The history file is usually temporary—when you exit from the browser program the history list is erased.

These browsers generally allow you to refresh, redraw, or reload the images to update them or correct the display errors.

Most of the GUI programs maintain a hotlist or list of bookmarks. These are sites that you have visited and have selected to be retained in a permanent file by the browser. These bookmarks are useful for pages you want to return to often, and for valuable pages that were originally hard to find.

Most of the graphical browsers allow you to look at the unprocessed HTML version of any Web page, variously calling it an unprocessed file, raw file, or source file. This lets you see the markup tags, the URLs, and other embedded items. This is useful for figuring out what kinds of

HTML tags were used to accomplish a given effect, and for getting the URL of a specific link.

The GUI browsers generally also have some other page-handling features:

- The ability to search for words or phrases in the page currently being viewed
- The ability to save the page on your computer system (embedded pictures usually aren't saved in this process)
- The ability to print out the page

Some of the browsers will let you e-mail a page to yourself or someone else. Some will even let you create and mail messages from within the browser.

Most of the GUI browsers work as interfaces for several protocols in addition to World Wide Web's HTTP. They will work with URLs that start with these prefixes:

- *gopher://*
- *ftp://*
- *telnet://*
- *news://*

Browsers are currently being developed and improved very rapidly. It's worthwhile to examine newly released versions as they appear.

What these GUI browser features add up to is a dramatically more powerful and easy way to use the Internet. Here are some of the advantages:

- Easy-to-use software—Because these GUI browsers operate under the same graphical systems you are used to (whether Windows, or Macintosh, or X-Windows), the screen appearance, menu options, and use of the mouse are familiar and intuitive. While the documentation for each program should be read, you'll probably be able to do some things with the program immediately. Also, because GUI browsers have menus, you don't need to memorize several dozen commands—just take a look at the menus, then "point and click."

- Easy-to-use Internet—Because these browsers can interact directly with most of the Internet's protocols, and because many other Internet systems and services have been made intelligible to browsers by Web server "gateways," almost all of the Internet's resources are now available to you through the operation of just one browser.

- Pictures, movies, and sound—While text-mode browsers can be used to download graphics and sound files for later playing or viewing using an appropriate program, the inconvenience of doing this deters all but the most highly motivated. With GUI browsers, full-color pictures, intermixed with text, can be displayed automatically, and on an appropriately equipped computer, sounds can be played automatically.

## Netscape, Mosaic, MS Internet Explorer, and More

Mosaic, the GUI Web browser created by NCSA at the University of Illinois, has, with the encouragement of its original developers, spawned many new programs based on the original Mosaic programming and concepts. One of these is the now very distant cousin, Netscape. In addition, Microsoft has the Internet Explorer.

### NCSA Mosaic

The "original" Mosaic, NCSA Mosaic is a classic Windows application with pull-down menus and mouse slider bars (Figure B.1). The menu bar has menus called File, Edit , Options, Navigate, Annotate, Starting, and Help. A stylized spinning globe lets you know that Mosaic is working.

The ribbon has buttons to click for opening a file, saving an item to disk, moving up and down your history list, reloading a page, going home, navigating, searching, printing, and going to your hotlist. Mosaic has tool tips, meaning that as you put your cursor over the tool icons, a small balloon will tell you the function of the tool.

The File menu gives you access to items to open a URL, open a local file, save and print a file, look at the source for the file, and exit.

The Edit menu is a fairly standard Windows editing menu for cutting and pasting text, and for searching for text in loaded pages.

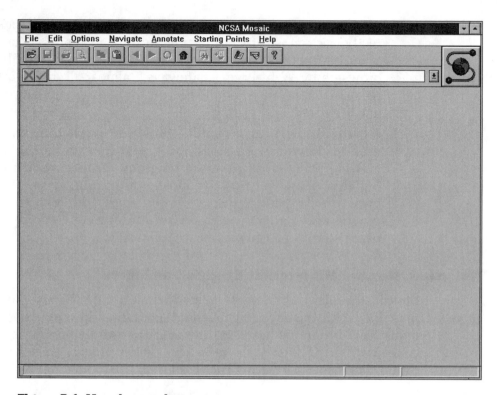

**Figure B.1  Mosaic opening screen.**

Under the Options menu item (Figure B.2) are numerous items governing the way Mosaic shows the toolbar, status bar, and URLs, and for controlling the cursor, and FTP directory browsing. It is the place where you can turn for the loading of inline images, or choose your on-screen font. It is also the location for choosing to load (save) to disk. This menu is very useful for turning the images off on the fly. NCSA Mosaic must load an entire image before you can view it, which can take some time; at some sites you will want to turn off image loading and selectively view images instead. You can usually abort the loading of a page by clicking on the spinning globe.

The Navigate menu is for moving around in your hotlist or up and down your history file, for reloading inline images, and to make an addition to your hotlist. It also has a menu editor for customization of the interface.

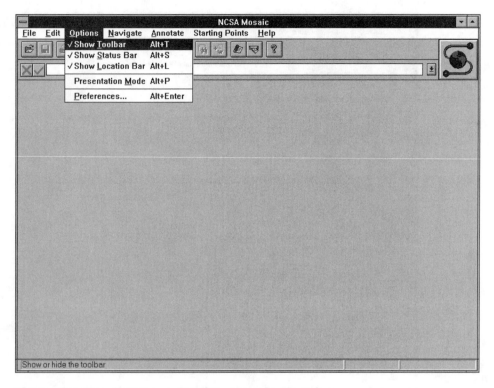

**Figure B.2 The Options pull-down menu in Mosaic.**

The Annotate menu is for editing and deleting document annotations.

NCSA has collected numerous interesting sites and placed them under the Starting Points menu item (Figure B.3). You will find the NCSA homepage, a collection of WWW documents and sites, interesting homepages, plus Finger, Gopher, and other gateways. This group of sites is worth exploring.

The Help menu can link you to online documentation, a FAQ, a bug list, and a feature page. These items only work while you are online, since they are links to NCSA.

NCSA Mosaic comes in three flavors—one for the PC, one for the Macintosh, and one for UNIX systems. In addition, new versions come along quite regularly, so you can anticipate new features.

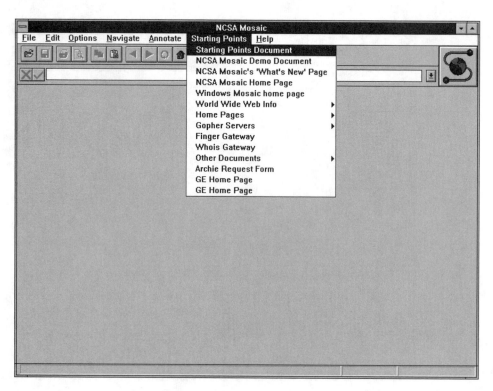

**Figure B.3 The Starting Points pull-down menu in Mosaic.**

### A Commercial Mosaic Browser—Quarterdeck

Mosaic has spun off numerous commercial Mosaics, such as AirMosaic and Spry. The Quarterdeck version included in the Internet Suite is typical of these (Figure B.4).

This version of Mosaic has the usual items as pull-down menus, including File, Edit, View, Navigate, Hotlist (bookmarks), Window, Tools, and Help.

The file menu is very familiar, covering the usual Windows items for opening, closing, and saving files, plus the Properties and Print menus. In addition it has a Reload item for reloading the current document.

Under the Edit menu are choices for cutting, pasting, copying, and deleting, and for searching. This is also the location of the Annotate feature for creating and editing items to be appended to the page.

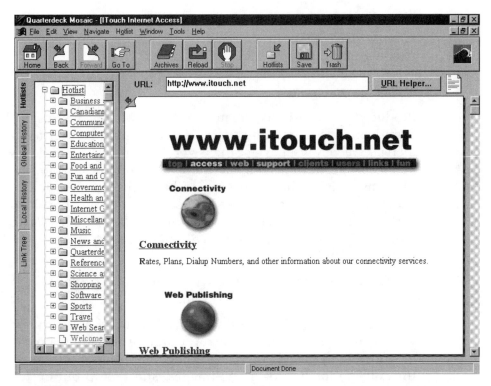

**Figure B.4  Quarterdeck's Mosaic with the browser window and hotlist window.**

Many versatile features reside in the View menu, including a variety of tools for working with the images on the page, viewing the document source, and turning the images off and on while surfing. It also lets you switch the view from page to listing of files.

The Navigate pull-down menu provides for going forward, backing up, stopping the current page from loading, and going to the home page. The Hotlist menu is very simple, used primarily for adding links and creating new lists.

The Window menu has the usual Windows management items for tiling and arranging windows on the screen. This is also where you may open a pane for your hotlists, and for editing those hotlists. Figure B.4 shows the main browser window with the hotlist window open as well.

The Tools menu houses the normal preferences area, and also provides for the configuration of Quarterdeck's FTP, Telnet, and e-mail clients.

In addition, Quarterdeck's browser has a ribbon with several frequently used items in easy reach: Home, Back and Forward, Go To,
Archives, Reload, Stop, Hotlists, Save, and Trash.

### Netscape Navigator

Produced by the original creators of NCSA Mosaic, Netscape Navigator
from Netscape Communications is a very popular full-featured commercial Web browser. Netscape is very feature-rich, complete with an e-
mail package, newsreader, and numerous options for configuration and
plug-ins. It is available in both 16-bit and 32-bit versions. Netscape
shows you the images as they load so that you can abort loading them
if they are not what you are looking for. It also permits concurrent
downloading of documents from different servers and support for JPEG
and other graphics.

The menu bar has pull-down menus called File, Edit, View, Go,
Bookmarks, Options, Directory, Window, and Help.

The ribbon has icons for stepping backward and forward through
your history (a left and right arrow), and for reloading a page, and buttons for opening and searching a page. In addition, it has a button to
turn off the loading of inline images, and a Stop button to abort the
loading of a page. The Netscape logo rotates to indicate that a page is
downloading.

It has a Location window showing the URL of the current document, and the usual Windows mouse scroll bars.

In addition, the Navigator has directory buttons for getting a
Guided Tour, to check What's New or What's Cool, to see the Hand-
book, to do a Net Search, and to get a Net Directory and Software.
These directory buttons are like a speed dialer—they quickly fetch related pages.

There is a small divider bar and key onscreen that shows as green
when you are visiting a Secure Server, and red when you are not at a secure site. This option permits businesses to provide a secure transaction
environment, and the Netscape browser user to know that immediately.
The small key in the lower left corner is "broken" when you are in an
insecure environment and "whole" when in a secure environment.

The File menu shown in Figure B.5 offers options for opening additional windows (or instances of the browser), opening a URL location,

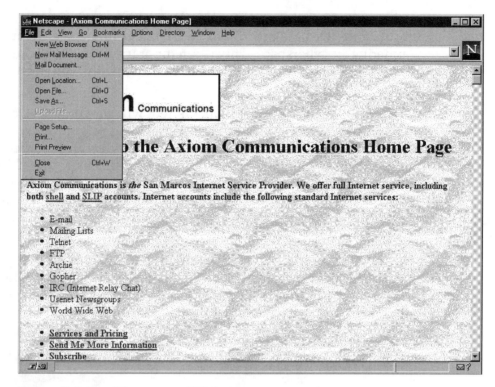

**Figure B.5 The File menu of Netscape.**

opening a local file, saving the downloaded page, and mailing a page, options for using the browser as a mailer (create mail), saving pages and images, and options to close the window and exit. The New Web Browser option is especially useful because it enables multiple simultaneous page display and retrieval.

The Edit menu contains standard document text manipulation options such as undo, cut, copy, and paste. In addition it has a Find Text feature useful for working with long documents.

The View menu has options for loading and reloading images, frames, and pages, a refresh option, and an item used to view the source document with the HTML tags visible. The Source command is very useful for examining a page to see the embedded HTML codings—it will let you see the URLs of links, the names of image files, and more.

The Go menu contains items for navigation—back, forward, and home. It is also where you can choose to stop the loading of a page, and to choose to view your session history. The history feature is especially useful, since it will allow you to go back and find a site if you get lost wandering in cyberspace. This is a temporary listing of the places you have been—if you want to keep a site permanently, you must add it to your Bookmarks file.

Clicking on the Bookmarks menu item will get you items for adding and editing your Bookmarks file, and a listing of your bookmarks for rapid navigation to favorite places. Choosing View Bookmarks opens a pane called the Bookmark List for viewing, finding, launching, and editing your bookmarks. The ability to manipulate and use bookmarks is critical to Web browsing, since it is very easy to follow links and lose the address of the page that was so interesting. Figure B.6 shows the Bookmarks pane.

The Options menu contains numerous items for selecting preferences, for choosing which screen elements are displayed (toolbar, location, directory buttons, FTP file information), and whether images are autoloaded or not, preferences for Mail and News, security preferences,

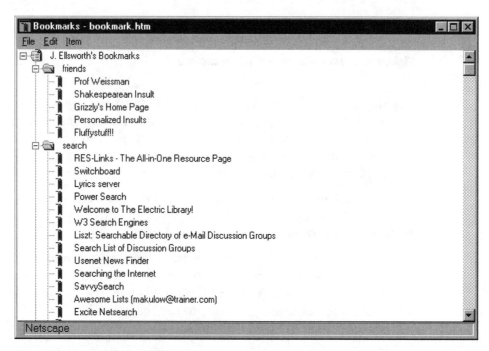

**Figure B.6 The Bookmarks pane.**

and a save options item. Under the Document encoding item, you may chose the character set, including Japanese, Chinese, and Korean.

The General Preferences submenu allows for the customization of styles, fonts, languages, helpers, applications, colors, and more. Considerable individualization is possible.

The Directory menu contains choices for rapid navigation to selected useful sites, including the Netscape homepage, What's New and What's Cool, the Internet Directory, and items about the Internet. These items are selected by Netscape Communications at their site.

The Help menu gives you access to a number of useful items, many of which must be obtained online—a guided tour, a manual, and a FAQ feedback and support. It also allows you to access the Netscape mailer and newsreader. From the Help menu you can get information about the version of browser you are using, and your history file.

The mouse buttons allow for highlighting and choosing links. The right mouse button menu, seen in Figure B.7, will save an image, add an address to the Bookmarks, move forward and backward, copy the link, view the image, save the image, and copy the image location.

### Microsoft Internet Explorer

The Internet Explorer from Microsoft is a classic Windows application—like Netscape, it is available in 16-bit and 32-bit versions, and supports numerous advanced features. The pull-down menus cover File, Edit, View, Go, Favorites, and Help, as seen in Figure B.8.

Under the File menu are document management items such as opening, saving, printing, page setup, properties, and a task list of the pages most recently visited. In addition, there is a feature to send mail.

The Edit menu is very traditionally configured for cutting, copying, pasting, selecting, and finding text.

The View menu is used to identify which screen components appear on the screen (toolbar, address bar, and status bar), as well as to stop the page loading and refresh the screen. It includes an item for font size defaults. Its Options submenu is very powerful. This is where you control the onscreen appearance, starting pages, news, proxy and advanced cache, and history control. File Types lets you identify the various image and sound viewers, as seen in Figure B.9.

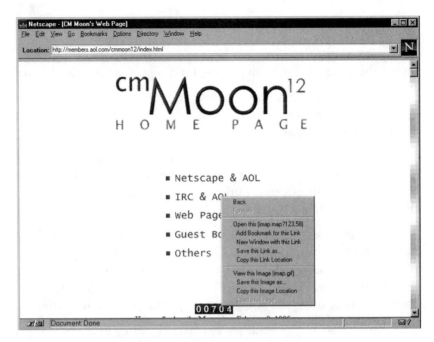

**Figure B.7  The Netscape right mouse button menu.**

**Figure B.8  The Microsoft Internet Explorer main screen.**

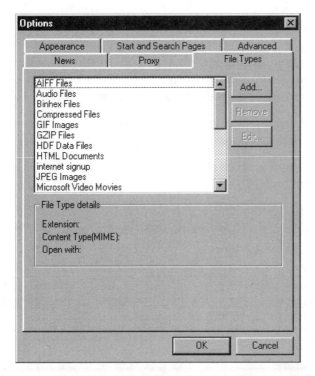

**Figure B.9 The Microsoft Internet Explorer, Options tabs.**

The Go menu is similar to many of the other browsers' Navigate menu—this is where you can step forward or backward through your history, or go to your start page or to a search page. In addition, it offers direct access to Microsoft's MSIE update page and to a Usenet news-reader.

The Favorites pull-down menu offers access to the MSIE bookmarks submenus, and keeps a hotlist of recent pages for easy backtracking. The Help menu is an index of topics.

The Ribbon is a quick one-button access to frequently used features including Favorites, cutting, copying, and pasting, font sizing, opening a page, printing, mailing, backing up and going forward, going to the homepage, refreshing the screen, searching, and getting updates.

The right mouse button is particularly useful—it provides for open-ing documents and windows, saving the page, copying images, and adding an item to the Favorites list.

### *Cello*

Cello is a GUI WWW browser from Cornell University. This interface is a bit plain in its presentation, and lags behind all the other graphical interfaces. It does have some features that are very useful to those browsing the WWW. Figure B.10 shows the main screen of Cello.

The menu bar includes File, Edit, Search, Configure, Jump, Bookmark, and Help.

On the simple button bar, there are just three options: Up (the Up arrow), Stop, and Home.

Clicking the triangular Up arrow icon will take you back one page, and continue stepping up through your history of pages. The Stop sign aborts the loading of a page, and the Home icon will take you to the

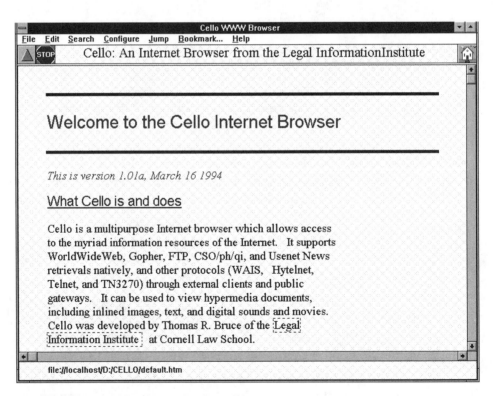

**Figure B.10 The main Cello window.**

Cornell-Cello top homepage. In addition, the ribbon shows the name of the file that is currently loaded.

The usual Windows mouse scrollbars for document navigation are present, and the current URL is displayed at the bottom of the window.

The File menu offers options for saving a file locally, sending (e-mailing) the currently loaded file to someone, printing the currently loaded page, reloading the file, and exiting the program.

The Edit menu offers just two choices—a chance to view the document source with all of its HTML markups plainly visible, to see "how they did it"; and the choice to simply see the file clean—without all of the markups.

The Search menu offers a simple keyword search of the currently loaded file which can be repeated, and a menu item for working with HTML indexing documents. The search option is particularly useful for long text files, or are hunting for a particular anchor.

There is a very full Configure menu option, covering files and directories, the default homepage, bookmarks, links, styles, and the size of the cache. You can decide here if you want the images to load automatically. You can control the look of Cello with options for the on-screen color and fonts. Further items that can be configured under this menu include the printer, your e-mail address, and how you access News and WAIS.

The Jump menu provides extensive navigation assistance, allowing you to move up through the recently loaded items, and launch items for Gopher, Telnet, TN3270, FTP, and URLs. This is also the location of the option for sending mail.

The Bookmarks menu opens a pane for entering, editing, adding, and using your bookmarks files.

Lastly, the Help menu takes you into context-sensitive help for Cello.

Overall the Cello browser is especially nimble, quickly moving through documents. While the look is a bit more austere than that of the Mosaics, Cello provides some useful features. At this time, Cello does not support the use of forms, a drawback for the business user who wants to provide for online data entry and/or purchases. Many users keep both their main browser and Cello handy for browsing.

### Other Net Browsers

An increasing number of companies are putting out Web browsers that can be used with some of the online commercial providers using SLIP or, in one case, a plain dial-up connection.

**Chameleon**    The Internet Chameleon from NetManage offers a suite of tools and utilities individually available from a window with icons, including WebSurfer, Gopher, NEWTNews, Mail, Telnet, Archie, FTP, Ping, Finger, and Whois. Each of these tools and utilities can be used independently at will.

In WebSurfer, the Chameleon icon changes color and moves its tail as documents load. The WebSurfer window is the NetManage WWW browser. The menus cover working with files, fetching pages, configuration settings, and help. The ribbon button bar has items for printing, a URL history item (small footprints), a hotlist of bookmarks, a button for reloading the image, arrows for loading the previous page and the next page, and one to go home.

The installation is relatively automated, and signing up for a provider is simple. Chameleon can be configured to use CSLIP, SLIP, or PPP.

**SlipKnot**    SlipKnot is an unusual WWW browser because unlike the others, it does not require any special kind of connection (like SLIP) to the Internet. (Get it? SLIP not?) It is designed to be used with a UNIX shell account, which is widely available.

SlipKnot begins in SlipKnot terminal mode to initiate a connection to your dial-up account. It has login scripts to get you online and into your account. When connected, you invoke SlipKnot WEB, a GUI for Web browsing.

The menu bar contains access for loading and saving files, configuring the WEB, navigating through URLs, a history and bookmarks file, and the status of the connection. Currently the WEB is strictly for browsing Web documents, but the terminal allows you to go into Telnet and Gopher.

The ribbon has a home button, a button to return to the previous page, a print button, and a goto button. The program icon is a colorful spider's web that changes color while documents load.

SlipKnot is currently very new, and it is anticipated that support for Gopher, FTP, and Telnet within the WEB will be added.

## System Requirements for Running Most Windows-based GUIs

Getting a GUI up and running requires that you have some particular hardware and software. The Windows versions of Mosaic, Netscape, and MSIE require:

- a 486 processor DOS computer with 8 MB RAM (more is better)
- Windows 3.1, or Windows 95 for 32-bit versions of these applications
- GUI software
- Winsock
- Viewers
- a Sound player
- a Modem or network connection
- a TCP/IP account such as PPP

You will need Windows, the GUI program, and some kind of network connection and/or Winsock (Windows socket) software to work with your account or provider. If you want to work with sound files, your computer must be multimedia capable, and you may also need external viewers for JPEG such as Lview, and MPEGPLAY to display MPEG movies.

You will need some kind of access to the Internet, be it direct through a company LAN, or through a dial-up PPP or pseudo-SLIP (like The Internet Adapter) connection through an ISP.

GUIs for Windows uses the Winsock (Windows Socket) standard for communicating with the network; one of the most popular versions is Trumpet Winsock (see how to get it below). If you get the 32-bit version of Mosaic, you need the Windows 32-bit extension software called Win32a.

Many of these programs come "zipped," so you will also need PKUNZIP or WinZip in some form to unpack these compressed files.

> **Note:**
>
> Netscape uses the same sockets programs and viewers as NCSA Mosaic, but does not require Win32a tools, although it can take advantage of them. Microsoft Windows 95 comes with a 32-bit Winsock.

The Macintosh version of Mosaic requires at least Mac with System 7, and 4 MB RAM. You will also need MacTCP 2.0.2. The associated viewers might include Anarchie, GIFConverter, JPEGView, and Sound Machine. Stuffit Expander is used to unzip the files.

## Where Can I Get a Browser?

NCSA Mosaic, MSIE, and Cello are all freeware. Netscape is providing an evaluation version of its package, but otherwise it must be purchased, unless you are eligible for the free version for educational use under its guidelines. Each of these are available via FTP at a minimum. All of the browsers mentioned here need to run under either Windows or Macintosh, and with the exception of SlipKnot, all of them will need to have a Winsock manager of some kind like Trumpet.

### NCSA Mosaic

You can obtain information about getting a copy of NCSA Mosaic from its homepage at *http://www.ncsa.uiuc.edu/SDG/Software/Mosaic/NCSA MosaicHome.html*.

Information on the various versions and platforms supported is available from the homepage. NCSA supports:

- NCSA Mosaic for the X-Windows system
- NCSA Mosaic for the Apple Macintosh
- NCSA Mosaic for Microsoft Windows

You can e-mail for more information or help:

- *mosaic@ncsa.uiuc.edu*—General information relevant to all Mosaic platforms
- *mosaic-w@ncsa.uiuc.edu*—Mosaic for Microsoft Windows help
- *mosaic-m@ncsa.uiuc.edu*—Mosaic for Macintosh help
- *mosaic-x@ncsa.uiuc.edu*—Mosaic for the X-Windows system

Access to the online user documentation is gained by going to *http://www.ncsa.uiuc.edu/SDG/Software/WinMosaic/Docs/2.1/index.html*.

Their FAQ is located at *http://www.ncsa.uiuc.edu/SDG/Software/WinMosaic/FAQ.htm*.

The NCSA FTP site is *ftp://ftp.ncsa.uiuc.edu*, and you will find the Windows version in the */Web/Mosaic/Windows* subdirectory. The Mac and X-Windows versions each have their own subdirectory as well.

## Quarterdeck

More information about the Internet Suite (which includes Quarterdeck Mosaic) is available from:

**Quarterdeck Corporation**

13160 Mindanao Way

3rd floor

Marina del Rey, CA 90292

Phone: (310) 309-3700

Fax: (310) 309-4219

e-mail: *info@quarterdeck.com*

Order directly from Quarterdeck: (800) 683 6696

*http://www.quarterdeck.com/*

## Netscape

You can get information about the latest version of Netscape from its page at *http://www.netscape.com*. Information about newer versions is maintained on this page, as is information on getting a copy using FTP via *ftp://ftp.netscape.com/*.

In addition, Netscape is available in the Internet Resources Forum on CompuServe, and at keyword "Netscape" on AOL.

## Microsoft Internet Explorer

Microsoft Internet Explorer is available for free from *http://www.micro soft.com/ie/*, or from the FTP site at *ftp://ftp.microsoft.com/msdownload/*.

## Cello

You can get information about Cello from its homepage at *http://www. law.cornell.edu/cello/cellotop.html*. You will find information about Cello itself, how to install it, and how to get it from the FTP site (*ftp://ftp.law. cornell.edu/pub/LII/Cello*).

## Trumpet Winsock

The Trumpet Winsock program by Peter Tattam is shareware. You may download it and try it out, but use requires registration. This required program is available from the URL *http://www.trumpet.com* or via FTP from *ftp://ftp.trumpet.com*.

Further information can be obtained by writing to *info@trumpet. com.au*.

## SlipKnot

SlipKnot is not free. You may try out a copy, but then to continue using it you will have to register. It is available via

*http://plaza.interport.net/slipknot/slipknot.html*,

*http://www.simtel.net/pub/simtelnet/win3/inet/slnot150.zip*, or

*ftp://oak.oakland.edu/pub/simtelnet/win3/inet/slnot/50.zip*.

## Other Useful Client Applications

In addition to your browser, there are some other applications that you as a business user will want to consider in creating a good working desktop of TCP/IP Internet applications.

## Client Software

While you can access FTP, Telnet, and News through most of the full-featured browsers, there are some free-standing programs that are useful:

- IRC chat
- FTP
- Telnet

### *IRC Chat*

IRC chat is getting more popular. It is for real-time interactive text-based discussions. Businesses use this for online conferences and customer interaction.

Netscape has an IRC chat client called Netscape chat (seen in Figure B.11). This is a full-feature chat interface, with options for servers, con-

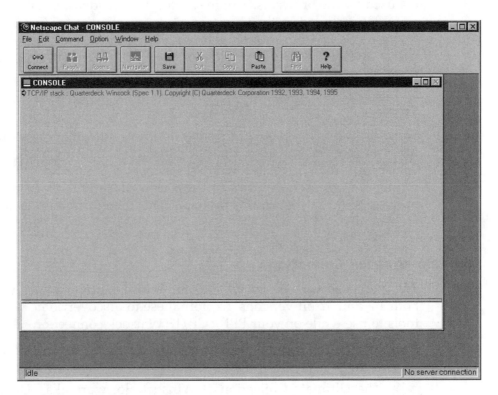

**Figure B.11 Netscape Chat.**

figurations for the user, nicknames, and channel commands. Information on obtaining Netscape Chat is available at *http://www.netscape.com*.

Another popular chat interface is mIRC. It has colored text for easy reading, numerous multilevel pop-up menus, and menus for configurations, nicknames, and commands. This program is freeware, and available at *http://www.shareware.com*.

The New IRC Users Page at *http://www.neosoft.com/~biscuits/niu.html* has lots of useful information on the various IRC chat networks including EFNet, Undernet, and DalNet. Another good source is CMMoon12's summary of IRC commands at *http://members.aol.com/cmmoon12/irc2.html*.

### FTP

Most browsers support FTP downloading through HTTP, but for long downloads, the FTP protocol is much more robust than the HTTP protocol used by the browsers. You may want to consider an FTP client such as QFTP, included in the Quarterdeck Internet suite, or CuteFTP (seen in Figure B.12). Both programs provide a visual display of the transfer, many options for file types, connection management, and viewing. CuteFTP is also available at *http://www.shareware.com*.

### Telnet

Some browsers have built-in Telnet abilities, but others need plug-ins like Trumpet Telnet, Quarterdeck's Telnet client called Qterm, Ewan, or Telnet included with Windows 95 (as shown in Figure B.13). These programs are often configured to drop into place when you are in the browser and use the *telnet://* protocol. The Telnet program is automatically invoked.

## Ultimate Winsock Collections

There are two very complete sites for Winsock applications, including both 16- and 32-bit versions. Explore these to discover some very useful tools to use while on your PPP TCP/IP Winsock connection.

- Stroud's Consummate Winsock Applications ( *http://www.cwsapps. com/*)

- The Ultimate Collection of Winsock Software aka TUCOWS by Scott Swedorski (*http://www.tucows.com/*)

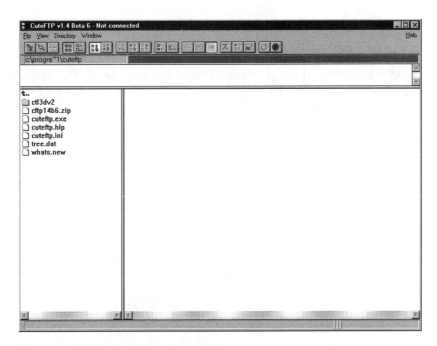

**Figure B.12  CuteFTP main screen.**

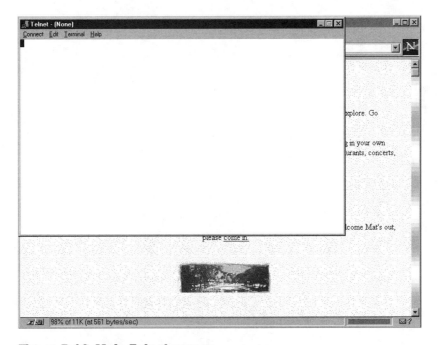

**Figure B.13  Main Telnet screen.**

Remember too, new browsers are springing up all the time, as are new plug-ins and helper applications. Use one of the search tools to have a look around frequently. Also check out some of the programs mentioned in Chapter 12.

# Lynx—A Text Browser

Lynx is the best of the text-based browsers. While text-based browsers have long been eclipsed by GUIs, many business users still go to Lynx from a home connection or when they want to do research and appreciate the blazing speed of a text connection.

Lynx requires a dial-up shell account, and access to the Lynx program itself. Most users dial in with a telecommunications program such as Procomm or Telix.

Lynx was developed at the University of Kansas, initially just as a campus-wide information system. After several upgrades it is now the most popular text-mode World Wide Web browser. Lynx is a Web browser that is usually run on UNIX or VMS systems. Your access to it is either via one of the terminals directly wired to one of these systems, or via a modem and phone line connected to one of these systems.

Phone line access does not require a SLIP or PPP account with an Internet service provider, just a basic "shell" account with Internet access, and the presence of the Lynx program on the service provider's system (ask the service provider if Lynx is available before signing up). A modem with 9600 baud speed or higher is recommended though not required. You can use Lynx from almost any type of personal computer that can run communications software with VT100 terminal emulation (check your communications software documentation to see if VT100 is available, and how to configure it). Monochrome monitors will work, but color or grayscale monitors are easier to use with Lynx.

## Basic Lynx Commands and Navigation Methods

Once you have logged on to your service provider's system, generally all you need to do to start Lynx is to type `Lynx` at your system's usual prompt and then press the Enter key. A screen similar to this will be displayed:

```
                    Overview of the Web
             WWW ICON GENERAL OVERVIEW OF THE WEB
   There is no "top" to the World-Wide Web. You can look at it from
   many points of view. Here are some places to start.
   Virtual Library by Subject
      The Virtual Library organizes information by subject matter.
   List of servers
      All registered HTTP servers by country
   by Service Type
      The Web includes data accessible by many other protocols. The
      lists by access protocol may help if you know what kind of
      service you are looking for.
   If you find a useful starting point for you personally, you can
   configure your WWW browser to start there by default.
      See also: About the W3 project.
Commands: Use arrow keys to move, '?' for help, 'q' to quit,
'<<-' to go back    Arrow keys: Up and Down to move. Right to
follow a link; Left to go back.  H)elp O)ptions P)rint G)o M)ain
screen Q)uit /=search [delete]=history list
```

Your screen may vary substantially from this, because each access provider can use a different favorite or custom HTML document as the default homepage that is displayed each time Lynx is started. Figure C.1 shows the opening screen of Lynx at my shell account.

Note also that some of the words are boldfaced, and some are boldfaced and underlined. These words or phrases are the anchors or links that link this document to other documents. Depending on your particular software, these bold and bold-underlined anchors may appear on your screen as different colors, reverse video, boldface, or italics. In some way, however, you should be able to see these differences on your screen. If all of the words look alike on the homepage that Lynx initially displays, check your communications software documentation on how

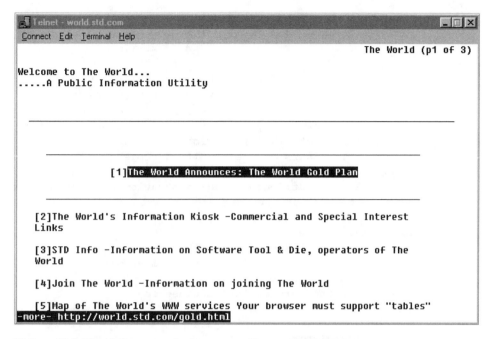

**Figure C.1 The Lynx opening screen shown via Telnet.**

to change colors, backgrounds, video intensity, display modes, reverse video, and so on. Be sure, if your communications software can display high and low intensity (brightness) characters, that your standard characters are from the low intensity group so that Lynx has a chance to use the high intensity colors for the anchors.

As a convention in this book, all of the "links" (anchors) on each screen will be boldfaced (there are four such links in the preceding example). One of the links on each screen will be "highlighted" by being boldfaced *and* underlined. The highlighted link is the currently selected link; others can be selected by using the Up and Down arrows to make the highlight jump from link to link.

Press the right arrow key to request the document indicated by the currently highlighted link. Lynx connects to whatever computer on the Internet has the document being requested, and sends commands to retrieve the file. Notification of the various steps involved in this will flash on the lower lines of the screen, and usually within a second or two the new document will be displayed.

If the currently highlighted document in the homepage shown above is requested by pressing the right arrow, this document will be displayed:

```
The World-Wide Web Virtual Library: Subject Catalogue (p1 of 6)
              VIRTUAL LIBRARY THE WWW VIRTUAL LIBRARY
This is a distributed subject catalogue. See Summary, and Index.
See also arrangement by service type ., and other subject
catalogues of network information.
Mail to maintainers of the specified subject or
www-request@info.cern.ch to add pointers to this list, or if you
would like to contribute to administration of a subject area.
See also how to put your data on the web. All items starting with !
are NEW! (or newly maintained).
Aboriginal Studies
    This document keeps track of leading information facilities in
    the field of Australian Aboriginal studies as well as the
    Indigenous Peoples studies.
Aeronautics and Aeronautical Engineering
Agriculture
Anthropology
Applied Linguistics
Archaeology
Architecture
Art
Asian Studies
Astronomy and Astrophysics
Aviation
Bio Sciences
Chemistry
Climate research
```

Again, in this document, to move the highlight from link to link, use the up and down arrow keys; to request a document, use the right arrow key.

---

### Hypertext Links

The links are ordered from left to right and from top to bottom on the screen; therefore, to move the highlight from "Summary" in the top line of this "Virtual Library" page to "Index," the *down* arrow would be used (using the right arrow would start a request for the "Summary" document).

To get back to the previous document (in this case, the homepage), press the left arrow. You can move backwards and forwards through the documents, branching off in a new direction at any time.

If you have made a number of document requests, you can repeat the use of the left arrow to work your way back to the homepage (if you want to go there), but you can also use the M key to go directly back (after answering a prompt about whether you really want to go back).

---

**Long Delays When Retrieving Documents**

Usually new documents are retrieved in a very few seconds. If the Internet is busy, or if there are some problems with a site you are accessing, you may wait a few minutes to get either an error report or the better-late-than-never document. If you run out of patience, however, press the letter Z or Ctrl-G to stop the transfer while it is in progress. You can then proceed in another direction or try for that document later.

---

At the top right of the Virtual Library screen is an indication that this is page 1 of 6. To move down a page, type a + (plus sign) or press the spacebar. To move back to earlier pages within a document, press - (minus sign), or the letter B.

To exit from the Lynx program, press Q (you will be asked if you really want to quit—answer with a Y); or for a quick departure, use Shift-Q and you will be returned immediately to the main system prompt.

---

**Lynx Command Letters**

Except as explicitly noted, all Lynx command letters are non-shifted (lowercase) letters.

---

## Navigation Aids

The default homepage offered by your ISP will probably have links to some large categorized lists of Web documents. Links from these documents can be followed to zero in subjects of interest to you, or you can use some of the Web search engines to delve more deeply. Also, at many sites an additional broad-based file is available by pressing the I (letter "i") key. You can follow the links from this file, or press the left arrow to return to the document you were just viewing.

If, in your wanderings through the links, you find a document that you find especially helpful, you can save its name and URL so that you can return directly to it later. Just press the = (equals key) to display the name and URL of the document you are currently viewing and the name and URL of the document whose link is currently highlighted. For example, on the homepage that was shown, with the highlight still on the first item, this is the information that would be displayed:

```
              Information about the current document
                 YOU HAVE REACHED THE INFORMATION PAGE
File that you are currently viewing
   Linkname: Overview of the Web
        URL: http://info.cern.ch/default.html
   Owner(s): None
       size: 20 lines
       mode: normal
Link that you currently have selected
   Linkname: Virtual Library by Subject
   Filename:
http://info.cern.ch/hypertext/DataSources/bySubject/Overview.html
```

In this example the document being viewed was the homepage (information about it is given at the top). The link of interest is the one that was highlighted (Virtual Library by Subject). Its URL as listed is *http://info.cern.ch/hypertext/DataSources/bySubject/Overview.html*. This information can be printed out or stored in a file for future use with the Go command. (To return to the document you were viewing before this information request, just press the left arrow as you would to return to any previous document.)

In this example, the Virtual Library page is only one link away from the homepage; but the gem you find related to your area of interest may be 10, 20, or even 50 links from that original homepage. Rather than try to remember every link you've selected and then try to repeat the path next time, you can use the information you obtained with the equals sign to jump directly to that document of interest.

To go directly to that document next time, start Lynx as usual and press the letter G (the Go command). A prompt "URL to open:" will appear at the bottom of the screen. Type in the URL and press Enter; the document will then be displayed.

## Bookmarks

Entering the URLs manually with the Go command is very useful if you received the URL information from some printed or other outside source; but Lynx provides a much easier way of keeping track of valuable documents and sites: Bookmarks.

When you have highlighted a link that you would like to be able to return to in the future, press the A key. A prompt at the bottom of the screen will ask whether you really want this link added to the Bookmarks. Respond with Y and Lynx will report "Done!" To confirm the addition of the link to the Bookmark file, press the letter V to display your list of bookmarks:

```
                    Bookmark file (p1 of 2)
You can delete links using the new remove bookmark command. it is
usually the 'R' key but may have been re-mapped by you or your
system administrator.
This file may also be edited with a standard text editor. Outdated
or invalid links may be removed by simply deleting the line the
link appears on in this file. Please refer to the Lynx
documentation or help files for the HTML link syntax.
  1. WebCrawler Top 25 List
  2. WebQuery search page
  3. W&L Menu: Subject
  4. W&L WWW (WorldWideWeb) Links
  5. dre-list.txt
  6. Cool Links Pages
  7. Net-Happenings
  8. Online Bookstore
  9. Commercial Sites on the Web
 10. BBC
 11. The Awesome
 12. Hypermail archive
 13. The INTERNET BUSINESS BOOK - Introduction
 14. Referenced Web Page Sources
 15. Austin City Limits
 16. Internet Resources Meta-Index
```

17. What's New With NCSA Mosaic
18. The Whole Internet Catalog
19. Business
20. Economy:Business:miscellaneous
21. Figure Skating Home Page
22. The World Wide Web Virtual Library: Literature
23. Dell Computer Home Page
24. Information Sources: the Internet and Computer-Mediated Communication
25. Internet Guide to Michigan
26. All USENET Newsgroups
27. Web Indexes
28. About Lynx
29. Hypertext Webster Interface
30. XFIND index of CERN

This bookmark page can be used like any other Web document: use the arrow keys to move the highlight, request a document, move back to the document you were viewing when you pressed the V key, and so on.

Shift-R can be used to remove a highlighted bookmark from the Bookmark file. If this does not work on your system, the line can be removed by removing the appropriate line from the bookmarks configuration file. The name of this bookmarks configuration file can be found in the Options menu (see next section).

## Keyboard Options

To display Lynx's user-configurable options, press the O key. A screen such as this will be displayed:

```
                        Options Menu
        E)ditor                 : NONE
        D)ISPLAY variable       : NONE
        B)ookmark file          : lynx_bookmarks.html
        F)TP sort criteria      : By Filename
        P)ersonal mail address  : NONE
        S)earching type         : CASE INSENSITIVE
        C)haracter set          : ISO Latin 1
        V)I keys                : ON
        e(M)acs keys            : ON
        K)eypad as arrows
            or Numbered links   : Numbers act as arrows
```

```
    U)ser mode              : Novice
Select first letter of option line, '>>' to save, or 'r' to return
to Lynx.
Command:
```

On this screen you can find the bookmarks configuration filename.

Also of value to navigating is the "Keypad as arrows or Numbered links" option. In its default setup, the only way to get to a particular link on the page is to use the up and down arrow keys. But you can change this option from "Keypad as arrows" to "Numbers act as arrows," so that each link is numbered (as was displayed in the bookmark screen). This sets up Lynx to automatically number all links in a document, allowing you to type in the number and press Enter to request that document's link. This can be particularly useful on a screen with (as is common) 50 or 60 links—if the item you want is about 40 links into the screen, that's a lot of arrow key tapping! With this new configuration, you can still use the arrow keys as before. About the only negative to the numbering is that it will slightly alter the layout of the document, since most are written without the use of the numbers in mind.

To turn on this option, press the O key to display the Options menu shown above. Now press K to display a prompt for the "Keypad..." options. Pressing the spacebar now will toggle back and forth between the two options. If you want the numbers to be added to the screen, stop at "Numbers act as arrows" and press Enter. To use the numbers in this Lynx session only, press R; to save this option so that Lynx will automatically start numbering in future sessions as well, type >> (the "greater than" sign).

The Virtual Library document that was shown earlier in this chapter is displayed this way with numbers:

```
The World-Wide Web Virtual Library: Subject Catalogue (p1 of 6)
            VIRTUAL LIBRARY THE WWW VIRTUAL LIBRARY
This is a distributed subject catalogue. See [1]Summary, and
[2]Index. See also arrangement by [3]service type ., and [4]other
subject catalogues of network information.
Mail to [5]maintainers of the specified subject or
www-request@info.cern.ch to add pointers to this list, or if you
would like [6]to contribute to administration of a subject area.
See also [7]how to put your data on the web. All items starting
with ! are NEW! (or newly maintained).
```

```
[8]Aboriginal Studies
    This document keeps track of leading information facilities in
    the field of Australian Aboriginal studies as well as the
    Indigenous Peoples studies.
[9]Aeronautics and Aeronautical Engineering
[10]Agriculture
[11]Anthropology
[12]Applied Linguistics
[13]Archaeology
[14]Architecture
[15]Art
[16]Asian Studies
[17]Astronomy and Astrophysics
[18]Aviation
[19]Bio Sciences
[20]Chemistry
[21]Climate research
```

To select a link, type its number (you can use the backspace key to make corrections). The numbers you enter will be shown at the bottom of the screen. After you type in a number, just press the Enter key. Lynx will now immediately request the document referred to by that numbered link.

## History Option

Another navigation aid is the History page. Lynx automatically keeps track of the documents you have viewed during the current session with Lynx. When the backspace key is pressed, the Lynx History page is displayed. The documents you have viewed are shown in reverse order (latest document first, first document last). This list will not always show all of the documents you have viewed. For example, if after viewing the "Talk N Toss" document (shown as number 4 below) you use the left arrow to go back to "Branch Information Services" (shown as item 3) and then request another document from "Branch Information Services," "Talk and Toss" will no longer show up in the History page.

You can use the History page just as a reminder of where you are (returning to the documents you were in previously, by using the customary left arrow key press); or use the History page just like any other Web page (move the highlight, request a document, check the URL, etc.).

```
                    Lynx History Page
            YOU HAVE REACHED THE HISTORY PAGE
4. —You selected:  Talk N Toss, Prepaid Calling Cards, Russell
Biaggne, Telephone cards, long distance phone service, calling
cards
3. —You selected:  Branch Information Services - flowers promotion
electronic mall storefront shopping advertising marketing zeeff
commercial catalogs
2. —You selected:  The World-Wide Web Virtual Library: Commercial
Services
1. —You selected:  The World-Wide Web Virtual Library: Subject
Catalogue
0. —You selected:  Overview of the Web
```

Using the History page allows you to explore one branch of links from a document and then go directly back to the document to explore another branch of links. It also allows you to, with the benefit of hindsight, go back to a particular document and add it to the bookmark file.

## Search Options

Lynx lets you do three basic types of searches:

- Searches within the current document
- Searches within an HTML database
- Searches of all of the Web-accessible Internet

The first two of these, discussed here, are accomplished via Lynx commands. The full Web search is explained in Chapter 9.

### Searching Documents

Individual documents that are being viewed can be searched for words, parts of a word, or phrases. To do a search, move to the top of the document, or at least note what page of the document you are viewing (searches start from your current position in the document, proceed toward the end, then wrap to the top of the document to continue the search). Now press the key with the right (forward) slash (/). A prompt and input line will appear. Type in the text you are searching for and press the Enter key. Lynx will stop at the first occurrence of the text you requested with that text on the top line of the screen. To go to the next occurrence of the text, press the N key, and continue pressing N for each next occurrence.

Unless you need to specify the uppercase-lowercase combination of letters (for example, to locate mention of the organization CARE, not the word "care"), it is usually better to have searches case-insensitive. Press O to display the options menu to verify or change the search case sensitivity.

## *Searching Databases*

Some HTML documents have been specially prepared to be databases. When these documents are requested, just an opening explanatory/ search-form screen is displayed. In this case, instead of using the forward slash, use the S key. Lynx will provide a prompt and an input line. Type in the word or words you are searching for and press Enter.

---

### Erasing Your Input

As with any Lynx input line, the backspace key can be used for erasing errors one letter at a time, or the Ctrl-U key combination can be used to erase the entire line.

---

A dictionary is a good example of how an HTML database can be used:

```
                   HYPERTEXT WEBSTER INTERFACE
The hypertext Webster interface provides a point-and-click client
interface (for xmosaic users) for accessing the Webster's
dictionary service. First, type the word for which you want the
definition in the search window and hit return. Words in the
resulting definition are hypertext linked back into the
dictionary, allowing you to use your mouse to access the
definition of those related (and unrelated) words.
If you misspell the word, the webster server may offer a list of
close matches as alternatives. If you know the prefix of the word,
a list of potential matches may be obtained by entering a * after
the prefix, e.g., alpha*.
The Web interface is rather simple-minded—all but very short words
are hyperlinked back to the dictionary. Because it doesn't know if
the words are actually in the dictionary, these links may fail. In
particular, prefix/suffix removal to find the root word is neither
performed by the Web interface nor the Webster server, so the link
```

```
for alphabetically doesn't work, since the webster server only has
an entry for alphabetic, and it is not smart enough to find the
root. The job of root extraction should be done in the Webster
server, just as spell correction feedback is done now for
alphabetic. Note that you can use cut-and-paste to extract the
root and paste it into the search window: you just have to
click-hold-drag instead of single-click.
The webster client used internally by this interface is
/afs/cs.cmu.edu/user/bsy/bin/webster, if you want to use it from
outside of the WWW. The webster database server that it contacts
is configurable via your ~/.webster file; see the man page for
details. The webster client uses either hopeless.mess.cs.cmu.edu,
nisc.sri.com, cs.indiana.edu, or mintaka.lcs.mit.edu as its
webster server, depending on which responds first.
The hypertext Webster interface was written by bsy@cs.cmu.edu
This is a searchable index.  Use 's' to search
```

After the S key is pressed, the line at the bottom of the screen, "This is a searchable index. Use 's' to search," changes to "Enter a database search string:" and waits for input. In this case the word "laser" was typed in and Enter was pressed. This is the document returned:

```
            Webster Definition for "laser"
          WEBSTER DEFINITION FOR "LASER"
la. ser \'la—z*r\ n [ light amplification by stimulate
emission of radiation : a device that utilizes the natural
oscillations of atoms for amplifying or generating
electromagnetic waves in the visible region of the spectrum
HTTP webster interface by bsy@cs.cmu.edu
```

Each of the bold items in this definition are links that can be highlighted and requested in the normal manner.

### Error Message

If you press the S key while viewing a normal, nondatabase document, Lynx will respond at the bottom of the screen with "Not a searchable index."

## Document Retrieval

Lynx provides two ways to retrieve documents:

- The Print command for retrieving documents currently being viewed
- The Download command for retrieving documents referred to by a highlighted link

### The Print Command

A document currently being viewed can be retrieved to your computer in several ways. To start the process, press the P key. Lynx will display a screen similar to this (the available menu items vary from site to site):

```
                Lynx Printing Options
                  PRINTING OPTIONS
There are 20 lines, or approximately 1 page, to print.
You have the following print choices
please select one:
[1] Save to a local file
[2] Mail the file to yourself
[3] Print to the screen
[4] Use vt100 print sequence to print from your local terminal
```

All of these methods are for ASCII text files. Binary files such as pictures, sound files, and formatted word processor files cannot be retrieved with these "Print" methods.

**Saving to a Local File**   This option allows you to put this document in a file on your access provider's system. It will place the file in whatever subdirectory you were in when you invoked Lynx (unless you changed it since logging into the system, this is the default directory assigned to your personal account). If you are accessing the account via a dial-up account, you may then want to download the file from your account to your personal computer.

To use this method, highlight this link and press the right arrow. The file's name will appear at the bottom of the screen. If the name is suitable, just press Enter and the file will be copied to your subdirectory. If you would like to rename the file, use the backspace key or Ctrl-U, as described previously, to delete the default name, and then type in the new name. Press Enter.

**Mailing the File to Yourself**   This option allows you to send the document as a normal e-mail message to yourself or to anyone else with an e-mail address. This is a good option if you want to evaluate the document later, don't have room on your hard drive right now, or want to share the find with a friend or business associate.

To use this method, highlight this link and press the right arrow key. A box will be displayed with an input line. Type in the full address and press Enter. Lynx will indicate that it is mailing the document and then return to the previously viewed document.

**Printing to the Screen**   This option "prints" the document to the screen without stopping at the end of each screen. If your communications software has some method for "logging" (recording) all text that is displayed to the screen, this can be a convenient way of getting text files.

To use this method, highlight this link and press the right arrow key. Now turn on your software's logging feature, and then press the Enter key. The document will scroll by on the screen. When it stops, turn off the logging feature and press Enter to complete the process.

**Printing a Hard Copy Directly**   If you have fully VT100-compatible terminal emulation in your communications software, and a printer connected to your personal computer, you may be able to directly print out the document you are viewing.

To use this method, first be sure the printer is turned on and ready to print. Now highlight this link and press the right arrow key. Your printer should now start printing the document.

### The Download Command

The Download command can be used to download text files as the Print command does, but it also can be used to download binary files such as picture files, sound files, and program-specific data files from word processors, spreadsheets, CAD programs, and other software. To start the process, press the D key. The following menu will be displayed:

```
                Lynx Download Options
                  DOWNLOAD OPTIONS
     You have the following download choices
     please select one:
     Save to disk
     Use Zmodem to download to the local terminal
```

```
Enter a filename: ibb-ch4.html
Arrow keys: Up and Down to move. Right to follow a link; Left to
go back.
 H)elp O)ptions P)rint G)o M)ain screen Q)uit /=search
[delete]=history list
```

The default filename is shown near the bottom of the screen. In this example, you can change "ibb-ch4.html" by deleting it with the backspace key or Ctrl-U key combination. Then type in a replacement name.

**Name Length**

If you are downloading to a DOS or Windows-based machine, you will be limited to filenames of eight-plus-three characters. The file you are downloading may be from a VAX or UNIX machine and thus have a much longer filename. It is a good idea to rename to file before downloading. Otherwise, your communications program will probably just truncate the name by removing all characters that it can't accommodate.

You have two options for saving the file. The first involves using the Save to disk option. This option operates in a manner similar to the Save to a Local File option described in the Print commands in the previous section of this chapter.

Your second option is to download the file to your local personal computer. The site in this example offers only the Zmodem download protocol. Some sites offer choices such as Kermit, Xmodem, and Ymodem protocols. In most cases the only concern is that your personal computer's communications software has the ability to use one of the transfer protocols offered by the Lynx site you are using.

To use this option, set your communications software to one of the transfer protocols offered by the Lynx site (each of hundreds of communications programs do this differently—you may need to consult your program documentation). Now highlight the download option and press the Enter key. At this point you need to give your software a command to start receiving the file (see your documentation). Some communications software can auto-detect the start of a download, and will therefore not need a receive command.

When the download is complete, the "Download Options" will still be displayed. The file is now in your personal computer, in whatever subdirectory your communications software was configured to place it. Press the left arrow key to return to the Lynx document you were viewing.

## Links to Information Outside of the World Wide Web

In addition to HTML documents, Lynx can be used to search for, display, and download files available via Gopher, FTP, Usenet news, and WAIS servers. It provides an easy-to-navigate, uniform user interface for these services. Gateway servers have also been set up that allow access to Telnet, X.500, WHOIS, and other protocols.

This ability of Lynx and many of the other Web browsers can be of real value to the new Internet user. Formerly, it was necessary to learn how to operate approximately 10 different client programs to have full use of the Internet; now learning how to use a browser and an e-mail program will give you access to most of the Internet's resources.

Here is how to recognize and use these various Internet services with the Lynx browser.

### Gopher Links

As you navigate through the Web, you will often encounter documents with links to Gopher servers (Gopher is a text-based organization of Internet material, now often supplanted by Web sites). Gophers present material as menus, which contain links to the site. When these links are selected, the resulting "document" will be a Gopher menu. Instead of the usual combination of paragraphs and lists, Gopher links will appear only as lists. It is usually a good idea to have the "Numbers as arrows" option turned on when retrieving Gopher menus. Here is a typical Gopher menu displayed by Lynx:

```
          All the Gopher Servers in the World (p1 of 50)
             ALL THE GOPHER SERVERS IN THE WORLD
(DIR)  [1]Search Gopherspace using Veronica
(DIR)  [2]1994 California Voter Information
(DIR)  [3]AACRAO National Office, Washington, DC
(DIR)  [4]AARNET
```

```
(DIR)  [5]A TF - American Association of Teachers of French
(DIR)  [6]ACADEME THIS WEEK (Chronicle of Higher Education)
(DIR)  [7]ACE GOPHER (American Council on Education)
(DIR)  [8]ACES - Educational Service Agency Gopher
(DIR)  [9]ACLU Free Reading Room
(DIR)  [10]ACM SIGDA
(DIR)  [11]ACM SIGGRAPH
(DIR)  [12]ACTLab (UT Austin, RTF Dept)
(DIR)  [13]AJCU Gopher (Jesuit Mission and Identity)
(DIR)  [14]ALADDIN Gopher
(DIR)  [15]< ALLDATA Corporation (car recall and technical service
            bulletins)
(DIR)  [16]AMI—A Friendly Public Interface
(DIR)  [17]ANS (Advanced Network Services)
(DIR)  [18]ANS gopher
(DIR)  [19]APK Gopher
(DIR)  [20]APS-Academic Physician and Scientist
(DIR)  [21]AREA Science Park, Trieste, (IT)
(DIR)  [22]ARPA Computing Systems Technology Office (CSTO)
(DIR)  [23]ASHI Gopher
(DIR)  [24]AT&T Global Information Solutions (formerly NCR) Info
            Server
(DIR)  [25]AbagOnline [Access to Bay Area Governments Online]
(DIR)  [26]Academia Sinica, Taiwan, ROC.
(DIR)  [27]Academic Physician and Scientist
(DIR)  [28]Academic Position Network
(DIR)  [29]Academy of Sciences, Bratislava (Slovakia)
(DIR)  [30]Acadia University Gopher
(DIR)  [31]AccessNet
(DIR)  [32]Achilles Internet Services
(DIR)  [33]Action for Blind People
(DIR)  [34]Active Living and Environment Program - Unibase Telecom
            Ltd.
(DIR)  [35]Active Window Productions, Cambridge, MA
(DIR)  [36]Adam Curry's Music Server (Gopher)
(DIR)  [37]Addison-Wesley Publishing Company
(DIR)  [38]Advantis Global Network Services, Applications &
            Outsourcing
(DIR)  [39]African National Congress Information
(DIR)  [40]AgResearch Wallaceville, Upper Hutt, New Zealand
```

While this menu format looks a bit different from the normal Lynx display, most of the Lynx features work the same way they do with

HTML documents. In this example, all of these links lead to further menus (directories or DIR). After following the links a layer or two down, you will start to see viewable documents and binary files that can be downloaded.

Gopher sites can also be used by Lynx with the Go command. Gopher URLs start with *gopher://* as in the URL for the screen shown above:

*gopher://gopher.tc.umn.edu/11/Other%20Gopher%20and%20Information %20Servers/all*

To search most of the Gopher menu items on the Internet at one time, use the Gopher equivalent of WebCrawler or Lycos: Veronica. Use Lynx's Go command (G) and enter this URL:

*gopher://gopher.tc.umn.edu:70/11/Other%20Gopher%20and%20 Information%20Servers/Veronica*

## FTP Links

FTP (File Transfer Protocol) is a system set up on the Internet that allows an individual using one computer system to look through some of the directories of another computer system on the Internet, and then download copies of files found in those directories.

FTP is normally one of the hardest services for new Internet users to learn about and operate well. Lynx, like other browsers, makes FTP much easier to use.

You will often note FTP sites listed as links in Web documents. You can also use Lynx's Go command with the FTP site's URL. For example, the site at *ftp://wuarchive.wustl.edu/* is an excellent source of software (software is in the "system" directory).

```
                                 Welcome   directory
                                       WELCOME
  Mar 13  1994   text/plain       [1].Links   792 bytes
  Nov 28  1990   text/plain       [2].notar
  Jan 14  1995   Directory        [3].tags
  Jun  6 12:16   Directory        [4]bin
  Nov  4 06:58   text/plain       [5]core   600Kb
  Aug  2 06:11   Directory        [6]decus
  Feb  7  1996   Directory        [7]doc
```

```
Jun 15 15:45   Directory        [8]edu
Nov  1 06:14   Directory        [9]etc
Jan 20  1994   Directory        [10]graphics
Jul  7 13:23   text/html        [11]index.html  1Kb
Nov  5 06:58   Directory        [12]info
Sep 28 13:21   Directory        [13]languages
Apr  6  1995   Directory        [14]mirrors
Jan 15  1994   Directory        [15]multimedia
Oct 19 15:32   Directory        [16]packages
Oct 24 07:48   Directory        [17]private
Nov  4 22:21   Directory        [18]pub
Oct 15 12:51   text/plain       [19]README   2Kb
Jun 29  1996   text/plain       [20]README.NFS  1Kb
Oct  7 08:31   Directory        [21]systems
Jun  3 09:46   Directory        [22]usenet
```

Lynx displays the directory at the remote computer, with each sub-directory and file shown as a highlightable link. These links can be followed up and down the directory tree using the usual Lynx arrow keys and commands. Documents can be viewed and downloaded, and directories or files can even be placed in the Lynx bookmarks file.

A list with links to FTP sites is available at *http://hoohoo.ncsa.uiuc.edu/ftp-interface.html*.

To search the directories of most of the FTP sites on the Internet for particular files, use Archie, the FTP equivalent of WebCrawler or Lycos. An excellent collection of Archie servers is available via *http://web.nexor.co.uk/archie.html*.

## Usenet Links

Most of the approximately 10,000 Usenet newsgroups can also be read and responded to via Lynx. The URLs for Usenet news have a special form. For example, to read the Usenet group *alt.business.misc,* use Lynx's Go command (G) and enter the URL *news:alt.business.misc*.

The screen Lynx displays is a list of postings to the group, with each posting's title marked as a highlightable link:

```
      Newsgroup alt.business.misc,  Articles 8579-8608 (p1 of 2)
([1]Earlier articles...) Articles in alt.business.misc
  * [2]"CHINA BUSINESS JL. 41030 Contents List" - "CBJ"
  * [3]"Ostriches for sale" - steve montroy
```

* [4]"Incorporate Without Legal Fees !!!!!" - Rick Fletcher
* [5]"Re: CASH IN On The BANKING CRISIS" - Moneybrokr
* [6]"9.7CPM LONG DISTANCE, 24 HOURS A DAY, NATIONWIDE$$$$" - HETENE
* [7]"====>> Wanted: your used scuzzy-to-scuzzy hard drive cable" - krazykev@panix.com
* [8]"Help!! Need info on reengineering the businessprocess" - SkeeterBDG
* [9]"Freight Costs" - Gowri Subramanian
* [10]"Sell to Eastern Europe" - Ross Hedvicek
* [11]"Pre-Launch of Clinically Proven Healthcare Products" - Garry Stroud
* [12]"Business contacts " - Charles Marais
* [13]"$$$$$$$ YOU CAN USE A 9.7CPM CALLING CARD $$$$$$$$$" - HETENE
* [14]"Advertising/marketing for start-up businesses" - BPomeroy
* [15]"Re: Freight Costs" - Alan Pearce
* [16]"Re: Business contacts" - Cosby A
* [17]"National Bank seeking secured credit card agents" - OUTRIGGER@DELPHI.COM
* [18]"WANTED: Software Engineer" - WFBMM
* [19]"Re: Network Marketing [SCAMWAY]" - D. Citron
* [20]"Help Needed _____ PRICE" - mironenko sergey ( bse ceng
* [21]"====>>How To Build Your Direct Mail Profits" - MichaelRgn
* [22]"CAPITAL MEDICAL EQUIPMENT DATABASE AVAILABLE TO ALL NET USERS" - David Spencer
* [23]"(Fwd) "MONEY FROM HOME"" - Walter Orochoski
* [24]"Research projects, reports." - OSAMA HEGGE
* [25]">>>>>> S U P E R R E S P O N S I V E N A M E S <<<<<<" - Scott
* [26]"Make Money Fast!!" - Peter Christoph Dorney
* [27]"Looking for Formulators and Researchers" - Chua Hock Heng
* [28]"PAS 16 bit/CM205 CD-ROM Drive Offer Previously Posted" - Paul
  H. Duval,paul@direct.ibm.ca,Internet2
* [29]"Re: 20% to 50+% travel discounts, Hotels, Cars, Trips etc." - aruta0tnt0@ins.infonet.net,Internet2
* [30]"9.7CPM IS EXPLODING, YOU HAD BETTER TAKE A LOOK NOW!" - HETENE
* [31]"Investors - South Africa" - Seagull Software

Lynx displays the postings with a very useful header. For example, if number 2, "CHINA BUSINESS JL," is requested, Lynx displays the posting in this manner:

```
        CHINA BUSINESS JOURNAL 41029 Contents List (p1 of 2)
 [1]Reply to: "CBJ"
             CHINA BUSINESS JOURNAL 41029 CONTENTS LIST
 30 Oct 1994 05:04:01 GMT
 China Business Journal
 Newsgroups:
         [2]misc.entrepreneurs,
         [3]alt.business.misc,
         [4]soc.culture.china,
         [5]soc.culture.taiwan,
         [6]soc.culture.hongkong
 [7]Reply to newsgroup(s)
                     ****      *****      *******
                    *    *    *     *            *
                   *          *     *            *
                   *          *****              *
                   *          *     *            *
                    *    *    *     *    *    *  *
                     ****      *****         **
 ###############################################################
                  CHINA BUSINESS JOURNAL ON-LINE
                       October  29, 1994
                          Saturday
                        Issue No.  41029
 ###############################################################
 China Business Journal(CBJ) is an on-line daily news published 5
 days a week. The subscriber can get the CBJ daily news by E-mail
 on the Internet, American On Line, Prodigy etc., network service.
 CBJ are trying to offer update economic news from China to let our
 readers have on-time informaton in hand to handle business with
 China. If you are intrested in subscribe CBJ, just send e-mail to
 p01570@psilink.com with your E-mail address and Name ,
 organization, and mailing address. We will send the CBJ by E-mail
 to you every day.
 ###############################################################
             Electronic News Editor:  Wei Shyu
                  China Business Journal
                    31-33 Market St.
                 New York, NY 10002
                 Tel: (212) 227-8620
                      (212) 227-6017
```

The header has links that allow you to respond directly to the individual that posted this message (in this case, **Reply to: "CBJ"**). The header also lists the groups that this posting was sent to (in this case, under "Newsgroups:" links 2-6). The **Reply to newsgroup(s)** will send your reply posting to all of the newsgroups that received the original posting.

# Other Useful Lynx Commands

There are several more commands that can be helpful in Lynx sessions.

## Comments

Lynx's Comments command allows you to send an e-mail message to the owner of the HTML document you are currently viewing. This feature will work only if the "owner" of the document is listed in the HTML document in the appropriate manner, with proper HTML syntax (this is the case for approximately 60 percent of current documents).

To send a comment, start by pressing the C key. You will be given a chance to cancel sending the message, then given a chance (optionally) to give your name, e-mail address, and subject of the message. Press Enter after each entry, or to ignore the question. You will then be prompted to type in your message. To end the message, press Enter, type a period (.), and press Enter again. The message will be sent and the previously viewed document will be redisplayed.

## Viewing Unprocessed HTML Files

Like GUI browsers, Lynx uses the HTML commands in a document to format it, mark certain words as links, and display information about the file. Lynx can also, however, retrieve the document without doing any processing or rendering. This is very useful for learning about how other HTML document authors accomplish various tasks.

To use this feature, press the backslash key (\). Lynx will retrieve the file without processing it. The first screen shown in this section, "Overview of the Web," looks like this in its raw form:

```
                    Overview of the Web
<<HTML>>
<<HEAD>>
<<TITLE>>Overview of the Web<</TITLE>>
<<!- Changed by: , 14-Jul-1996 —>>
```

```
<<NEXTID N="z5">>
<</HEAD>>
<<BODY>>
<<H1>>
<<IMG ALT="WWW Icon"
SRC="http://info.cern.ch/hypertext/WWW/Icons/WWW/WWWlogo.gif
<</H1>>There is no "top" to the World-Wide
Web. You can look at it from many
points of view. Here are some places
to start.
<<DL>>
<<DT>><<A
NAME="z0" HREF="http://info.cern.ch/hypertext/DataSources/
bySubject/Overview.html
<<DD>> The Virtual Library organises
information by subject matter.
<<DT>><<A name="z4" href="http://info.cern.ch/hypertext/
DataSources/WWW/Servers.html List of servers<</a>>
<<DD>>All registered HTTP servers by country
<<DT>><<A
NAME="z1" HREF="http://info.cern.ch/hypertext/DataSources/
ByAccess.html">>by Ser
<<DD>> The Web includes data accessible by many other protocols.
The lists by access protocol may
help if you know what kind of service you are looking for.
<</DL>>
If you find a useful starting point for you personally,
you can configure your WWW browser to start there by default.<<p>>
See also: <<A
NAME="z2" HREF="http://info.cern.ch/hypertext/WWW/TheProject.
html">>About the W3 project<</A>> .<</BODY>>
<</HTML>>
```

There are, of course, no highlightable links in this display, since it is just being shown as a standard text file. Other normal Lynx commands and features are still available.

## Configuration Options

Several of the user-configurable options have been mentioned previously along with an explanation of how to change and save the configuration. The Options menu contains these configurable options:

```
                          Options Menu
E)ditor                        : NONE
D)ISPLAY variable              : NONE
B)ookmark file                 : lynx_bookmarks.html
F)TP sort criteria             : By Filename
P)ersonal mail address         : NONE
S)earching type                : CASE INSENSITIVE
C)haracter set                 : ISO Latin 1
V)I keys                       : ON
e(M)acs keys                   : ON
K)eypad as arrows
or Numbered links    : Numbers act as arrows
U)ser mode             : Novice
```

At this point, you can select first letter of option line, '>>' to save, or 'r' to return to Lynx.

**Editor:** Enter the name of one of the editors available on your access provider's system (e.g., pico, vi). This will be used for sending messages and for editing files on your system. If no editor is specified, Lynx's own editor is used.

**Display variable:** Only of concern for some UNIX users who are using X-Windows.

**Bookmark file:** See the "Bookmarks" section earlier in this appendix.

**FTP sorting criteria:** Determines what criterion is used for sorting FTP site files and directories before displaying them: filename, size, type, or date.

**Personal mail address:** The default address for sending documents to yourself, and to appear as the return address for comment messages. It is also included in all document requests.

**Searching type:** See "Search Options" earlier in this appendix.

**Character set:** Allows use of character sets for several languages other than English.

**VI keys:** Allows use of H, J, K, and L keys instead of arrows keys (for terminals without arrow keys).

**eMacs keys:** Allows use of Ctrl-P, Ctrl-N, Ctrl-F, and Ctrl-B key combinations instead of arrow keys (for terminals without arrow keys).

**Keypad as arrows:** See "Navigation Aids" earlier in this appendix.

**User mode:** Allows you to choose between three types of screen display:

Novice—All help and status lines are displayed (as shown in the examples in this appendix).

Intermediate—The status report/entry line is displayed, but the two help lines at the bottom of the screen are turned off. This allows for more lines of data on the screen.

Advanced—The URL of the currently highlighted link is displayed at the bottom of the screen.

## Refreshing the Screen

Lynx provides two ways to "refresh" the screen. This can be helpful if noise on the phone line causes errors in printing the screen, or when incoming mail announcements are printed on the screen right over the document you are viewing.

The Ctrl-W key combination is for a quick reprinting of the screen using the file that was retrieved to your service provider's machine.

Use Ctrl-R instead if you suspect the file received at your system was corrupted. This command requests a new copy of the same file and then prints the screen using this new copy of the file.

## Lynx Commands Quick Reference

**Frequently Used Program Commands**

| | |
|---|---|
| Up | Move highlight to previous link |
| Down | Move highlight to next link |
| Left | Request previously viewed document |
| Right (or Enter key) | Request highlighted link's document |
| + (or spacebar) | Move to next screen |
| - (or B) | Move to previous screen |
| Z (or Ctrl-G) | Cancel a request or file transfer while it is taking place |

| | |
|---|---|
| H (or ?) | Display a list of help files |
| Q | Leave the Lynx program (asks whether you really mean to leave) |
| Shift-Q | Leave Lynx (no questions asked) |

### Commands Affecting Input Lines (in Searches, Comments, etc.)

| | |
|---|---|
| Backspace | Erase one character at a time |
| Ctrl-U | Erase all characters on the line |

### Navigation Aids

| | |
|---|---|
| G | Display an input line for retrieval of a specific document by entering its URL on the line |
| I | Display many good starting documents (varies from site to site) |
| M | Return to the homepage displayed when Lynx was first started |
| = | Display information on current file and highlighted link |
| Backspace | Display list of documents you have viewed during the current Lynx session |

## Document Retrieval

| | |
|---|---|
| D | Download the currently highlighted link's document—select from: |
| |     To your current directory on your Internet access provider's system |
| |     To your personal computer |
| P | Print the currently viewed document—select from: |
| |     Print to screen (does not pause when screen is full) |
| |     Save to local file (sends file to your directory at provider's site) |
| |     Mail file (to yourself or others) |
| |     Print document on your own printer (if using VT100 emulation) |

### Bookmarks

| | |
|---|---|
| A | Add highlighted link to bookmark list |
| V | View the bookmark list |
| Shift-R | Erase the currently highlighted bookmark (doesn't work at all sites) |

## Searches

| | |
|---|---|
| / | Search for a word or phrase within the currently viewed document |
| N | Search for next occurrence of same word or phrase |
| S | Search for a word or phrase within a database |

## Other Useful Commands

| | |
|---|---|
| C | Send a comment (e-mail message) to the owner of the file being viewed |
| \ | Display currently viewed file as an unprocessed, un-rendered HTML file |
| O | Display Options screen to reconfigure how Lynx performs some tasks |
| Ctrl-W | Reprint the screen using the previously requested file |
| Ctrl-R | Request current file again and reprint screen |

If you have never given Lynx a try, you might be surprised how swift it is, and how full-featured.

# Selected Marketing-Related Discussion and Announcement Groups

There are numerous useful resources for online marketers, and one of the most useful for finding appropriate discussion lists is Marketing Lists on the Internet from Kim Bayne. It identifies lists and forums of use for those interested in joining the on-going dialogs about Internet business, marketing, advertising and public relations. Kim has graciously allowed us to reproduce her listing in this appendix.

Kim Bayne's Marketing Lists on the Internet
a.k.a. Selected Marketing-related Discussion and Announcement
Groups on the Internet and Commercial Online Services
by Kim M. Bayne, wolfBayne Communications
Volume 3, Issue 3. March, 1996
ISSN 1084-7391

Used with permission

```
-  ------
```

```
There are currently over 90 marketing-related groups referenced in
this issue of 'Marketing Lists on the Internet.' Both current and
discontinued lists are included for reference purposes. The most
updated version of this directory can be found at
http://www.bayne.com/wolfBayne/htmarcom/mktglist.html.
```

```
- ------
```

Marketing discussion groups come and go. They change servers,
change owners and even change format. wolfBayne Communications is
in no way responsible for the operation of lists, newsgroups or
forums other than our own. For assistance in subscribing,
unsubscribing or changing your list options, please contact the
individual list owners.

```
- ------
```

```
- ------
```

Descriptions of Selected Marketing Lists, Newsgroups and Other
Forums

HTMARCOM
(High Tech MARketing COMmunications, Computer and Electronics
Products - Discussions -
Moderated)
Subscriptions: listserv@listserv.rmii.com

4SaleList
(New and Used Items For Sale - Moderated)
Subscriptions: 4salebot@teletron.com

ACTIVE_MARKETER
(Weekly Web Site Report on Sales and Marketing - Newsletter -
Moderated)
Subscriptions: listserv@listserv.mktplace.com

ADFORUM
(Advertising Education - Discussions)
Subscriptions: listserv@unc.edu

AFMNet
(Market Research, French Language - Discussions - Unmoderated)
Subscriptions: MXserver@CRISV1.univ-pau.fr

AIM
(Asian Internet Marketing)
Subscriptions: majordomo@apic.net

AMODLMKT
(Applied Modeling Issues in Marketing - Discussions)
Subscriptions: LISTSERV@UMSLVMA.UMSL.EDU

ANN-LOTS
(Indexing Forum for Annotated Lists-of-Things - Announcements -
Moderated)
Subscriptions: LISTSERV@VM1.NODAK.EDU

BA315
(Marketing Management - Discussions)
Owner: BA315-Request@UMSLVMA.UMSL.EDU

BIOMARKET
(Human BIOtechnical and Biomedical MARKETing - Discussions)
Note: This list ceased 4/1/95.

BIZ-MARKETING-CONSULTING
(Performing Marketing as a Consultant - Discussions)
Subscriptions: MAJORDOMO@world.std.com

BizOpList
(Business Opportunities - Announcements)
Note: Subscription requests for this list are returned. No current
address on file.

BOOKMKT
(Book Marketing - Discussions)
Subscriptions: majordomo@ttx.com

BUSCOM-L
(Business Communication Students, Classes and the Internet -
Discussions)
Subscriptions: LISTSERV@UTEPVM.UTEP.EDU

CAN-IMARKET
(Canadian Internet Marketing - Discussions)
Subscriptions: can-imarket-request@idirect.com

CIO MarketTalk
Information: lbrown@cio.com

CNI-ADVERTISE
(Advertising on the Internet)
Note: This list is inactive but the archives are still available.
CNI-ADVERTISE will refer you to:
CNI-MODERNIZATION
Subscriptions: LISTPROC@cni.org

CommInfo
(Commercial Advertisements - Announcements - Moderated)
Subscriptions: automailer@teletron.com

COMMERCIAL-REALESTATE
(Commercial Real Estate for Sale or Lease - Announcements -
Moderated)
Subscriptions: listserv@property.com

Customer Support
(Customer Support - Discussions)
Subscriptions: majordomo@lists.infoboard.com

CRM-L
(Relationship Marketing, Academic - Discussions)
Subscriptions: LISTSERV@emuvm1.cc.emory.edu

(The) Delphi Group
(Internet Marketing, Advertising and Sales - Discussions)
Discussions: http://www.cam.org/~delphig

DIRECTMAR
(Direct Marketing - Discussions)
Note: Subscription requests for this list are returned. No current
address on file.

DLD
(Discount Long Distance Telephone Resale - Newsletter - Moderated)
Subscriptions: dld-request@webcom.com

DM-DIGEST
(Database Marketing and Relationship Management)
Subscriptions: dm-digest@iafrica.com

EEUROPE-BUSINESS
(Doing Business in Eastern Europe - Discussions - Unmoderated)
Subscriptions: listmanager@hookup.net

E-LIST
(Advertising Age - Discussions)
Note: This list has not yet been formed. Email Advertising Age
magazine at
list@AdAge.com to express your interest.

ELMAR
(Academic Research in Marketing - Discussions)
Subscriptions: ELMAR- REQUEST@columbia.edu
Message text: subscribe ELMAR-LIST
- or -
subscribe ELMAR-DIGEST

Esearch
(Internet Market Research - Surveys - Moderated)
Subscriptions: esearch@esearch.com

FREE-MARKET
(Marketing on the Internet - Discussions - Unmoderated)
Subscriptions: LISTSERV@ar.com

GINLIST
(Global Interactive Network/Int'l Bus & Mktg Issues - Discussions)
Subscriptions: LISTSERV@msu.edu

GLOBALMC
(Global Marketing Consortium - Discussions)
Subscriptions:LISTSERV@TAMVM1.TAMU.EDU

GLOBMKT
(Applied Global Marketing - Discussions)
Subscriptions: LISTSERV@ukcc.uky.edu

Guerrilla-Weekly
(Guerrilla Marketing - Newsletter - Moderated)
Subscriptions: majordomo@listserv.gmarketing.com

HEP2-L
(Marketing with Technology Tools - Discussions)
Note: see MT-L

HTMNEWS
(Ideas and Resources for High Tech Marketing Communicators -
Newsletter -
Moderated)
Merged with HTMARCOM. Copies archived. Published irregularly.
Web: http://www.bayne.com/wolfBayne/htmarcom/htmnews.html

IC
(Inside Connections, Business on the Internet)
Note: Subscription requests for this list are returned. No current
address on file.

IMALL-CHAT
(Internet Malls - Discussions)
Subscriptions: LISTSERV@netcom.com

InBusiness
(Making Money on the Net - Interviews - Moderated)
Discussions: on America Online, enter Keyword: InBiz

INTERNET-MARKETING
(Internet Marketing Discussions - Discussions - Moderated)
This list has been discontinued. Archives available at
www.popco.com.

INTERNET-SALES
(Internet Sales - Discussions)
Subscriptions: IS-SUB@MMGCO.COM

International Business
(International Business - Discussions)
Subscriptions: woolford@trip.net

ISI-L
(Marketing Simulations)
Subscriptions: Simul8r@aol.com

JOBS-SLS
(Sales and Marketing Jobs - Announcements - Moderated)
Subscriptions: JOBS-SLS@EXECON.METRONET.COM

JunkMailList
Note: Subscription requests for this list are returned. No current
address on file.

KAWASAKI
(Clients and Fans of Guy Kawasaki, Marketer and Author -
Discussions)
Subscriptions: listserv@umslvma.umsl.edu

L-CUPRAP
(College and University Public Relations - Discussions)
Subscriptions: LISTSERV@PSUVM.PSU.EDU

MARKET-L
(General Marketing - Discussions - Unmoderated)
Subscriptions: listproc@mailer.fsu.edu

MARKETING
(General Marketing, Micromuse PLC, United Kingdom - Discussions)
Subscriptions: Majordomo@micromuse.co.uk

MARKETING
(General Marketing - Discussions)
Subscriptions: majordomo@usa.net

MARKETING-L
(General Marketing, Prague University of Economics - Discussions)
Subscriptions: listproc@pub.vse.cz

MARKETNET-L
(Marketing in Portuguese - Discussions)
Subscriptions: MAJORDOMO@AX.APC.ORG

Marketing Tools
(Demographics, Marketing Research, Database Marketing, Advertising
and Media
- Discussions)
Discussions: http://www.marketingtools.com/

MARTECH
(the original Marketing with Technology Tools - Discussions -
Unmoderated)
Originally a spin-off of HTMARCOM, MARTECH ceased 8/1/94.
INTERNET-MARKETING, HEP2-L (now MT-L) and FREE-MARKET were created
to fill the MARTECH void.

Mavenconference
(The Marketing Mavens Conference Room - Discussions)
Subscriptions: listserv@mail.Telmar.Com

misc.business.marketing.research
(proposed newsgroup - Discussions)
Note: Creation of this newsgroup has not yet been approved.

MKTALUM
(Marketing Alumni of Miami University, Ohio USA - Discussions)
Subscriptions: LISTSERV@MIAMIU.ACS.MUOHIO.EDU


MediaPlan
(Media Planning - Discussions)
Subscriptions: listserv@amic.com

MKTSEG
(Market Segmentation Issues - Discussions)
Subscriptions: listserv@mail.telmar.com

MKTSHARE
(Emergent Issues in Integrated Marketing Communications -
Discussions)
Subscriptions: listserv@piranha.acns.nwu.edu

MKTTEACH
(Marketing Education - Discussions)
Subscriptions: MAJORDOMO@hawk.depaul.edu

MRKT-PHD
(Doctoral Students in Marketing - Discussions)
Subscriptions: LISTSERV@univscvm.csd.scarolina.edu

MT-L

(Marketing with Technology Tools, formerly HEP2-L - Discussions - Unmoderated)
Subscriptions: listserv@uhccvm.uhcc.hawaii.edu

MUMME
(Miami Marketing Enterprises)
Subscriptions: LISTSERV@MIAMIU.ACS.MUOHIO.EDU

NetNews
(Marketing Issues on the Internet)
Note: This list has been discontinued.

Net.Value
(Net Value Forum, Internet Marketing - Discussions)
Discussions: http://owi.com/forum/data/msgs.html

NEWPROD
(New Product and Service Development - Discussions)
Subscriptions: MAJORDOMO@world.std.com

OSF-BUS
(Open Software Foundation, Business and Marketing Mailing List - Discussions)
Subscriptions: LISTSERV@LISTSERV.RL.AC.UK

OUT-OPTS
(Output Options; Artists, Publishers, Marketers - Discussions)
Subscriptions: majordomo@TreeO.com

PRFORUM
(Public Relations and Corporate Communications - Discussions - Unmoderated)
Subscriptions: LISTSERV@indycms.iupui.edu

PRODUCT_DEV
(New Product Development - Discussions)
Subscriptions: PRODUCT_DEV-REQUEST@msoe.edu

PROJECT-MANAGEMENT
(Project Management - Discussions)
Subscriptions: Project-Management@smtl.demon.co.uk

PRSIG
(PR and Marketing Forum - Discussions)
Discussions: on CompuServe, enter GO PRSIG

PRSSA-L
(Public Relations Student Society of America - Discussions)
Subscriptions: listproc@cornell.edu

RESELLER
(Computer Reseller Mailing List - Discussions)
Subscriptions: majordomo@shore.net

RITIM-L
(Telecommunications and Information Marketing - Discussions)
Subscriptions: LISTSERV@uriacc.uri.edu

SERVNET
(Multidisciplinary Service - Discussions)
Subscriptions: LISTSERV@asuvm.inre.asu.edu

SHOWBIZM
(Show Business Marketing and Publicity - Discussions - Moderated)
No current information on file.

SOC
(Selective Online Classifieds - Announcements - Moderated)
Subscriptions: Pangaea@eworld.com
Warning: you will receive MANY advertisements upon subscribing to
this list!

STUEPAP
(Student Electronic Papers Marketing - Discussions)
Subscriptions: LISTSERV@VM.TEMPLE.EDU

STUMARK-L
(Student Marketing)
Subscriptions: listproc@scu.edu.au

TELECOMREG
(Telecommunications Market Regulation - Discussions)
Subscriptions: LISTSERVER@relay.adp.wisc.edu

TELEMKT
(Telemarketing and Call Center Industry - Discussions)
Discussions: http://www.syn.net/telemkt/tel_for.html

TRADENET
(TradeNet World Service; International Traders - Announcements - Moderated)
Subscriptions: membership@TradeNet.org
Warning: you will receive MANY advertisements upon subscribing to this list!

TRADESHO
(Improving Sales Results at Trade Shows - Discussions)
Note: This list has not yet been formed. Eemail Bill Steinmetz at CyberStein@aol.com to
express your interest.

WEBCRIT
(Web Critiques - Discussions)
Note: This list has been discontinued.

www_marketing
(World Wide Web Marketing - Discussions)
Subscriptions: www_marketing-request@xmission.com

YELLOWPAGES
(Small Business Internet Advertising - Discussions)
Subscriptions: YELLOWPAGES-REQUEST@WEBCOM.COM

If you find that any of the above lists have ceased, changed location or owner, your assistance in updating us would be appreciated. Please email
webmaster@wolfBayne with the Subject line: MARKETING LISTS UPDATE.

Marketing Lists on the Internet' is researched, updated and published by:
Kim M. Bayne, president
wolfBayne Communications
P.O. Box 50287
Colorado Springs, CO 80949-0287
Tel. (719) 593-8032
email: kimmik@wolfBayne.com
http://www.bayne.com/wolfBayne/

Note: To join a list using the listserv software, send a message to:

*listserv@node.name*

with a message of:

*subscribe nameoflist YourRealName*

To join a list run on listproc the process is similar, except you send the same message to:

*listproc@node.name*

For lists running on majordomo software send a message to:

*majordomo@node.name*

with a message of

*subscribe nameoflist*

# *Glossary*

*Address (network address)*—Internet site addresses come in two forms: as a set of numbers such as *192.74.137.5*, and as alphanumerics such as *world.std.com* (as it happens, these are addresses to the same site, and either could be used, for example, with Telnet). Ben Franklin's e-mail address at this site might look like this: *bfranklin@world.std. com*.

*ADSL (Asymmetric Digital Subscriber Line)*—A technology under development that may offer dramatic improvements in the speed of data transmission over normal phone lines.

*Anonymous FTP*—The use of the FTP protocol with Internet sites that offer public access to their files without requiring personal IDs or passwords. Usually, after making a connection with the FTP site the user responds to the login prompt with the word "anonymous," and then to the password prompt with the user's full Internet address.

*Applets*—small downloadable Java applications that can be run on the fly from a Web page. (See also *Black Widows*.)

*Archie*—A service which can be used to search network-wide for FTP-accessible files and directories.

*ASCII (American Standard Code for Information Interchange)*—Now a worldwide standard in which the numbers, uppercase letters, lowercase letters, some punctuation marks, some symbols, and some control codes, have each been assigned a number from 0 to 127. This number can be stored digitally as a 7-bit binary number. For instance, using ASCII, the letter "a" is always stored as binary number 1000001. Plain text files are usually stored in this manner, and the Internet e-mail system primarily uses ASCII.

*AU*—The file extension for one type of audio file originally common on UNIX machines, but now used throughout the Internet. It can be played by most types of sound-ready computers if the proper software is obtained.

*Authentication*—Any of several methods used to provide proof that a particular document received electronically is actually from the individual it claims to be from, and is unchanged.

*Avatar*—A graphical image that you select to represent yourself in virtual reality worlds. It is used to interact with the virtual environment, and to interact with other individuals' avatars. An avatar can be a scanned-in photographic image or a more cartoon-like graphic.

*AVI*—A video-with-sound file format used primarily on computers with the Windows operating system. Other video formats used on the Internet include QuickTime and MPEG.

*B channel (Bearer channel)*—An ISDN data-carrying channel that can handle 64 kbps. Two such channels are available with most basic ISDN hookups.

*Bandwidth*—The data transferring capacity of a system—how much information can be sent from one place to another in a given period of time. There are many technical ways to measure this—for example, the number of megabytes transferred per second.

*Banner ads*—Graphical advertisements placed on various Web pages, similar to newspaper ads. These can be keyed to searches in the search engines so that the banner ad is targeted at the search results. For example, an athletic shoe maker might purchase a banner to come up when someone searches on sports or athletic shoes.

*Baud*—Technical term concerning modem audio frequency modulation that is used interchangeably, by everyone except engineers, with bps (bits per second) as a measure of a modem's speed (e.g., 28,800 baud modem).

*Binary data*—In its broadest sense, any data stored or transferred in digital form. In more common use, binary refers to data stored in 8-bit groups (which in decimal number terms provides 256 different possible numbers). Unlike 7-bit ASCII files, binary files have no standard way of being interpreted. Instead, they are used for software and for data files that are only meaningful when used with a compatible program. For example, a word processing data file from WordPerfect is not readable by most other types of word processor programs.

*Bitmap image*—The most commonly used images on the Internet such as GIF and JPEG are forms of bitmap. These are made of colored dots displayed in rows and columns to form a picture. By contrast, see *Vector image.*

*BBS (Bulletin-Board System)*—Computer system that predated the popularity of the Internet, consisting of a computer which can be reached directly by phone (by use of a computer modem). Most BBSs are small, menu-oriented sites which offer a variety of services such as e-mail, ways to post public messages in various topical "discussion groups," ways to offer files to the public and receive files from the public, and sometimes access to other remote computers and services. Increasingly, BBSs are accessible from the Internet, and provide access to the Internet for those who dial in to the BBS.

*Black Widows*—Destructive or harmful Java applets. These applets are analogous to some viruses in that that they may be both damaging and self-replicating.

*Boolean*—In Internet parlance, Boolean refers to online search systems that use the terms AND, OR, or NOT (and often particular syntax and punctuation) to write more accurate database queries. Most search sites offer help files to explain their particular flavor of Boolean search.

*Bounce*—When e-mail is undeliverable it is sent back to you (bounced) so that you will know it was not delivered, and be able to determine what the problem was.

*Browser*—Any of many programs used for retrieving and viewing HTML documents.

*Campus-Wide Information Systems (CWIS)*—A navigation and information retrieval tool which provides data from a variety of campus sources accessed through one user interface.

*CGI (Common Gateway Interface)*—A standardized way for Web servers to provide access to information and programs outside of the normal Web system and protocols.

*Chat*—Broadly, any text-based real-time interactive talking via the keyboard. (See also *Web chat*.)

*Click-through*—A click-through occurs when a user actually clicks on a banner or icon ad and arrives at the advertiser's page.

*Client/Server*—A way of distributing information on a network which involves using a small number of server programs to provide data to client programs installed on many computers throughout the network. The server program maintains a database and provides information to the client programs through the network, when requested. Also, some of the server programs have the ability to collect data and update their database files themselves. The client programs provide a user-friendly and consistent interface. Examples of Internet client/server systems include Gopher and the World Wide Web.

*Cookie*—In Internet parlance, a text file that stores information, on your own computer's hard drive, about your browser's interaction with certain Web sites. This information is then available to Web sites each time you visit.

*Command line*—On a PC without a graphical operating system, and with a shell account on an Internet access provider's computer, when you are at the system's main prompt you are on its command line (prompts often end in symbols such as $ or % or >). More broadly, any time that you must type in commands to the computer, whether you are at the operating system's prompt, or within a program, you are at the "command line." Command line programs often require you to remember and type in commands. These programs are usually harder to learn to use than programs that offer menus or lists of commands from which to select. (See also *GUI*.)

*Communicon (communication + icon)*—Combinations of letters and symbols used in Internet e-mail and public postings to provide emphasis, perspective, or clarification. These include very loosely standardized "smileys," "emoticons," abbreviated phrases, underlining methods, and parenthetical phrases.

*Communications software*—Usually used in reference to programs that run on a personal computer which allow the computer to communicate with a modem, and thus through the phone lines. These programs also allow the personal computer to "look like" a particular type of terminal to the computer it is connected to through the phone lines.

*Cross-links*—Mutual HTML pointers between two Web sites. Essentially, each site lists the other in its hotlinks.

*Cross-post*—Sending the same message to more than one mailing list or discussion group. This is usually discouraged unless the posting is specifically appropriate for each list it is sent to, and there is reasonable expectation that each mailing list has a substantially different audience.

*CSO*—A system for retrieving data from simple database files such as phone books. Named after the University of Illinois's Computing Services Organization (CSO).

*Cybermall*—A collection of virtual storefronts offered online by one Web access provider, usually with some similarity in appearance and functions, and usually listed on one top page. Through a cybermall, a group of businesses uses one Web access provider to do sales online.

*D channel (Data channel)*—The portion of an ISDN connection used for various setup and signaling functions. This can keep the B channels completely free for data transferring. On Basic Rate Interface systems, the D channel is a 16 kbps channel.

*Daemon*—A UNIX program that will, among other things, report errors in delivering your e-mail messages.

*Domain Name System (DNS)*—An Internet addressing system which uses a group of names that are listed with dots (.) between them, in the order of most specific to the most general group. In the United States the top (most general) domains are network categories such as edu (education), com (commercial), and gov (government). In other countries a two-letter abbreviation for the country is used, such as ca (Canada) or au (Australia).

*Download*—To receive on your local computer a copy of a file that currently exists on some remote computer. Many protocols for doing this have been devised, such as Zmodem, Xmodem, Ymodem, and Kermit, each with its own commands and syntax. With most browsers the user need not be aware of which protocols are being used.

*E-journal (electronic journal)*—A publication distributed on the Internet at regular intervals. Distribution may be by active means such as e-mail mailing lists, or by placing the publication on an FTP site, Web page, or other public location for people to retrieve. Most e-journals are distributed in standard ASCII text, though some are offered as formatted text with graphics and pictures in specific formats such as PostScript. Some are offshoots of paper-based publications, but most are purely electronic and are distributed free.

*E-mail (electronic mail)*—Private messages delivered via networks to another individual's e-mail account. Used with automatic group mailing list software, e-mail is the basis for discussion groups and many other Internet services. "E-mail" is used both as a noun and verb (" I received his e-mail three days after I e-mailed him.")

*Emoticons (emotion + icon)*—One group of communicons which include both "smileys" and expressions of surprise, annoyance, sarcasm, etc. Tilt your head left to view smile :) or frown :(   or wink ;)

*External images*—Images that are linked to an HTML file, but are only loaded and displayed when their anchor is activated. Compare *Inline images*.

*FAQs (Frequency Asked Questions)*—Because newcomers are always arriving at Usenet newsgroups and on topical mailing lists, the same questions can be asked repeatedly (to the dismay of more advanced, long-time members of the group). Therefore, volunteers will often assemble a document which presents, in question-and-answer format, the basic facts about the topic and group. This FAQ is revised and posted to the group at regular intervals and is also stored, for access at any time, at a public location such as an FTP site.

*Finger*—An Internet system that allows you to find out about who the person is behind an e-mail address, when he or she last checked in for mail, and several other items. If that person has written a ".plan" or ".project" file, that will also be displayed. For example, to see the account information and .plan file for the address *oakridge@world. std.com*, just type *finger oakridge@world.std.com* at your access provider's main prompt (with shell account).

*Firewall*—A hardware and/or software method to protect a network from unauthorized use by those outside of a network. Businesses and organizations that have connected their computers to the Internet often install a firewall to protect their data from theft and alteration.

*Flame*—To send e-mail or make public postings with harsh, provocative tirades. This can result in flame wars and other unpleasantness.

*Forms*—Data entry areas on Web pages supported by CGI scripts to allow for data gathering and online ordering.

*Frame relay*—A fast data transfer system (56 kbps to 1.5 mbps) that works well for linking business sites. It can have some economic advantages over full-time leased lines because the data is sent in packets over the phone system on shared common phone systems.

*Freeware*—Software available from many locations on the Internet (often via FTP and the Web) which is totally free.

*FTP (File Transfer Protocol)*—A system used to transfer copies of files from one computer to another on the Internet. (See also *Anonymous FTP*.)

*Gateway*—A computer that connects two or more networks or types of systems. Especially in the past, before TCP/IP protocols were so widely used, gateway computers often had to pass data between incompatible network systems.

*GIF (Graphics Interchange Format)*—A type of picture storage file developed by CompuServe, and now widely used on the Internet. Files in this format have an extension of ".gif" as in *mars.gif*. GIF files vary greatly in size depending on their height and width, and the number of colors they depict.

*GIS (Geographic Information System)*—a digital location system based on land-based references.

*Gopher*—An Internet tool for finding and retrieving files of all kinds throughout the Internet. It is a menu-oriented client/server system with a top menu at each Gopher site leading to many submenus and files throughout the Internet.

*GUI (graphical user interface)*—Any of a number of programs and operating systems, such as Windows and Macintosh systems, which are operated by using a mouse input device to move a pointer to various graphics, icons, and menus (in contrast to command-line or other text-based methods).

*Helper applications*—Programs that a browser can call up to display or process files that it was not originally programmed to handle itself. The filename's extension indicates to the browser which external program should be used. A file ending in .avi, for example, would load the movie viewer for avi files. These are sometimes called plug-ins.

*Hit*—A request made to a Web server for any file. For a single Web page that has five pictures, the Web server would count six hits—one for the HTML document and five for the inline pictures. Hits should not, therefore, be confused with counts of the number of individuals that have visited a Web site, or a particular Web page. (See also *Impression*.)

*Host*—Your Internet access provider's computer. You may use one of its hard-wired terminals if you are at an institution with a mainframe computer connected directly to the Internet, or you may dial up and use a modem to connect with the Internet access provider's host computer. (As computer systems have changed, the term "host" has changed in meaning, so do expect some confusing references to "host" at times.)

*HTML (HyperText Markup Language)*—A standardized (but evolving) set of commands and syntax rules used for encoding text files with formatting and document linking information, for use on the World Wide Web. HTML documents are viewed using a Web browser.

*HTTP (HyperText Transfer Protocol)*—A standardized set of rules for transferring and processing HTML and other documents on networks.

*Hypertext*—Text in an HTML document that is coded to provide a link (hyperlink) to other locations within the document, or to other documents. Hypertext within a document is highlighted, to indicate to viewers that they can, with just a few keystrokes or clicks of a mouse, view these other documents. These other documents may also have links to still other documents. . . .

*Hypermedia*—Documents with links to and from images, sound, video, and interactive elements.

*Impression*—The smallest *useful* measure of access to a Web page: the whole single page unit, including the text, images, icons, etc. as viewed by a user. Internet advertising is often charged based on impression rates.

*Inline images*—Graphics and pictures that are automatically downloaded and displayed when viewing an HTML file. Compare *External images*.

*Information Superhighway*—A vaguely defined term sometimes referring to the Internet, and sometimes referring to the entire collection of new communications technologies.

*Internet*—A digital communications network connecting other smaller networks from many countries throughout the world. It transfers data using a standardized protocol called TCP/IP.

*Internet Backbone*—The collection of top-level data transfer networks through which local Internet service providers route traffic to and from the Internet.

*Intranet*—A private network that uses Internet-like protocols, but is not connected to the Internet. It allows business employees to use the user-friendly document sharing, displaying, and searching technologies of the Internet without providing access to confidential information to the Internet community at large.

*IRC (Internet Relay Chat)*—An Internet system which allows Internet users to "chat" (via keyboard) in "real time." Separate channels are available with various options for privacy, filtering out unwanted messages, and one-to-one messages.

*IP address*—The groups of numbers (e.g., *101.23.121.3*) used by Internet routers to direct packets to the right sites. Individuals can alternately use the much easier to remember domain names (such as *yahoo.com*) in e-mail addresses and Web URLs.

*ISDN (Integrated Services Digital Network)*—A phone service that allows much faster transfer of data than is currently available with POTS (Plain Old Telephone Service) and modems. It comes in various forms, such as BRI, which provides two 64 kbps data lines and a 16 kbps control line.

*ISP (Internet service provider)*—A business or institution connected to the Internet which provides Internet access to others (usually via phone lines).

*Java*—A system designed by Sun Microsystems to allow extra features to be added to Web displays, such as animations and interactive elements, by adding small programs (applets) to Web documents that can be processed by Java-compatible browsers.

*JPG, JPEG*—The filename extension used for JPEG (Joint Photographic Experts Group) graphics/pictures files (e.g., *moon.jpg*). This file format can be much more compressed than, for example, GIF, but high compression causes some loss of detail. JPG is among the three most popular picture file formats on the Internet, along with GIF and PCX.

*Listserv*—A program that provides automatic processing of many functions involved with mailing lists (discussion groups). E-mailing appropriate messages to it will automatically subscribe you to a discussion list or unsubscribe you. A listserv will also answer requests for indexes, FAQs, archives of the previous discussions, and other files.

*Log file*—In PC communication programs, a feature that allows you to save in a file everything that is displayed to the screen, thus providing a full recording of the activity for a full or partial online session. Web site administrators also use log files which record Web server activity.

*Login*—When one computer seeks to establish a connection to another computer, there will be a login process on the remote computer which usually involves some user steps beyond those things taken care of by the computer software. This may be as simple as pressing Enter, or may require a specific login word and a password to be entered. (Usually used interchangeably with "logon".)

*Logoff*—To leave or disconnect from a computer system. Often accomplished by selecting a menu item for disconnecting, or typing *exit*, *bye*, *quit*, or *logout* at the command line prompt .

*Lurk*—To read messages from discussion groups or Usenet newsgroups without contributing any.

*Mailing lists*—Discussions carried on by sending e-mailing messages to an automated re-mailer, which then sends a copy of each message via e-mail to every one who has subscribed to the list for that particular discussion group. Also known as "lists," "discussion lists," or "discussion groups."

*Marquee*—A line of text that scrolls across the bottom or top of a Web page, often used for advertising, or to feature a particular item. Sometimes called a crawl.

*Micropayment*—a very small payment (sometimes only a few cents or dollars) enabled by some of the various digital cash systems.

*MIME (Multipurpose Internet Mail Extensions)*—An improvement on the Internet mail system standards that allows binary files to be sent as e-mail through the Internet. Formerly only ASCII files could be sent. This system is not available on all sites yet.

*Mirror site*—Popular FTP sites often get too much traffic. This causes slowed reactions, inability to access the site, and sometimes, more system load than a site can spare. When this happens, mirror sites are sometimes set up, with exact copies of the files and the directories in which they are stored, at other locations.

*Modem (MOdulator/DEModulator)*—An electronic device that converts computer signals into audio (sound) signals so that they can be sent over normal phone lines and received by another modem, which will convert the sound back into computer signals. Virtually all modems combine the send and receive functions in one circuit.

*Moderator*—In discussion lists (groups) which are moderated, the moderator watches the postings as they come in to be sure, for example, that they relate to the topics and goals of the list and that the language and nature of the messages are suitable for public posting. The types and extent of moderating ranges widely from merely re-stating the goals and limits occasionally, to actual editing of incoming messages.

*Mosaic*—A graphical user interface browser program that works as client software for FTP, Gopher, Usenet news, WAIS, and WWW servers.

*Mov (.mov)*—The extension used on graphics/movie filenames that require a QuickTime viewer.

*MPEG (Motion Pictures Experts Group)*—A standard for storing and compressing video/sound files. Mac and Windows programs are available for viewing these files, which have an .mpg filename extension.

*MPPP (Multilink Point-to-Point Protocol)*—A standard for data transfer with ISDN that allows both data channels to be used simultaneously, and their use to be re-assigned dynamically as voice and data communication needs change.

*Netiquette (network + etiquette)*—Customs and socially accepted behavior for using networks.

*Netscape*—A commercially available World Wide Web GUI browser.

*Network*—A group of computers connected together in any way that allows data to be sent among computers.

*Newbie*—Anyone new to the Internet. Due to the rapid growth of the Internet, most people on the Internet are newbies, and therefore this is not considered a particularly negative term.

*Newsgroups*—Not news in the traditional sense, these are public postings message groups that cover thousands of topics.

*NIC (Network Information Center)*—A site designated to provide information services about the network to network users.

*NSFnet (National Science Foundation (NSF) + net)*—The system of high-speed data transfer links and nodes that used to form the backbone of the Internet in the United States.

*Offline*—Anything that happens when your computer is not connected to another computer. For instance, a communications program may download many messages and files quickly and then allows you to read them offline in order to save on connect charges and long distance phone charges.

*Online*—Any activity carried out while your computer is connected to another computer or network.

*PCX*—A bitmap graphics file format developed by Zsoft. The standard includes file compression.

*PGP (Pretty Good Privacy)*—A data encryption/deciphering system which uses two digital "keys" (similar to passwords) to protect messages or other information from being read by anyone other than the intended recipient.

*Pixels*—The individual dots of light that make up the images on a computer screen. (Not the same as "dot-pitch," which refers to the distribution of phosphor dots on a screen.) A standard VGA screen has 480 rows of 640 pixels each.

*Plan file (.plan)*—A file that you create and store in your home directory on your Internet access provider's computer, telling anything you want about yourself or your business, or any other subject. A copy of it can be obtained by anyone who uses the Finger program to check your e-mail account (rarely used now).

*Plug-in*—Small program designed to add features to a specific larger program. On the Internet some browsers such as Netscape have been designed to be used with plug-ins such as Shockwave. Movie and image viewers and sound players are plug-ins for browsers. When specifications of a program are made public, third parties can develop plug-ins.

*PoP (Point of Presence)*—Dial-in site maintained by an Internet service provider at a location that would normally require a toll call for customers to connect with the ISP. This allows an ISP to attract customers from a much larger area.

*Post*—To send an e-mail message to one of the public discussion groups.

*Postmaster*—The person at each site who is responsible for handling e-mail problems at that site. Send e-mail to the postmaster at a site if you are having some difficulties getting a message through, or need other information about the site. E-mail messages to this person are addressed to *postmaster@(site name)*—for example, *postmaster@world.std.com*.

*POTS (Plain Old Telephone Service)*—A new name for normal phone service, used to distinguish it from the many newly available services such as T1 and ISDN.

*PPP (Point-to-Point Protocol)*—A standardized set of rules describing the procedures for one computer to connect with another and exchange TCP/IP packets. This procedure allows a user of a dial-up connection to an Internet service provider to directly interact with the Internet. PPP has replaced an earlier protocol, SLIP, at many ISPs.

*Prompt*—What is displayed when a computer system is waiting for some sort of input from you.

*Protocol*—A formal, standardized set of operating rules governing the format, timing, error control, etc. of data transmissions and other activities on a network.

*Proxy server*—A system that stores frequently used information closer to the end-user to provide faster access, or reduce the load on another server.

*QuickTime*—A movie/sound/graphics file format originally developed by Apple Computer. Viewers for these files (with the filename extension .mov) are also available for Windows and other systems.

*README files (or READ.ME)*—At FTP sites, files commonly named READ.ME are used to direct the newcomer to index files or other useful information about the files in that directory. READ.ME files are also often included with software for last-minute instructions or important notices.

*Referring site*—When a user enters a Web site by way of a link from another site, the other site is the referring site. This is used in tracking site visitors to understand their path into a given site.

*RFC (Request for Comments)*—Documents relating to the Internet system, protocols, proposals, etc.

*RJ-11*—The official designation for the normal 4 conductor phone jack/plug used in homes and small businesses throughout the United States.

*Search engines*—The true Web search tools such as Excite. These engines search out pages and create a database for searching. (See also *Web catalogs*.)

*Secure container* —- An electronic "envelope" or "box" that holds encrypted data and encrypted authentication information which can only be opened by the designated recipient.

*Secure transactions*—Financial or other business transactions carried out using procedures with adequate privacy and authentication given the nature and risks of the transaction. In general, on the Internet, this means using, Secure HTTP, Secure MIME, encryption, or other procedures to protect privacy and prevent theft of credit card numbers and other personal information.

*Server*—See *Client/Server.*

*Shareware*—Software available from many locations on the Internet. It is initially free, but the authors expect payment to be sent voluntarily after an initial test period. Quality varies from bad to better than some commercial software. Prices are usually excellent. Some initial versions are limited in function in some way, with an upgrade available if you pay the fee.

*S/HTTP (Secure HyperText Transfer Protocol)*—An HTTP-compatible protocol that adds security features to Web documents.

*SIG (signature)*—A short message placed at the bottom of an e-mail message or a discussion group posting which identifies the sender and includes items such as phone number, fax number, address, information about the person's occupation or company, and even a philosophical saying or humorous message. Most e-mail programs have some provision for adding prewritten SIGs automatically to outgoing e-mail.

*SLIP (Serial Line Internet Protocol)*—A standardized set of rules describing the procedures for a computer to connect with another and exchange TCP/IP packets. This procedure allows a user of a dial-up connection to an Internet access provider to directly interact with the Internet. (See also *PPP*.)

*Smiley*—Any of several smiling faces created by various keyboard letters and symbols such as :) and 8-). (See also *Communicon* and *Emoticon*.)

*S/MIME (Secure Multipurpose Internet Mail Extensions)*—A MIME-compatible protocol that adds authentication to documents sent via e-mail. (See also *MIME*.)

*Snail mail*—An irreverent reference to standard paper-based postal mail from those on the Internet who have become accustomed to the speed of e-mail.

*Spam*—In Internet parlance, to send unsolicited e-mail to large groups of people, or post messages on large numbers of newsgroups or discussion lists. Most networks and ISPs have policies against spamming. Some back up their policies by terminating service to the spammer.

*Sponsorship*—Some companies choose to sponsor a whole Web site as the sole advertiser. They offer substantial support with services, hardware, or cash for a site in exchange for exclusive visibility as the sponsor.

*STT (Secure Transactions Technology)*—A system providing for secure transactions.

*Streaming (data streaming)*—The processing or use of a data file by the site downloading it before the full file has been received. Web browsers, for example, start to display a Web page before the main file and all the supporting documents have arrived. Data streaming is likely to become important for online audio and video distribution as well.

*Sysop (SYStem OPerator)*—The individual who does the hands-on work of being sure a computer system, or some portion of, it is operating correctly. Sometimes called "sysgod" in jest.

*Tag spamming*—The practice of including commented-out descriptors dozens of times within a Web page, in order to make it more likely that the page will appear prominently in a Web search on those repeated words. This practice is on the wane.

*TCP/IP (Transmission Control Protocol/Internet Protocol)*—The agreed-on set of computer communications rules and standards that allows communications between different types of computers and networks that are connected to the Internet.

*Telnet*—Also called remote login, a system that allows access to remote computers on the Internet. Many of the features of the remote computer can then be used as if your personal computer or terminal were directly connected to it.

*Terminal emulator*—Communications software that can make itself "appear" to another computer as if it were a specific type of terminal. Some common terminals that are emulated are VT100, VT52, and ANSI.

*Thread*—Within Usenet newsgroups and topical discussion groups, one of several sub-discussions. For instance, in a forestry discussion group there may be on-going discussions of old growth forests, the spotted owl, forest fires, etc. Each thread is started with an original posting which others can respond to using the same subject name preceded by "RE:".

*TN-3270*—Telnet software that provides IBM full screen support.

*UNIX*—An operating system, widely used on the Internet, developed by AT&T Bell Laboratories, that supports multiuser and multitasking operations.

*Uploading*—File transfers from your local computer to a remote one.

*URL (Uniform Resource Locator)*—An addressing system that can uniquely name most files found on the Internet. It includes a protocol name (such as *gopher, ftp,* or *http*), plus a site name (such as *world.std.com*) and subdirectory path (such as */pub/oakridge/*) and a filename (such as *newsletter.html*). Example: *ftp://ftp.std.com/pub/ oakridge/newsletter.txt*

*Usenet newsgroups (Netnews)*—Thousands of discussion groups based on public postings of messages. Newsreader software interacts with Usenet servers and allows messages to be read by topic and discussion thread, and provides provisions for responding to particular messages. (This is a different system than the listserv discussion group system, which is based on e-mail).

*User name*—A short name (usually with no spaces allowed), unique to you on your Internet access provider's system. Sometimes this is assigned and sometimes you can select your own. The user name (or ID), followed by your Internet service provider's site name, becomes your e-mail address. For example, if Ben Franklin had an account at *world.std.com*, and he chose a user name of *bfranklin*, his e-mail address would be *bfranklin@world.std.com*.

*UUCP (Unix-to-Unix Copy Program)*—A protocol used for communication between consenting UNIX systems.

*VAX*—Hardware produced by the Digital Equipment Corporation, in use by some sites on the Internet. The VMS operating system is used on VAX computers.

*Vector image*—An image made up of sets of instructions which direct the viewer program to draw various shapes, fill them with color, etc. Commonly used in CAD programs and formatted files such as PostScript. In contrast, see *Bitmap image.*

*Veronica*—A client/server system that provides a way to search for a particular word or topic of interest in all Gopher menus, at all Gopher sites known to the veronica server database.

*Virtual reality*—Any of various combinations of user interface features that permit a user to interact with a computer or system in a manner which more closely mimics how humans normally operate in the real world—may include use of speech synthesis, speech recognition, three-dimensional graphics, hand and head position sensors, etc.

*Virtual storefront*—An online business presence for online sales. This is usually accomplished through use of Web pages. The pages display information about the products, often including pictures. Information on ordering is also given, and an on-screen input form , may be displayed to take the customer's order.

*VRML (Virtual Reality Modeling Language)*—A document-encoding protocol that provides for three-dimensional navigation among sites on the Internet.

*VT100*—Originally, a type of terminal used by DEC (Digital Equipment Corporation); now, a widely used terminal standard for communicating with Internet service providers that offer shell accounts (command-line interaction with the host computer, rather than SLIP or PPP protocols).

*Web catalogs*—Pages such as Galaxy that categorize and organize sites much like a catalog in a library might. See also *Search engines.*

*Web chat*—Real-time interactive talk, based from a Web site. This may be text-only or may use graphics, avatars, animation, etc. to create a richer, more visual environment.

*WWW (World Wide Web)*—Initially created in Switzerland, WWW is a client/server system designed to use hypertext and hypermedia documents via the Internet. It uses *HTTP* (hypertext transfer protocol) to exchange documents, images, and other data. The documents are formatted in *HTML* (hypertext markup language).

# Index

## C

cable TV, 327
camcorders, 152-153
cameras, 152-153
    digital, 153
CAN-IMARKET, 386
capture, 151
catalogs, 196-199. *See also* searching
    Galaxy, 198
    Xplore, 198-199
    Yahoo, 196-197
CDnow, 15-16
Cello, 344-346
    obtaining, 350
CERN (European Laboratory for Particle
        Physics), 31-32
CERT (Computer Emergency Response
        Team), 101-102
Chameleon, 346
Channel One Internet Services, 324
chat, 27, 303-304
    The Chat Server, 303
    IRC chat, 351-352
The Chat Server, 303
checks, 96. *See also* security
    NetCheque, 98-99
CIO MarketTalk, 386
Cisco Systems, 100
click-through pricing, 87
Clorox, 19
CmMoon12, 352
CNI-ADVERTISE, 386
CNI-MODERNIZATION, 386
codes, countries on the Internet, 7-13
color
    balance, 155
    and file size, 154-155
comments, 128
CommerceNet, 225-226
commercial online services, 325

COMMERCIAL-REALESTATE, 386
Commercial Sites Index, 84-85
CommInfo, 386
communication, 43
Computer Emergency Response Team
        (CERT), 101-102
computer-generated graphics, 153
conferences
    list of conferences, 255
    real-time, 287-291
    videoconferencing, 292-295
connections, 317-321
    for marketing, 326
Connectix, 295
contests, 106
converting files, 155-156
cookies files, 108
CoolTalk, 289-291
copyrights, 105-106
corporate
    connections, 318
    identity, 89-90
    sponsorship, 54-55
cost containment, 51
countries on the Internet, 7-13
coupons, NetCash, 98
creating an account, 96
credit cards, cyber, 96
    CyberCash, Inc., 101
    First Virtual, 98
CRM-L, 386
cross-links, 87
culture of the Internet, 21
curiosity, 63
CU-SeeMe, 292-293
customer service, 46-48
Customer Support, 386
customs, good practices 93-95
CuteFTP, 352
CyberCash, Inc., 101